Lecture Notes in Computer Scienc

T0237962

Commenced Publication in 1973
Founding and Former Series Editors:
Gerhard Goos, Juris Hartmanis, and Jan van Leeuwen

Editorial Board

Abdelkader Hameurlain   A Min Tjoa (Eds.)

Data Management in Grid and Peer-to-Peer Systems

Second International Conference, Globe 2009
Linz, Austria, September 1-2, 2009
Proceedings

 Springer

Volume Editors

Abdelkader Hameurlain
Paul Sabatier University
Institut de Recherche en Informatique de Toulouse (IRIT)
118, route de Narbonne, 31062 Toulouse CEDEX, France
E-mail: hameur@irit.fr

A Min Tjoa
Vienna University of Technology
Institute of Software Technology
Favoritenstraße 9-11/188, 1040 Wien, Austria
E-mail: amin@ifs.tuwien.ac.at

Library of Congress Control Number: 2009931958

CR Subject Classification (1998): D.2, C.2.4, D.1.3, H.2.4, E.1

LNCS Sublibrary: SL 3 – Information Systems and Application, incl. Internet/Web
and HCI

ISSN   0302-9743
ISBN-10   3-642-03714-3 Springer Berlin Heidelberg New York
ISBN-13   978-3-642-03714-6 Springer Berlin Heidelberg New York

springer.com

© Springer-Verlag Berlin Heidelberg 2009
Printed in Germany

Typesetting: Camera-ready by author, data conversion by Scientific Publishing Services, Chennai, India
Printed on acid-free paper   SPIN: 12737710   06/3180   5 4 3 2 1 0

Preface

The synergy and convergence of research on grid computing and peer-to-peer (P2P) computing have materialized in the meeting of the two research communities: parallel systems and distributed systems. The main common objective is to harness Internet-connected resources (e.g., CPU, memory, network bandwidth, data sources) at very large scale. In this framework, the Globe Conference tries to consolidate the bidirectional bridge between grid and P2P systems and large-scale heterogeneous distributed database systems.

Today, the grid and P2P systems hold a more and more important position in the landscape of the research in large-scale distributed systems, and the applications which require an effective management of voluminous, distributed and heterogeneous data. This importance comes out of characteristics offered by these systems: autonomy and dynamicity of peers, decentralized control for scaling, and transparent sharing large-scale distributed resources.

The second edition of the International Conference on Data Management in Grid and P2P Systems was held during September 1-2, 2009 in Linz, Austria. The main objective of this conference was to present the latest results in research and applications, to identify new issues, and to shape future directions.

This year, we had the pleasure and honor of welcoming Anastasios Gounaris (Aristotle University of Thessaloniki, Greece), Leo Bertossi (Carleton University, Ottawa, Canada), and Zoe Lacroix (Arizona State University, Tempe, USA) to present a part of their research activities concerning: "A Vision for Next-Generation Query Processors and an Associated Research Agenda," "Designing, Specifying, and Querying Metadata for Virtual Data Integration Systems," and "Customized and Optimized Service Selection with ProtocolDB," respectively.

In response to the call for papers, 18 papers were submitted from around the world. Of these, 9 papers were accepted for publication in the proceedings. The selected papers represent recent development in the field, which provide the opportunity to discuss requirements, problems and proposed solutions.

I would like to express thanks to the authors who submitted papers, and to the Program Committee for the thorough review process. Special thanks go to Roland Wagner and Gabriela Wagner (FAW, University of Linz).

June 2009

Abdelkader Hameurlain
A Min Tjoa

Organization

Conference Program Chairpersons

Abdelkader Hameurlain   IRIT, Paul Sabatier University, Toulouse, France
A Min Tjoa   IFS, Vienna University of Technology, Austria

Program Committee

Frederic Andres   University of Advanced Studies, Tokyo, Japan
Philippe Balbiani   IRIT, Paul Sabatier University, Toulouse, France
Djamal Benslimane   LIRIS, Universty of Lyon, France
Leopoldo Bertossi   Carleton University School of Computer Science, Ottawa, Canada
Lionel Brunie   LIRIS, INSA of Lyon, France
Qiming Chen   HP Labs, Palo Alto, California, USA,
Alfredo Cuzzocrea   ICAR-CNR, University of Calabria, Italy
Bruno Defude   Telecom INT, Evry, France
Kayhan Erciyes   Ege University, Izmir, Turkey
Shahram Ghandeharizadeh   University of Southern California, USA
Tasos Gounaris   Aristotle University of Thessaloniki, Greece
Ismail Khalil   Johannes Kepler University, Linz, Austria
Zoe Lacroix   Arizona State University, Tempe, USA
Anirban Mondal   University of Tokyo, Japan
Franck Morvan   IRIT, Paul Sabatier University, Toulouse, France
Kjetil Nørvåg   Norwegian University of Science and Technology, Trondheim, Norway
Claudia Roncancio   LIG, Grenoble University, France
Salvatore Orlando   University of Venice, Italy
Florence Sedes   IRIT, Paul Sabatier University, Toulouse, France
Fabricio A. B. Silva   University of Lisbon, Portugal
Mário J.G. Silva   University of Lisbon, Portugal
David Taniar   Monash University, Australia
Ngoc Thanh Nguyen   Wroclaw University of Technology, Poland
Genovevav Vargas-Solar   LIG, Grenoble University, France
Roland Wagner   FAW, University of Linz, Austria
Wolfram Wöß   FAW, University of Linz, Austria

External Reviewers

Francisco Couto   University of Lisbon, Portugal
Florence Perronnin   University of Grenoble, France
Catia Pesquita   University of Lisbon, Portugal

Table of Contents

Invited Talk

4 Semantics for P2P Systems and Applications

A Vision for Next Generation Query Processors and an Associated Research Agenda

Anastasios Gounaris

Aristotle University of Thessaloniki
Department of Informatics
541 24 Thessaloniki, Greece
gounaria@csd.auth.gr

Abstract. Query processing is one of the most important mechanisms for data management, and there exist mature techniques for effective query optimization and efficient query execution. The vast majority of these techniques assume workloads of rather small transactional tasks with strong requirements for ACID properties. However, the emergence of new computing paradigms, such as grid and cloud computing, the increasingly large volumes of data commonly processed, the need to support data driven research, intensive data analysis and new scenarios, such as processing data streams on the fly or querying web services, the fact that the metadata fed to optimizers are often missing at compile time, and the growing interest in novel optimization criteria, such as monetary cost or energy consumption, create a unique set of new requirements for query processing systems. These requirements cannot be met by modern techniques in their entirety, although interesting solutions and efficient tools have already been developed for some of them in isolation. Next generation query processors are expected to combine features addressing all of these issues, and, consequently, lie at the confluence of several research initiatives. This paper aims to present a vision for such processors, to explain their functionality requirements, and to discuss the open issues, along with their challenges.

1 Introduction

The success of databases and the reason they play such a key role in data management lies largely in their ability to allow users to specify their data retrieval and update tasks declaratively, relieving them from the burden of specifying how these tasks should be processed; the responsibility of the latter aspect rests with the query processor. To this end, query processing involves the phases of translation, optimization and execution, which have been the topic of investigation for many decades, resulting in a broad range of effective and efficient techniques (e.g., [8,25,30]). In conventional static query processors, the three phases of query processing occur sequentially, whereas adaptive query processing (AQP) solutions differ in that they interleave query optimization with query execution [12].

A. Hameurlain and A M. Tjoa (Eds.): Globe 2009, LNCS 5697, pp. 1–11, 2009.

Since it is rather unusual for all the data of a single organization to reside at a single physical place, distributed query processing (DQP) has received considerable attention mainly with a view to supporting transactional tasks over geographically spread data resources. Distributed query execution involves the same three phases as centralized query processing, but considers more issues than in traditional centralized systems, such as dynamic data placement, replica management and communication cost [34,43]. Consequently, optimization of distributed queries is inherently more complex than when applied to a single-node setting [56] and this is aggravated by the fact that different distributed environments may shape it towards different, and potentially contradicting goals [42]. For example, in some environments accuracy is not as important as returning the first results as early as possible (e.g., [31]), or the economic cost may be an issue (e.g., [53]). A typical optimization criterion is the minimization of a query's response time; this problem is often reduced to the problem of minimizing the communication cost under the assumption that communication is the dominant cost and there exist several proposals that try to address it [6,17,39]. This type of DQP is suitable for short transactional tasks requiring strong guarantees on the ACID properties [43].

Nevertheless, modern applications are often characterized by different needs. Conventional query processing techniques are tailored to settings where data reside on disk, appropriate indices have been built and metadata have been collected, whereas, nowadays, data sources, either in the form of sensors or not, may continuously produce data to be processed on the fly. There are several complications stemming from that, including the unavailability of the metadata that are typically fed to the optimizer and the applicability of one-pass algorithms only. In addition, more and more data management applications do not comprise transactional tasks. They rather focus on decision support, analysis and data driven research, and as such, they tend to comprise particularly data- and computation-intensive tasks requiring relatively high degrees of parallelism. The emergence of new computing paradigms, such as grid and cloud computing, has enabled the runtime pooling of hardware and software resources, whereas technologies such as web services facilitate the reuse and sharing of remote complex analysis tools called from within database queries (e.g., as in [3,38]) or generic workflows (e.g., [50]). Finally, in modern applications, economic cost, energy consumption, network utilization, quality of analysis tools employed, accuracy of results, data quality and other QoS criteria may be equally if not more important than query response time, throughput and communication cost.

In this paper, we make a statement that next generation query processors should evolve so that they can efficiently and effectively support scenarios addressing all the afore-mentioned issues. Note that not all of these issues are new, however, until now, they have tended to be investigated in isolation. For instance, AQP techniques try to deal with the unavailability of statistics mostly when processing takes place in a centralized manner [12], and programming frameworks such as MapReduce [10,11] and PigLatin [41] offer massive parallelism at the expense of less declarative task definition and lack of sophisticated optimization. Also, there have been significant advances in stream data management (e.g., [19,9]), and multi-objective optimization (e.g., [45]), but without considering wide-area heterogeneous computation platforms with arbitrarily high degrees of parallelism. The surveys in [27,44,55], which focus on data-management on grid computing infrastructures, and the discussion in [52] about the future of database are relevant to this work, too.

In the remainder of this paper, we present our vision for next generation query processors in more detail (Section 2). Next, in Section 3, we discuss three of the most important open research areas in order this vision to be fulfilled, namely the programming and execution model, the optimization process and the need for advanced autonomic techniques. Section 4 concludes the paper.

2 The Vision and Its Requirements

Our vision is in line with the suggestion of the recent Claremont report that *"database researchers should take data-centric ideas (declarative programming, query optimization) outside their original context in storage and retrieval, and attack new areas of computing where a data-centric mindset can have major impact"* [2]. Recently, some scepticism has been expressed about the suitability of a single database engine for meeting the afore-mentioned modern needs [52]. This scepticism is mostly grounded on the diversity of characteristics and requirements of modern applications, although there have been some efforts in developing unifying systems (e.g., [14]). Orthogonally to any architectural choices, the query processors envisaged in this work have extended functionality, so that they become capable of supporting scenarios involving arbitrary data sources requiring arbitrary computational and analysis resources while benefitting from the significant advances in and the maturity of database technologies in the last decades. More specifically, the query processors envisaged are characterized by:

– *Declarative task statement:* Assuming that there are catalogues (either centralized or distributed) of (i) the computational, (ii) data, and (iii) analysis resources, users can define complex data analysis tasks in a both expressive (e.g., SQL-like as opposed to simple keyword searches) and declarative manner. These tasks may be mapped not simply to traditional query plans, but also to workflows comprising calls to web services (e.g., [50]), or combination of both, (e.g. [38]). Note that the corresponding language may be lower level than SQL in order to benefit from a richer type system and programming patterns such as iteration, which are necessary for several read only, data-intensive analysis tasks that are typical in data driven research (e.g., [41,57]).
– *Declarative statement of optimization objective(s):* Nowadays, query processors typically operate on a best-effort basis, trying to minimize fixed system-wide metrics such as total work, throughput, query response time and time to deliver early results. These metrics still apply, but, in addition, metrics such as economic cost [53] and energy consumption [28,36] are becoming

increasingly important. Clearly, there is a need for data management systems firstly to provide support for multiobjective query optimization [45], and secondly, to allow users to decide which are the preferred optimization criteria for a given task. In other words, apart from describing the task, users should also describe the aspects that they are more interested in (perhaps along with their weights), with a view to guiding the optimization process. The proposal of the ripple joins, which are initially proposed in [26] and enhanced later in [37], can be deemed as an early example of such an approach. This type of joins constitute a family of physical pipelining operators that maximize the flow of information during processing of statistical queries that involve aggregations and are capable of adapting their behavior during processing according to user preferences about the accuracy of the partial result and the time between updates of the running aggregate. More importantly, these preferences can be submitted and modified during execution. In [45], an efficient optimization algorithm is presented for the case where the system enables users to supply a function describing the desired trade-off between contradicting parameters. Similar functionality is of significant importance for modern query processing engines.

– *Massively parallel execution (and optimization):* Parallelism is now well understood in databases, both in terms of architectures, where the shared-nothing model seems to be the most attractive [51], and query processing; parallel query processing can be further divided in independent, pipeline and partitioned parallelism [13]. Although partitioned parallelism can lead to the most significant performance improvements, it is typically employed to a limited extent in wide area heterogeneous settings (e.g., [9,40,49]). Data analysis tasks may require exceptionally high degrees of parallelism [11,14,57] and next generation query processors should evolve to support this requirement, even in the case where the execution environment is remote, non-dedicated and potentially significantly different from fully controlled homogeneous clusters. In addition, since wide area optimization is computationally demanding, optimization may take place in a distributed and parallel manner, as well. Finally, massive parallelism should be applicable to both stream and stored data.

– *Autonomic execution:* This property is becoming increasingly important as tasks are becoming more complex and long running. Two aspects of autonomic computing [32] that are particularly relevant are self-optimization and self-healing. The former strongly relates to AQP, and the latter to fault-tolerance. Today, the vast majority of AQP techniques tackle the problem of unavailable, inaccurate and/or changing data statistics; however there is also a need to be capable of adapting to changing resource characteristics (e.g., [21]).

The characteristics above will render query processors more suitable for online, inbound [52], high performance data analysis in grid and cloud computing environments. In order to develop such a query engine, several features of existing research initiatives should be combined, and open research issues should be investigated, as outlined in the next section.

3   A Research Agenda

In order to efficiently and effectively support scenarios involving complex analysis of sheer data volumes in remote, non-dedicated environments with flexible optimization criteria, next generation query processors should be equipped with mechanisms to process tasks and optimization criteria submitted declaratively, benefit from massive parallelism and improve their autonomic behavior. Given that partial solutions to some of these requirements have been proposed, the development of the envisaged next generation query processors lies at the confluence of several paradigms and a question arises as to how these partial solutions can be combined and in which areas further research should be conducted. In this section, we deal with this problem focusing on three complementary aspects, namely the programming and execution model, the optimization process and the autonomic execution at runtime.

3.1   Unifying Programming and Execution Model

The combination of stream, parallel and distributed databases yields database systems that can scale to thousands of nodes and numerous data sources, may employ both push and pull execution model, and exhibit good performance for lookup tasks that require reading part of the data (due to the presence of indices); also parallel and distributed databases can effectively employ pipeline parallelism [25], incorporate sophisticated optimization techniques, modify the execution plan at runtime and, in principle, support multiple optimization criteria. Developing efficient integrated systems combining features from stream, parallel and distributed databases is a promising research direction, and may require radical changes in the way DBMSs are designed and implemented [52].

However, integrated systems based solely on database technologies suffer from inherent limitations. They lack efficient fault tolerance mechanisms; typically queries are re-executed in case of failure, which is not desirable in long running tasks. Also, several analysis tasks cannot be easily expressed as user-defined functions so that they can be called from within queries. On the other hand, execution paradigms based on, or inspired by, MapReduce offer built-in fault-tolerance capabilities, a user-convenient way to express complex analysis tasks, and good performance when these tasks involve the reading of complete sets of either structured or unstructured data, even in heterogeneous settings [58].

Non-surprisingly, the development of hybrid engines combining the strong points of both approaches has already been suggested [1]. According to [1], the integration should be at both the language level and the system and engine level. At the language level, efforts such as PigLatin [41], and DryadLINQ [57] can be deemed as an important initial step to this direction. However, developing a unifying execution model seems to be a more challenging research issue.

Current query processors receive as input a query in a high level language and transform it to a query execution plan, which, in most of the cases, is in the form of a directed acyclic graph (DAG), and more specifically, of a binary tree. In the case of SQL, for example, the tree nodes are query operators, such as joins, scans, projections and so on. Interestingly, workflows consisting of calls to web services, which is a common means of expressing data analysis tasks, are typically represented as DAGs, as well [50]. MapReduce jobs can also be regarded as simple single-input two stage workflows. Although in both databases, and workflow management and MapReduce-like paradigms the tasks can be expressed as DAGs, the vertex semantics and the execution logic in each case are different. So, it is unclear how integrated and unifying engines can be developed. In database query plans, the order of operators may change without affecting the quality of results with a view to improving the efficiency of the execution, and there exist well established rules to determine when such re-orderings should take place. This is not the case in generic workflows. Also, database technologies may adopt an adaptive execution model, like Eddies [4], which, in essence, corresponds to different DAGs for each data item; this feature, again, is not supported by today's workflow management systems and MapReduce implementations. Finally, stream query processing, apart from specific primitives [52], requires effective pipelining.

Perhaps, an intermediate goal is to develop integrated systems that can compile and execute database queries, workflows and MapReduce-like tasks in a common environment, without actually developing a unifying execution engine. Clustera [14] is an early example of such initiatives.

3.2 Optimization

Optimization of parallel data-intensive query plans involves several important open research issues. In general, query optimization problems in distributed settings are intractable, even in the case where partitioned parallelism and scheduling issues are ignored [56]. Frameworks such as [14,41,57] either do not perform any optimization or apply a limited set of greedy heuristics. The degree of parallelism in these settings is configured in an ad-hoc manner, which may deviate from (near) optimal solutions significantly. A promising research direction is to develop more sophisticated, cost based optimizers in this context both for the execution plan and the order of operations, and the number of machines.

However, even when only traditional database queries are considered, solutions should be developed for the multi-objective cases and for the resource allocation and scheduling problem. For the later, efficient solutions have been proposed only for homogeneous settings [18]. In heterogeneous settings, not only the degree of parallelism must be decided, but also the exact resources participating in the execution must be selected (e.g., [20]); the challenge here is that any solution should be as close to optimal as possible without being too complex with respect to the number of candidate nodes, as, in grid and cloud settings, this number may be too high. Borrowing solutions from generic workflow scheduling does not fully help; typically, in DAG scheduling, partitioned parallelism is not considered [35].

Nevertheless, there exist interesting proposals that do consider economic cost [7] and heterogeneity [47].

When high level optimization criteria apply, e.g., energy consumption and economic cost, there is a need to establish how these criteria impact on the execution and what is their exact correlation with the decisions taken during optimization; i.e., there needs to be a mapping between high level objectives and lower level metrics directly manipulated by the system. Furthermore, in the case of multi-objective optimization further research is required for establishing a standard efficient way to describe the trade-offs (e.g., [45]). The optimization process may also differ according to whether the objectives are specified as utility functions or not [33], and until now, the exact consequences of such a decision are not well understood.

To summarize, the envisaged query processors require optimizers that can handle arbitrary combinations of objectives and provide optimal or near optimal parallelized execution plans in reasonable time. Note that the whole optimization process may be interactive: the users may submit some criteria the exact configuration of which can be negotiated, in order to reach a Service Level Agreement (SLA). This mode of optimization has not been adequately explored in database query processors.

3.3   Runtime Execution

Operating on data that may have not been preprocessed in a non-dedicated environment consisting of numerous nodes calls for more advanced AQP techniques. We have already mentioned the need to further emphasize on changing resources in combination with volatile data characteristics; e.g., adapting the degree of parallelism in heterogeneous environments on the fly or investigating the interplay between resource allocation and load balancing [54] are issues that have been largely overlooked. In addition, more attention should be placed on the theoretical analysis of adaptive solutions and investigation of properties such as stability, accuracy, and settling time. To this end, AQP can benefit from control theory techniques, which are well-established in engineering fields and are typically accompanied by theoretical investigations of such properties [29]. Interesting examples of applications of control theory to data management systems have been proposed in [15,16,22,23,24]. Another open research area is the development of AQP techniques in which actions are driven by utility functions (e.g., [46]).

Efficient fault tolerance is equally important to runtime re-optimization. Fault tolerance features are built-in in platforms such as MapReduce; also some proposals exist also in the database field, mainly for continuous queries and data streams (e.g., [5,48]). However, all these solutions are based on different protocols and concepts, so there is a need to reach a consensus as to which approach is more appropriate in each case.

Finally, data analysis and data driven research may be processed in a way that early results are delivered as soon as possible, in case users choose to cancel their queries if, for example, realize that the results are not interesting or the task has not been specified appropriately. Pipelining execution addresses to an adequate extent this need. Pipelining may be employed by database engines in a straightforward manner, but this may not be the case for other computing paradigms, such as MapReduce.

4 Conclusions

This work aims at specifying the requirements of modern applications and presenting a vision for next generation query processors, so that they are more tailored to data analysis and data driven research, benefit from declarative task and objective statement and are capable of being highly parallelized while exhibiting advanced autonomic behavior to cope with the volatility of the environment. In addition, this work discusses important areas in which further research is required in order to fulfill the vision. These areas include the development of integrated execution engines, advanced wide-area optimization and autonomic runtime execution.

Acknowledgements. The author would like to thank his colleagues Apostolos Papadopoulos and Constantinos Tsichlas for their insightful comments and help during the preparation of this work.

References

1. Abadi, D.J.: Data management in the cloud: Limitations and opportunities. IEEE Data Eng. Bull. 32(1), 3–12 (2009)
2. Agrawal, R., Ailamaki, A., Bernstein, P.A., Brewer, E.A., Carey, M.J., Chaudhuri, S., Doan, A., Florescu, D., Franklin, M.J., Garcia-Molina, H., Gehrke, J., Gruenwald, L., Haas, L.M., Halevy, A.Y., Hellerstein, J.M., Ioannidis, Y.E., Korth, H.F., Kossmann, D., Madden, S., Magoulas, R., Ooi, B.C., O'Reilly, T., Ramakrishnan, R., Sarawagi, S., Stonebraker, M., Szalay, A.S., Weikum, G.: The claremont report on database research. SIGMOD Record 37(3), 9–19 (2008)
3. Alpdemir, M.N., Mukherjee, A., Paton, N.W., Watson, P., Fernandes, A.A.A., Gounaris, A., Smith, J.: Service-based distributed querying on the grid. In: Orlowska, M.E., Weerawarana, S., Papazoglou, M.P., Yang, J. (eds.) ICSOC 2003. LNCS, vol. 2910, pp. 467–482. Springer, Heidelberg (2003)
4. Avnur, R., Hellerstein, J.M.: Eddies: Continuously adaptive query processing. In: Proceedings of the ACM SIGMOD International Conference on Management of Data, pp. 261–272. ACM, New York (2000)
5. Balazinska, M., Balakrishnan, H., Madden, S., Stonebraker, M.: Fault-tolerance in the borealis distributed stream processing system. ACM Trans. Database Syst. 33(1) (2008)
6. Bernstein, P.A., Goodman, N., Wong, E., Reeve, C.L., Rothnie Jr., J.B.: Query processing in a system for distributed databases (sdd-1). ACM Trans. Database Syst. 6(4), 602–625 (1981)
7. Buyya, R., Abramson, D., Giddy, J., Stockinger, H.: Economic models for resource management and scheduling in grid computing. Concurrency and Computation: Practice and Experience 14(13-15), 1507–1542 (2002)

8. Chaudhuri, S.: An overview of query optimization in relational systems. In: Proceedings of the Seventeenth ACM SIGACT-SIGMOD-SIGART Symposium on Principles of Database Systems, pp. 34–43. ACM Press, New York (1998)
9. Cherniack, M., Balakrishnan, H., Balazinska, M., Carney, D., Çetintemel, U., Xing, Y., Zdonik, S.B.: Scalable distributed stream processing. In: CIDR (2003)
10. Dean, J., Ghemawat, S.: Mapreduce: Simplified data processing on large clusters. In: OSDI, pp. 137–150 (2004)
11. Dean, J., Ghemawat, S.: Mapreduce: simplified data processing on large clusters. Commun. ACM 51(1), 107–113 (2008)
12. Deshpande, A., Ives, Z.G., Raman, V.: Adaptive query processing. Foundations and Trends in Databases 1(1), 1–140 (2007)
13. DeWitt, D.J., Gray, J.: Parallel database systems: The future of high performance database systems. Commun. ACM 35(6), 85–98 (1992)
14. DeWitt, D.J., Paulson, E., Robinson, E., Naughton, J.F., Royalty, J., Shankar, S., Krioukov, A.: Clustera: an integrated computation and data management system. PVLDB 1(1), 28–41 (2008)
15. Diao, Y., Hellerstein, J.L., Storm, A.J., Surendra, M., Lightstone, S., Parekh, S.S., Garcia-Arellano, C.: Incorporating cost of control into the design of a load balancing controller. In: IEEE Real-Time and Embedded Technology and Applications Symposium, pp. 376–387 (2004)
16. Diao, Y., Wu, C.W., Hellerstein, J.L., Storm, A.J., Surendra, M., Lightstone, S., Parekh, S., Garcia-Arellano, C., Carroll, M., Chu, L., Colaco, J.: Comparative studies of load balancing with control and optimization techniques. In: Proceedings of the American Control Conference, pp. 1484–1490 (2005)
17. Epstein, R.S., Stonebraker, M., Wong, E.: Distributed query processing in a relational data base system. In: Lowenthal, E.I., Dale, N.B. (eds.) Proceedings of the ACM SIGMOD International Conference on Management of Data, pp. 169–180. ACM, New York (1978)
18. Garofalakis, M.N., Ioannidis, Y.E.: Parallel query scheduling and optimization with time- and space-shared resources. In: VLDB, pp. 296–305 (1997)
19. Golab, L., Özsu, M.T.: Issues in data stream management. SIGMOD Record 32(2), 5–14 (2003)
20. Gounaris, A., Sakellariou, R., Paton, N.W., Fernandes, A.A.A.: A novel approach to resource scheduling for parallel query processing on computational grids. Distributed and Parallel Databases 19(2-3), 87–106 (2006)
21. Gounaris, A., Smith, J., Paton, N.W., Sakellariou, R., Fernandes, A.A., Watson, P.: Adaptive workload allocation in query processing in autonomous heterogeneous environments. Distrib. Parallel Databases 25(3), 125–164 (2009)
22. Gounaris, A., Yfoulis, C., Sakellariou, R., Dikaiakos, M.D.: A control theoretical approach to self-optimizing block transfer in web service grids. TAAS 3(2) (2008)
23. Gounaris, A., Yfoulis, C., Sakellariou, R., Dikaiakos, M.D.: Robust runtime optimization of data transfer in queries over web services. In: Proc. of ICDE, pp. 596–605 (2008)
24. Gounaris, A., Yfoulis, C.A., Paton, N.W.: An efficient load balancing LQR controller in parallel databases queries under random perturbations. In: 3rd IEEE Multi-conference on Systems and Control, MSC 2009 (2009)
25. Graefe, G.: Query evaluation techniques for large databases. ACM Comput. Surv. 25(2), 73–170 (1993)
26. Haas, P.J., Hellerstein, J.M.: Ripple joins for online aggregation. In: SIGMOD 1999, Proceedings ACM SIGMOD International Conference on Management of Data, pp. 287–298 (1999)

27. Hameurlain, A., Morvan, F., El Samad, M.: Large Scale Data management in Grid Systems: a Survey. In: IEEE International Conference on Information and Communication Technologies: from Theory to Applications, ICTTA (2008)

28. Harizopoulos, S., Shah, M., Ranganathan, P.: Energy efficiency: The new holy grail of data management systems research. In: CIDR (2009)

29. Hellerstein, J.L., Diao, Y., Parekh, S., Tilbury, D.M.: Feedback Control of Computing Systems. John Wiley & Sons, Chichester (2004)

30. Ioannidis, Y.E.: Query optimization. ACM Comput. Surv. 28(1), 121–123 (1996)

31. Ives, Z.G., Florescu, D., Friedman, M., Levy, A.Y., Weld, D.S.: An adaptive query execution system for data integration. In: SIGMOD 1999, Proceedings ACM SIGMOD International Conference on Management of Data, Philadelphia, Pennsylvania, USA, June 1-3, pp. 299–310. ACM Press, New York (1999)

32. Kephart, J.O., Chess, D.M.: The vision of autonomic computing. IEEE Computer 36(1), 41–50 (2003)

33. Kephart, J.O., Das, R.: Achieving self-management via utility functions. IEEE Internet Computing 11(1), 40–48 (2007)

34. Kossmann, D.: The state of the art in distributed query processing. ACM Comput. Surv. 32(4), 422–469 (2000)

35. Kwok, Y.-K., Ahmad, I.: Static scheduling algorithms for allocating directed task graphs to multiprocessors. ACM Comput. Surv. 31(4), 406–471 (1999)

36. Lang, W., Patel, J.M.: Towards eco-friendly database management systems. In: CIDR (2009)

37. Luo, G., Ellmann, C., Haas, P.J., Naughton, J.F.: A scalable hash ripple join algorithm. In: Proceedings of the 2002 ACM SIGMOD International Conference on Management of Data, pp. 252–262. ACM, New York (2002)

38. Lynden, S., Mukherjee, A., Hume, A.C., Fernandes, A.A.A., Paton, N.W., Sakellariou, R., Watson, P.: The design and implementation of ogsa-dqp: A service-based distributed query processor. Future Generation Comp. Syst. 25(3), 224–236 (2009)

39. Mackert, L.F., Lohman, G.M.: R* optimizer validation and performance evaluation for distributed queries. In: VLDB 1986 Twelfth International Conference on Very Large Data Bases, pp. 149–159. Morgan Kaufmann, San Francisco (1986)

40. Ng, K.W., Wang, Z., Muntz, R.R., Nittel, S.: Dynamic query re-optimization. In: SSDBM, pp. 264–273 (1999)

41. Olston, C., Reed, B., Srivastava, U., Kumar, R., Tomkins, A.: Pig latin: a not-so-foreign language for data processing. In: SIGMOD Conference, pp. 1099–1110 (2008)

42. Ouzzani, M., Bouguettaya, A.: Query processing and optimization on the web. Distributed and Parallel Databases 15(3), 187–218 (2004)

43. Ozsu, M., Valduriez, P.: Principles of Distributed Database Systems, 2nd edn. Prentice-Hall, Englewood Cliffs (1999)

44. Pacitti, E., Valduriez, P., Mattoso, M.: Grid data management: Open problems and new issues. J. Grid Comput. 5(3), 273–281 (2007)

45. Papadimitriou, C.H., Yannakakis, M.: Multiobjective query optimization. In: Proceedings of the Twentieth ACM SIGACT-SIGMOD-SIGART Symposium on Principles of Database Systems. ACM, New York (2001)

46. Paton, N.W., Aragão, M.A.T., Lee, K., Fernandes, A.A.A., Sakellariou, R.: Optimizing utility in cloud computing through autonomic workload execution. IEEE Data Eng. Bull. 32(1), 51–58 (2009)

47. Sakellariou, R., Zhao, H.: A hybrid heuristic for DAG scheduling on heterogeneous systems. In: 18th International Parallel and Distributed Processing Symposium (IPDPS 2004). IEEE Computer Society, Los Alamitos (2004)

48. Shah, M.A., Hellerstein, J.M., Brewer, E.A.: Highly-available, fault-tolerant, parallel dataflows. In: Proceedings of the ACM SIGMOD International Conference on Management of Data, pp. 827–838. ACM, New York (2004)
49. Smith, J., Gounaris, A., Watson, P., Paton, N.W., Fernandes, A.A.A., Sakellariou, R.: Distributed query processing on the grid. International Journal of High Performance Computing Applications 17(4), 353–367 (2003)
50. Srivastava, U., Munagala, K., Widom, J., Motwani, R.: Query optimization over web services. In: VLDB, pp. 355–366 (2006)
51. Stonebraker, M.: The case for shared nothing. IEEE Data Engineering Bulletin 9(1), 4–9 (1986)
52. Stonebraker, M.: Technical perspective - one size fits all: an idea whose time has come and gone. Commun. ACM 51(12), 76 (2008)
53. Stonebraker, M., Aoki, P.M., Litwin, W., Pfeffer, A., Sah, A., Sidell, J., Staelin, C., Yu, A.: Mariposa: A wide-area distributed database system. VLDB J. 5(1), 48–63 (1996)
54. Tian, F., DeWitt, D.J.: Tuple routing strategies for distributed eddies. In: VLDB, pp. 333–344 (2003)
55. Venugopal, S., Buyya, R., Ramamohanarao, K.: A taxonomy of data grids for distributed data sharing, management, and processing. ACM Comput. Surv. 38(1) (2006)
56. Wang, C., Chen, M.-S.: On the complexity of distributed query optimization. IEEE Trans. Knowl. Data Eng. 8(4), 650–662 (1996)
57. Yu, Y., Isard, M., Fetterly, D., Budiu, M., Erlingsson, Ú., Gunda, P.K., Currey, J.: Dryadlinq: A system for general-purpose distributed data-parallel computing using a high-level language. In: OSDI, pp. 1–14 (2008)
58. Zaharia, M., Konwinski, A., Joseph, A.D., Katz, R.H., Stoica, I.: Improving mapreduce performance in heterogeneous environments. In: OSDI, pp. 29–42 (2008)

AGiDS: A Grid-Based Strategy for Distributed Skyline Query Processing

João B. Rocha-Junior*, Akrivi Vlachou**, Christos Doulkeridis**,
and Kjetil Nørvåg

Norwegian University of Science and Technology
{joao,vlachou,cdoulk,noervaag}@idi.ntnu.no

Abstract. Skyline queries help users make intelligent decisions over complex data, where different and often conflicting criteria are considered. A challenging problem is to support skyline queries in distributed environments, where data is scattered over independent sources. The query response time of skyline processing over distributed data depends on the amount of transferred data and the query processing cost at each server. In this paper, we propose AGiDS, a framework for efficient skyline processing over distributed data. Our approach reduces significantly the amount of transferred data, by using a grid-based data summary that captures the data distribution on each server. AGiDS consists of two phases to compute the result: in the first phase the querying server gathers the grid-based summary, whereas in the second phase a skyline request is sent only to the servers that may contribute to the skyline result set asking only for the points of non-dominated regions. We provide an experimental evaluation showing that our approach performs efficiently and outperforms existing techniques.

1 Introduction

Skyline queries [1] have attracted much attention recently, mainly because they help users to make intelligent decisions over data that represent many conflicting criteria. The skyline of a given set of d-dimensional points S is the set of points which are not dominated by any other point of S. A point p is dominated by another point q if and only if q is not worse than p in any dimension and q is better than p in at least one dimension.

During the last decades, the vast number of independent data sources and the high rate of data generation make central assembly of data at one location infeasible. As a consequence, data management and storage become increasingly distributed. Skyline query processing in a distributed and decentralized environment has received considerable attention recently [2,3,4,5,6,7,8,9,10,11,12]. Distributed information systems are applications that can benefit from this query

---

* Ph.D. student at NTNU, on leave from Universidade Estadual de Feira de Santana.
** This work was carried out during the tenure of an ERCIM "Alain Bensoussan" Fellowship Programme.

A. Hameurlain and A M. Tjoa (Eds.): Globe 2009, LNCS 5697, pp. 12–23, 2009.

type. Consider a hotel reservation system, consisting of a large set of independent servers geographically dispersed around the world, each of them storing its own data about hotels. Such a system could potentially provide booking services over the universal hotel database, by allowing users to find suitable hotels based on skyline queries.

In this paper, we propose a novel way to process skyline queries efficiently in a distributed environment. We make no assumption on the existence of an overlay network that connects servers in an intentional manner, thus a querying server directly communicates with other servers. We assume horizontal partitioning of data to servers. Furthermore, each server stores a lightweight data structure, which enables obtaining summary information about the data stored at each server. Each participant is responsible to maintain its own data structure with information about its local data. Based on this information, we are able to process skyline queries only at the servers and regions in the d-dimensional data space, which have data points belonging to the skyline result set. By means of an experimental evaluation, we show that our solution reduces both response time through higher parallelism and the amount of data transferred.

This paper makes the following contributions: First, we present an overview of the current research on distributed skyline query processing. Then, we propose a new strategy to compute skyline queries efficiently in a distributed environment, where data is horizontally distributed to servers and no overlay network exists. Further, we propose the use of a data structure to maintain summary information about the data stored at each server. Finally, we perform an experimental evaluation in order to demonstrate the effectiveness of our approach. The paper is organized as follows: Section 2 presents an overview of the related work. In Section 3, we provide the necessary preliminaries and definitions. In Section 4, we describe our approach for distributed skyline computation. The experimental evaluation is presented in Section 5 and we conclude in Section 6.

2   Related Work

Skyline computation has recently attracted considerable attention both in centralized [1] and distributed domains [2,3,4,5,6,7,8,9,10,11,12]. One of the first algorithms in the distributed domain, by Balke *et al.* [2], focuses on skyline query processing over multiple distributed sources, with each source storing only a subset of attributes (vertical data distribution). Later, most of the related work has focused on highly distributed and P2P environments, assuming all sources store common attributes (horizontal data distribution). In the following, we provide a brief survey of existing P2P skyline processing algorithms. A comparative overview of distributed skyline literature is presented in Table 1.

Approaches that assume horizontal data distribution can be classified in two main categories. In the first category, the proposed methods assume space partitioning among peers, thus each peer is responsible for a disjoint partition of the data space. Towards this goal, a structured P2P or tree-based network overlay is employed. The system controls the location of each data point and splits the

Table 1. Summary of approaches for P2P skyline processing

Papers	P2P overlay	Skyline query type	Partitioning
MANETs [4]	no overlay	global	data
QTree [7]	unstructured	approximate	data
DSL [5]	DHT (CAN)	constrained	space
SKYPEER [3]	super-peer	subspace	data
BITPEER [8]	super-peer	subspace	data
PaDSkyline [6]	no overlay	constrained	data
iSky [9]	BATON	global	space
SkyFrame [10,11]	CAN and BATON	global, approximate	space
FDS [12]	no overlay	global	data

data in a way that the system can visit first the peers with higher probability of having skyline points. DSL was proposed by Wu *et al.* [5] and it is the first paper that addresses constrained skyline query processing over disjoint data partitions, which are assigned to peers using CAN. Wang *et al.*[10] propose the SSP algorithm based on the use of a tree-based overlay (BATON) for assigning data to peers. They use a one-dimensional mapping of data based on z-order and then data is assigned to peers. Later, the authors present SkyFrame [11] as an extension of their work. SkyFrame is a framework that comprises two methods: GSS (Greedy Skyline Search) and RSS (Relaxed Skyline Search). GSS and RSS can run on top of either CAN or BATON. GSS achieves low bandwidth consumption, whereas RSS reduces the overall response time. Chen *et al.* [9] propose the iSky algorithm, which employs another transformation, namely iMinMax, in order to assign data to BATON peers.

In the second category, data partitioning is assumed and each peer autonomously stores its own data. Huang *et al.* [4] study skyline query processing over mobile ad-hoc networks. The aim is to reduce communication costs as well as processing costs on the individual device. In SKYPEER [3], each super-peer computes and stores the extended skyline of its associated peers. Then, when a super-peer processes a skyline query, the query is forwarded to neighboring super-peers, processed locally using the extended skyline set, followed by in-network merging of results. Fotiadou *et al.* [8] propose BITPEER that uses a bitmap representation, in order to improve the performance of query processing. Hose *et al.* [7] use distributed data summaries (QTree) about the data stored by the peers. During skyline query processing, the QTree is used as routing mechanism to determine the peers, which need to be processed, in order find the skyline points. The approach supports approximate result sets for reducing the processing cost and provides guarantees for the completeness of the result.

Cui *et al.* [6] study skyline query processing in a distributed environment, without the assumption of an existing overlay network, where a coordinator can directly communicate with all peers (servers). They propose the use of MBRs (Minimum Bounding Regions) to summarize the data stored at each server. The proposed PaDSkyline algorithm works in two steps. In the first step, the MBRs of all servers are collected and assigned to incomparable groups, which can be queried in parallel, while specific plans are used within each group. Subsequently, servers are queried and the results are returned back to the coordinator. Recently, in [12], a feedback-based distributed skyline (FDS) algorithm is proposed, which also assumes no particular overlay network. The algorithm is efficient in terms of bandwidth consumption, however it requires several round-trips to compute the skyline, thus it may incur high response time.

Our framework, similar to the ones presented in [6,12], assumes no particular network topology. In contrast to [12], our approach requires only two round trips, thus avoiding high latency caused by multiple round trips. Differently than [6], we use grid-based summary information instead of MBRs. Therefore, the data space is split into non-overlapping regions, which makes easier to identify and discard dominated regions across different servers, whereas MBRs may have high overlap and cannot be discarded.

3   Preliminaries

Given a data space D defined by a set of d dimensions $\{d_1, ..., d_d\}$ and a dataset P on D with cardinality $|P|$, a point $p \in P$ can be represented as $p = \{p_1, ..., p_d\}$ where p_i is a value on dimension d_i. Without loss of generality, let us assume that the value p_i in any dimension d_i is greater or equal to zero ($p_i \geq 0$) and that for all dimensions the minimum values are more preferable. Figure 1 offers an overview of the symbols that are used throughout this paper.

Definition. *Skyline Query (SQ).* A point $p \in P$ is said to *dominate* another point $q \in P$, denoted as $p \prec q$, if (1) on every dimension $d_i \in D$, $p_i \leq q_i$; and (2) on at least one dimension $d_j \in D$, $p_j < q_j$. The *skyline* is a set of points $SKY_P \subseteq P$ which are not dominated by any other point in P. The points in SKY_P are called skyline points.

Consider a database containing information about hotels where each tuple of the database is represented as a point in a data space consisting of different characteristics of the hotel. In our example, the y-dimension represents the price of a room, whereas the x-dimension captures the distance of the hotel to a point of interest such as the beach (Figure 2). According to the dominance definition, a hotel dominates another hotel because it is cheaper and closer to the beach. Thus, the skyline points are the best possible tradeoffs between price and distance. In our example, the hotels that belong to the skyline are a, i, m and k.

In this work, we assume a set of N servers S_i participating in the distributed skyline computation. Each server S_i stores a set of points P_i that is a fraction of the dataset P such that $P_i \subseteq P$ and $\bigcup_{1 \leq i \leq N} P_i = P$. The data partitions are not necessarily disjoint and they may overlap. We also assume that each server S_i can directly connect to any other server S_j. Thus, we do not make an explicit assumption about the availability of an overlay network that assigns regions of the data space to specific peers intentionally. Moreover, each server S_i is able to compute the local skyline set SKY_{P_i} (mentioned also as local skyline points)

Symbol	Description
d	Dimensions
P	Dataset
$|P|$	Cardinality of the dataset
p, q	Data points
S_i	Server i
N	Number of servers
P_i	Dataset of server S_i
SKY_P	Skyline points of dataset P

Fig. 1. Overview of symbols

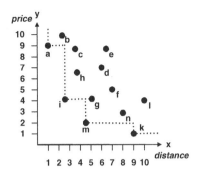

Fig. 2. Skyline example

based on the locally stored points P_i. Similarly, we refer to the skyline set SKY_P of the dataset P as global skyline set.

Observation. A point $p \in P$ is a skyline point $p \in SKY_P$ if and only if $p \in SKY_{P_i} \subseteq P$ and p is not dominated by any other point $q \in SKY_{P_j}, j \neq i$.

In other words, the skyline points over a horizontally partitioned dataset are a subset of the union of the skyline points of all partitions. Therefore, aggregating and merging the local skyline points produces the skyline result set SKY_P. In the following, we propose an algorithm that computes the exact skyline result set SKY_P by transferring only a subset of the local skyline points.

4   AGiDS Algorithm

In a distributed environment, a skyline query can be initiated by any server, henceforth also called query originator (S_{org}). The naive approach to process a skyline query is to send the query to all the servers S_i, which in turn process the skyline locally, and report the local skyline result to S_{org}. Then, S_{org} merges all received results to obtain the global skyline set. This approach requires transferring an excessive amount of data and processing the complete skyline query at each server. Instead, we present an algorithm (AGiDS) that improves the overall performance, aiming at reducing both processing and communication cost.

AGiDS is divided in two phases: planning and execution. To this end, we propose the usage of a grid-based data structure that captures the data distribution of each server (Section 4.1). During the planning phase (Section 4.2), S_{org} contacts all servers S_i and obtains information about which regions contain data that belong to the local skyline result set. The assembled regions enable two improvements during the subsequent execution phase (Section 4.3): S_{org} queries only the servers that contain at least one non-dominated region, and more importantly S_{org} requests only a subset of local skyline points, namely the local skyline points that

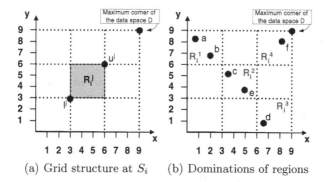

(a) Grid structure at S_i (b) Dominations of regions

Fig. 3. Information at P_{org} after receiving the important regions from all the servers

belong to non-dominated regions. After gathering the relevant points, S_{org} computes the skyline result set by merging only the necessary regions.

4.1 Grid-Based Data Summary

AGiDS employs a grid-based data summary for describing the data available at each server. We assume that all servers share a common grid and the partitions cover the entire universe D. Optimizing the grid is out of the scope of this paper and in the following we assume that the partitions are created by splitting each dimension d_i in a predefined number of slices. Therefore, each partition has the form of a d-dimensional hypercube. In the following, we refer to a partition of the server S_i as the j-th data region R_i^j of server S_i. Obviously, the regions of a server S_i are non-overlapping d-dimensional data regions R_i^j. A region R_i^j is defined by two points l^j and u^j indicating the lower left and upper right corner of the region respectively.

Consider for example Figure 3(a), that depicts the data structure maintained by each server S_i and a data region R_i^j. We define a region of R_i^j of server S_i as *populated*, if there exists at least one point $p \in P_i$ enclosed in region R_i^j, i.e. for each dimension $d_i \in D$, $l_i^j \leq p_i < u_i^j$. For instance, in Figure 3(b), the populated regions are R_i^1, R_i^2, R_i^3 and R_i^4. Furthermore, given two populated regions of R_i^j and R_i^k, we define the following dominance relationships. Notice that all the examples used in the definitions below can be found at Figure 3(b).

Definition. R_i^j *dominates* R_i^k, if the right upper corner u^j of R_i^j dominates the left lower l^k corner of R_i^k. For example, R_i^2 dominates R_i^4, which means that any point of R_i^2 dominates all the points of R_i^4. Notice that point f is dominated by both points c and e of region R_i^2.

Definition. R_i^j *partially dominates* R_i^k, if R_i^j does not dominate R_i^k, but the left lower corner l^j of R_i^j dominates the right upper corner u^k of R_i^k. For example, R_i^1 partially dominates R_i^4. Therefore, some points of R_i^1 may dominate some or all points of R_i^4. In our example point b dominates point f, but a does not dominate f.

Definition. R_i^j and R_i^k are *incomparable*, if there is no point in R_i^j able to dominate any point in R_i^k and vice versa, e.g. R_i^1 and R_i^2. This means that R_i^j does not dominate nor partially dominate R_i^k, and also R_i^k does not dominate nor partially dominate R_i^j.

Finally, we define as *region-skyline* of a server S_i the skyline of the populated regions of S_i, based on the aforementioned definition of region dominance. Thus, the region-skyline contains all regions that are not dominated by another region. Moreover, it can be easily computed in a way similar to the traditional skyline query on the data points. In Figure 3(b), for example, the regions R_i^1, R_i^2 and R_i^3 define the region-skyline of peer S_i in the data space D.

   Using the grid-based data summary common for all servers enables determining regions that are dominated by other servers in an efficient way. Also, the grid regions are easily and uniquely identified with a small cost. Furthermore, local skyline points can be easily merged based on the region that they belong. Having a common grid makes the regions directly comparable, which means that each server can uniquely identify a region in the entire universe D. Moreover, a compact representation of regions is feasible, usually just a small number of bits, which avoids the use of two d-dimensional points. Thus, each server S_i just needs to send an identifier of the populated regions R_i^j.

4.2   Phase 1: Planning

The planning phase starts with S_{org} requesting the region-skyline of each server S_i in parallel. We assume that S_i has a grid-based data structure, which is used to answer queries of S_{org}. The message sent by S_i back to S_{org} returns the region-skyline of S_i. In Figure 4, for example, B is the single region sent to S_{org} by S_2, because all other populated regions in S_2 are dominated by region B and are not part of the region-skyline of S_2.

   After receiving the region-skyline from all the servers, S_{org} computes the global region-skyline. The global region-skyline is the skyline of the populated regions of all servers contacted by S_{org}. The objective of computing the global region-skyline is eliminating all the regions of a server, which are dominated by other regions of another server. For example, in Figure 4, region H is dominated by region A and does not belong to the global region-skyline. Computing the global region-skyline is much cheaper than computing the entire skyline over data points, because the number of populated regions is much smaller than the number of points. After computing the global region-skyline, S_{org} has information about all the regions in the entire data space D, which have points that may be part of the global skyline. In the current example, S_{org} computes as global region-skyline the regions A, B and F.

4.3   Phase 2: Execution

The execution phase starts after S_{org} has computed the global region-skyline. Then, S_{org} can determine the servers that may contribute to the global skyline result set. Furthermore, S_{org} knows which regions of each server S_i are necessary

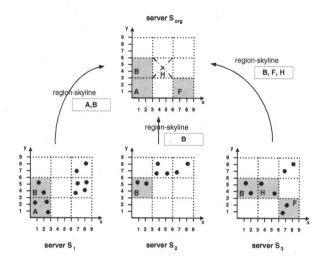

Fig. 4. Planning phase of AGiDS

for the skyline computation. Therefore, before sending a skyline query to a server S_i, S_{org} attaches the identifiers of the regions that need to be examined for the query. For example, in order to process the skyline query at the server S_3, only the skyline points at the regions B and F are requested, since region H was eliminated in the previous phase. Thus, a server S_i receives a message requesting the skyline of the regions that are relevant for the global skyline. S_i processes the skyline of the regions requested, discarding points dominated by points of other requested regions. Then, S_i reports its result to S_{org}, which comprises the local skyline points of the requested regions, after discarding the dominated points.

The local skyline points returned to the S_{org} are grouped based on the region they are enclosed in. S_{org} receives the points of each server S_i and merges them into the global skyline. Merging of the local skyline points is performed efficiently based on the information of the regions. Only the points enclosed into regions which are partially dominated have to be merged. Therefore, S_{org} is able to return immediately to the user the points enclosed in a region R_i, if there is no other server which has a region R_j that partially dominates R_i. Thus, the skyline points are reported progressively by S_{org} to the user.

5   Experimental Evaluation

In this section, we study the performance of our distributed processing strategy in a simulated environment. For this purpose, we compare our approach against the PaDSkyline algorithm proposed by Cui *et al.* [6]. Both approaches were implemented in Java, while the network aspects were simulated using DesmoJ[1], an event-based simulator framework. We consider two main performance aspects:

---

[1] http://desmoj.sourceforge.net/home.html

(1) the response time and (2) the total amount of data transferred. The experiments were conducted in a 3GHz Dual Core AMD processor equipped with 2GB RAM.

We compare our approach against PaDSkyline, because both approaches assume no overlay network and S_{org} can directly communicate with all servers. Furthermore, both approaches have a first phase in which some summary information about all the servers is collected. This information is used to define the strategy adopted on the second phase, where the skyline points are collected. In the following, we explain the implementation of PadSkyline in more detail.

After collecting the MBRs of all the servers, PaDSkyline identifies incomparable groups of MBRs (and servers) and processes each group of servers in parallel. Within each group, servers are organized in a sequence for processing the query, thus a way to order the servers is necessary. The servers with MBRs closer to the minimum corner of the universe are accessed first. At each server, the local skyline is computed, using filter points received from the previous server. The filter points are selected based on maximizing the dominated volume (maxSum heuristic in [6]) and they are used to reduce the amount of data transferred.

Then, the local sever computes the new filter points, which are a percentage of the points of the local skyline. We use the default value of 10%. The servers in the group that are dominated by the new filter points are discarded. After that, the query is forwarded to the next server with the new filter points attached. The process within each group finishes when the group becomes empty. This is the *linear approach* for intra-group processing, as described in [6].

5.1   Experimental Settings

In the experiments, we have used three types of synthetic datasets: uniform, correlated, and anti-correlated. The settings used in the simulator are listed in the Table 2. Unless mentioned explicitly, we have used as default setup a 3-d dataset, distributed to 50 servers with each server storing 25K points.

The network communication was simulated based on events; therefore, the time required to transfer data is computed by dividing the size of the data transferred with the network speed. Filter points are used only in the simulation of PaDSkyline, thus the percentage of filter points applies only for PaDSkyline.

Table 2. Settings used in the experiments

Parameter	Values
Dimensions	2, **3**, 4, 5
Number of servers	**50**, 100, 150, 200, 250
Cardinality of each server	10K, **25K**, 50K, 75K, 100K
Network speed	0.2 Mbit/s
Filter points percentage	10%
Maximum number of regions	1024

Similarly, the maximum number of regions R_{max} is used only in the simulation of AGiDS. This number is used to compute the number of slices s of each dimension of the grid, as: $s=R_{max}^{1/d}$, where d is number of dimensions.

5.2   Experimental Results

The response time achieved with AGiDS is better than the response time obtained with PaDSkyline in all evaluated setups, as shown in Figure 5. Figures 5(a), 5(b), and 5(c) provide comparative results for uniform, anti-correlated and correlated datasets respectively. We study the scalability of the algorithms with increasing dimensionality d. In all cases, the response time increases more rapidly in PaDSkyline than in AGiDS. In particular, notice the excessive response time required by PaDSkyline for the anti-correlated dataset.

The main reason for the better response time achieved by AGiDS is the higher parallelism during the second phase. After collecting the region-skyline, AGiDS processes in parallel the skyline points at regions of each server which can contribute to the global skyline. In contrast, the linear approach of PaDSkyline achieves parallelism in the second phase only between incomparable groups. During the intra-group processing, PaDSkyline uses sequential execution on servers, thereby spending much time to produce the global skyline result. Another reason for achieving better response time with AGiDS is the reduced processing time at each server. While PaDSkyline computes the entire skyline, AGiDS computes only the skyline at the regions requested by S_{org}, which are the only regions that can contribute to the global skyline.

Figure 6 depicts the total amount of transferred data for the two algorithms, for different data distributions. This amount corresponds to the number of bytes transferred during query processing for all required communications. Only in the case of uniform data (Figure 6(a)) PaDSkyline transfers less data than AGiDS. Both in the anti-correlated (Figure 6(b)) and correlated (Figure 6(c)) data distributions, AGiDS performs better. PaDSkyline transfers less data in the case of uniform data distribution, because the MBRs of the servers are completely overlapping, and one filter point located near the minimum corner can prune several servers within a group. However, notice that despite the higher amount of transferred data in the case of the uniform dataset, AGiDS achieves much better response time. In any case, for anti-correlated and correlated datasets, AGiDS is better in both measures.

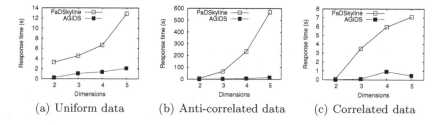

(a) Uniform data   (b) Anti-correlated data   (c) Correlated data

Fig. 5. Evaluation of response time for various data distributions

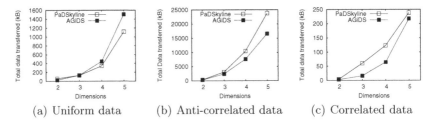

(a) Uniform data   (b) Anti-correlated data   (c) Correlated data

Fig. 6. Evaluation of the total data transferred for various data distributions

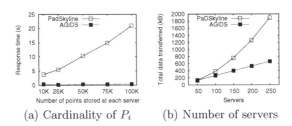

(a) Cardinality of P_i (b) Number of servers

Fig. 7. Scalability study of AGiDS

Then, in Figure 7(a), we test the effect of increasing the cardinality of the data stored at each server from 10K to 100K points, following a uniform data distribution. We observe that the response time of AGiDS is not affected by the increasing number of points stored at each server. The main reason is that the number of regions in the region-skyline is the same, irrespective of the number of points stored. Therefore, the performance of the planning phase is not affected. Only the number of local skyline points transferred at the second phase changes slightly, but this does not have a significant impact on the response time. However, notice that the response time of PaDSkyline increases significantly with the number of points stored at each server.

Finally, in Figure 7(b), we conduct a scalability study with the number of participating servers. In this setup, AGiDS benefits from the fact that it requires only two steps to finalize the query processing, while PadSkyline may have to access many servers within a group sequentially. Therefore, the amount of data transferred by PaDSkyline grows much faster than with AGiDS.

6   Conclusions

Distributed skyline query processing poses inherent challenges, due to the distribution of content and the lack of global knowledge. In this paper, we presented AGiDS, a skyline query processing algorithm for distributed environments. AGiDS processes skyline queries efficiently by applying a two phase approach. In the first phase, it uses a grid-based data summary on each server, in order to discard regions that cannot contribute to the skyline result. In the second phase, local skyline points that belong to non-dominated regions are selectively collected, in order to produce the global skyline. By means of an experimental evaluation, we have demonstrated the superiority of AGiDS compared to an existing approach that is appropriate for our context.

References

1. Börzsönyi, S., Kossmann, D., Stocker, K.: The skyline operator. In: Int. Conf. on Data Engineering (ICDE), pp. 421–430 (2001)
2. Balke, W.T., Güntzer, U., Zheng, J.X.: Efficient distributed skylining for web information systems. In: Bertino, E., Christodoulakis, S., Plexousakis, D., Christophides, V., Koubarakis, M., Böhm, K., Ferrari, E. (eds.) EDBT 2004. LNCS, vol. 2992, pp. 256–273. Springer, Heidelberg (2004)
3. Vlachou, A., Doulkeridis, C., Kotidis, Y., Vazirgiannis, M.: SKYPEER: Efficient subspace skyline computation over distributed data. In: Int. Conf. on Data Engineering (ICDE), pp. 416–425 (2007)
4. Huang, Z., Lu, C.S.J.H., Ooi, B.C.: Skyline queries against mobile lightweight devices in MANETs. In: Int. Conf. on Data Engineering (ICDE), p. 66 (2006)
5. Wu, P., Zhang, C., Feng, Y., Zhao, B.Y., Agrawal, D., Abbadi, A.E.: Parallelizing skyline queries for scalable distribution. In: Ioannidis, Y., Scholl, M.H., Schmidt, J.W., Matthes, F., Hatzopoulos, M., Böhm, K., Kemper, A., Grust, T., Böhm, C. (eds.) EDBT 2006. LNCS, vol. 3896, pp. 112–130. Springer, Heidelberg (2006)
6. Cui, B., Lu, H., Xu, Q., Chen, L., Dai, Y., Zhou, Y.: Parallel distributed processing of constrained skyline queries by filtering. In: Int. Conf. on Data Engineering (ICDE), pp. 546–555 (2008)
7. Hose, K., Lemke, C., Sattler, K.U.: Processing relaxed skylines in PDMS using distributed data summaries. In: Int. Conf. on Information and Knowledge Management (CIKM), pp. 425–434 (2006)
8. Fotiadou, K., Pitoura, E.: BITPEER: Continuous subspace skyline computation with distributed bitmap indexes. In: Int. Workshop on Data Management in Peer-to-Peer Systems (DAMAP), pp. 35–42 (2008)
9. Chen, L., Cui, B., Lu, H., Xu, L., Xu, Q.: iSky: Efficient and progressive skyline computing in a structured P2P network. In: Int. Conf. on Distributed Computing Systems, pp. 160–167 (2008)
10. Wang, S., Ooi, B.C., Tung, A.K.H., Xu, L.: Efficient skyline query processing on peer-to-peer networks. In: Int. Conf. on Data Engineering (ICDE), pp. 1126–1135 (2007)
11. Wang, S., Vu, Q.H., Ooi, B.C., Tung, A.K.H., Xu, L.: Skyframe: A framework for skyline query processing in peer-to-peer systems. VLDB Journal 18(1), 345–362 (2009)
12. Zhu, L., Tao, Y., Zhou, S.: Distributed skyline retrieval with low bandwidth consumption. Transactions on Knowledge and Data Engineering (TKDE) (to appear, 2009)

A Virtual Data Source for Service Grids

Martin Husemann and Norbert Ritter

University of Hamburg, Information Systems,
Vogt-Kölln-Straße 30, 22527 Hamburg, Germany
{husemann,ritter}@informatik.uni-hamburg.de
http://vsis-www.informatik.uni-hamburg.de

Abstract. Service Grids allow providing all kinds of resources ranging from simple storage space to complex functionality. Provision of data, however, is usually limited to connecting data sources to the Grid via service- or document-oriented interfaces. This approach hardly implements the idea of virtualized, easy-to-use resources. We propose a virtual data source that provides structured data according to user demands instead of forcing users to adapt to existing data sources. To this end, existing data sources are selected by their suitability for a given query. Their individual results are then dynamically integrated into the overall result presented to the user. In this paper, we present the background, the main concepts and the architecture of our virtual data source.

Keywords: virtual data source; dynamic mediation; dynamic data integration; source selection; data source catalog.

1 Introduction

Today, Grid Computing forms the basis of rapidly evolving topics such as Service-Oriented Computing or Cloud Computing. Nevertheless, considering the comprehensive implementation of fundamental Grid concepts, many challenges still lie ahead. Storage Grids were among the first use cases for Grid Computing, but efforts so far have been concentrated on data-intensive applications in scientific settings, where the emphasis is on high throughput and capacity, and the scope of employed Grids is relatively small and static.

At the same time, the vast number of databases connected to the Internet is generally difficult to exploit. Such databases are mostly accessible through query interfaces on Web pages, which form a severe bottleneck on the way to the data for Web users and even more for generic direct access. Our research interest is the transparently integrated use of distributed sources of structured data from a user's point of view. Users today are accustomed to certain sources of information, i.e., they usually have their favorite Web sites to look up consumer prices, stock quotes, bus timetables, travel bookings and so on. With all those Web sites, they have come to terms with the individual interfaces and the limited scopes of information. On the other hand, users resort to generic search engines for all remaining needs of information. Querying a search engine results

A. Hameurlain and A M. Tjoa (Eds.): Globe 2009, LNCS 5697, pp. 24–35, 2009.

in pointers to probable sources of the desired information. Users thus need to follow the pointers and evaluate the sources behind them regarding their utility. Only then the actual information can be queried from the newly found sources, which again implies having to cope with individual interfaces.

We argue that to fully leverage the potential of data sources, they should not only be equipped with comprehensive, well-defined query interfaces. In order to provide actual virtualization of data as a resource, individual data sources can only be the back-end of data provision services which provide data according to user demands. Following this insight, we designed a virtual data source for Service Grids which can be used as a single place to address queries to and which processes data from original sources into the form required by the user. In the remainder of this paper, we present this virtual data source and the concepts behind it. Section 2 gives details of the notion of demand-oriented data provision. Section 3 depicts underlying aspects of data integration, especially dynamic integration. Section 4 introduces our DynaGrid virtual data source, and Section 5 concludes the paper.

2 Demand-Oriented Data Provision

As outlined in Section 1, two fundamental types of retrieving information can be distinguished. Interacting with an original data source (or with an information system that conventionally integrates original data sources) allows posing direct and precise queries and delivers direct result data. A user, however, first has to find a data source with suitable content, learn about its specific structure to pose a precise query, and accept the result data in the given form. If the scope of a data source is limited, several data sources with differing structures may have to be found and queried, and the individual results need to be aggregated by the user.

On the other hand, search engines are typically versatile to use and disregard concrete content. A user can thus pose queries regarding any content to one and the same search engine, whose interface is plain and well known. Those queries, however, cannot be as specific or precise as with original data sources, but are limited to keywords. Search engines do not return direct result data, but only lists of sources which contain the query keywords. The user has to evaluate these sources manually and usually has to access sources found suitable directly to retrieve actual result data.

In practice, these two approaches are used in combination. As a first step, a relatively simple keyword query to a search engine is used to find data sources potentially suitable for a given need for information. In a second step, the actual detailed queries are posed to the sources listed by the search engine. Search engines thus present a tool for the *discovery* of data sources. However, the overall process to acquire concrete data for a given demand is tedious and has to be executed mostly manually by the user: Initial keywords need to be deduced, the list of potential sources needs to be reviewed, individual sources need to be made acquainted and queried, and their individual results need to be aggregated.

In cases of static, repetitive information demands, this process can be performed once and results either in finding a suitable data source which complies with the demands directly or in the construction of an integration system that aggregates and integrates data from original sources into the demanded form and can subsequently be used as a data source. Either way, queries have to be posed compliant with the structures of the addressed data source, i.e., users still have to adapt to existing resources and formulate their demands accordingly. In cases of varying demands, the process needs to be performed again when the demands change, and the construction of integration systems becomes increasingly expensive with growing frequency of changes. With individual short-term demands, users are therefore left to their own devices, i.e., manual work.

Building on this insight, demand-oriented data provision should combine aspects of search engines and direct data source access as well as additional functionality to reduce manual work as far as possible while maintaining full query expressiveness, directness, and precision. In concrete, these six requirements result:

D1 Support of precise queries
D2 Delivery of direct, current result data
S1 Single point of contact; abstraction from the location of data
S2 Single interface; abstraction from the native structure of data
P1 Transparent aggregation and integration of data from several sources
P2 Transformation of results into the form defined by the user

Requirements D1 and D2 are obviously fulfilled by direct access to data sources. Requirement S1 is fulfilled by search engines by indexing data sources with the help of crawlers. Data sources are thus listed in a single catalog, but the information gathered by the crawlers may be outdated. The creation of a single catalog from differently structured sources lets search engines also fulfill requirement S2, but at the same this flattening of structures prevents precise queries. Requirements P1 and P2 are neither fulfilled by search engines nor by data sources. Search engines at best provide a very simple form of aggregation by generating cohesive lists of individual data sources. Integration systems, however, transparently aggregate and integrate results from several sources and are therefore a starting point for the design of a demand-oriented data provision service. In any case, though, users have to adapt to the form of results delivered by data sources or search engines.

In order to implement requirement P2, native result data from data sources needs to be transformed depending on the current query. If data is to be aggregated and integrated from several sources, this process also needs to produce results corresponding to the current query. Since transformation and aggregation can be regarded as parts of the integration process, the generalized procedure of delivering results in the desired form and thus the implementation of requirements P1 and P2 can be subsumed in a suitable integration process. Such an integration process is consequently at the heart of a demand-oriented data provision service.

3   Data Integration

The most common approaches to integration of structured data are centered on the creation of a *global schema* which comprises the schemas of the participating data sources and allows accessing the distributed data as if it was contained in a single data source. Integration systems that implement such an approach and transform the queries to the global schema into queries to the original data sources are called *mediators* [1]. A demand-oriented data provision service that employs dynamic integration acts as a *dynamic mediator*, which performs the mediation depending on the query.

The creation of the global schema is commonly based on an analysis of the correspondences between the individual schemas of the participating data sources (*schema matching*). Research efforts in data integration have been focused on automatic schema matching [2,3]. Various designs of integration systems which can automatically integrate data sources at run-time have been proposed [4,5,6,7]. While some approaches in this context mention a notion of dynamic integration or dynamic attachment of data sources, this does not refer to data integration depending on the current query, but merely to the integration of new or changed data sources into the running integration system. The mediation between a given query and the data sources in these cases is still static in terms of its independence of the query.

In order to provide a clearly defined set of terms for the various types of data integration, we devised a taxonomy of approaches to data integration, which is depicted in Figure 1. At the first level of the taxonomy, data integration is distinguished into *fixed integration*, where mediation takes place at the design-time of an integration system only, and *adaptive integration*, where mediation can also be performed at run-time of an integration system. Fixed integration systems are consequently not capable of managing changes in their original data base, i.e., in the participating data sources, at run-time. Adaptive integration systems can handle changes in their data base at run-time, but they differ greatly in the exact way of handling such changes.

At the second level of the taxonomy, adaptive data integration is therefore distinguished into *static integration* and *dynamic integration*. In static integration systems, mediation is performed before a query can be posed. In dynamic integration systems, mediation is performed depending on and specifically catering for the current query. Static integration systems are similar to fixed integration systems. The automation degree of mediation in fixed and static integration can range from fully manual procedures to tool-supported or completely automated procedures. Mediation comprises the selection of participating data sources, the construction of the global schema, and the creation of integration directives for the schemas of the participating data sources toward the global schema. It can be *target-driven*, i.e., the global schema is predefined and data sources are selected and integrated to best contribute to the global schema, or *source-driven*, i.e., the data sources are predefined and their integration is performed as closely and completely as possible, with the global schema emerging as the result of the integration process.

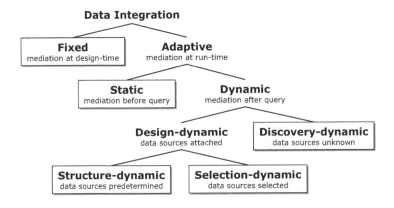

Fig. 1. Taxonomy of approaches to data integration

Obviously, source-driven mediation cannot cater for user demands on the part of queries and is therefore no suitable basis of a demand-oriented data provision service. Target-driven mediation facilitates integration systems that best possibly support user demands as expressed in the predefined global schema. Static integration systems with automatic mediation can maintain this support in cases of changes to their data base, e. g. by repeating the mediation in the event of schema changes or data sources becoming unavailable. Despite this adaptivity with regard to varying supply conditions, however, they are still static with regard to demand, since queries have to meet the global schema. As a solution, a new global schema can be defined and the mediation performed accordingly whenever a new class of queries is to be posed. Such a pseudo-dynamic procedure enables integration systems to cater for changing user demands, but becomes increasingly awkward with growing frequency of the changes.

We therefore propose *dynamic integration* as a new type of integration where mediation is performed directly between the query and the original data sources instead of predefining a global schema. Consequently, mediation takes place after a query has been posed. The process steps in static and dynamic integration are depicted in Figure 2. In both cases, a query is posed and data sources are accessed to answer the query, but the mediation steps differ. With static integration, mediation takes place before the query is posed (steps 1 and 2). With dynamic integration, posing the query is the first step in the integration process. Since there is no predefined global schema, the query can be posed freely as an expression of the user's data demands (requirement S2). In contrast to search engines, however, queries are not limited to keywords, but can be precise queries with the same expressiveness as direct queries to the original data sources (requirement D1).

From the information contained in the query, a *query schema* is built in step 2. The more expressive the query language, the more precise demands regarding both content and form of the results can be defined. The query can contain definitions of attribute names and data types, constraints regarding values,

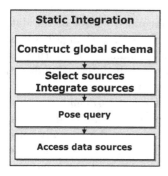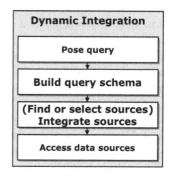

Fig. 2. Process steps in static and dynamic data integration

comparisons with literals or other query items, and so on. The query schema is then constructed as a schema to which the query can be directly posed, i.e., it contains tables and attributes whose names and data types match those in the query. Through the use of a query schema, the order of defining the global schema and posing a query is reversed compared to static integration. This procedure eliminates the need of manually and explicitly defining a global schema and is the decisive difference between dynamic integration and automated, target-driven static integration.

The further steps in dynamic integration are structurally similar to those in static integration. After suitable data sources to support the query schema have been selected and the appropriate integration directives have been created in step 3, the data sources are accessed and their individual results are integrated in step 4. These steps are performed automatically and are transparent to the user, who thus does not need to interact with the original data sources directly, but is provided with direct and current results (requirements S1 and D2). The integration system, if appropriate, selects several data sources to answer the query and integrates the individual results into the form defined by the user in the query (requirements P1 and P2).

As depicted in Figure 1, we identified three kinds of dynamic data integration, which are distinguished by their methods of attaching data sources to the integration system in general and to answer a given query in particular. With *discovery-dynamic integration*, there are no predetermined data sources attached to the integration system. The third step of the integration process as shown in Figure 2 therefore implies discovering data sources suitable for answering the current query from a previously unexplored search space. These data sources are then used to answer the query and afterward detached. While this approach theoretically offers maximum currency and specificity for the selection of data sources, it is impracticable for practical application since exploring a search space at a large scale is of incalculable complexity.

Practical applications of dynamic integration therefore operate on known sets of data sources. With *design-dynamic integration*, dynamic mediation is limited to designing the integration directives over a given data base depending on the current query. In case of *structure-dynamic integration*, the set of data sources taking part in query answering is a predetermined subset of the data sources attached to the integration system. This subset may change between queries, but is independent of the current query and remains static during its processing. Dynamic mediation performs the creation of the integration directives from the data sources in the subset to the query; differing queries may thus result in differing integration directives. In case of *selection-dynamic integration*, the definition of the query-answering subset is part of dynamic mediation, i.e., the data sources taking part in answering a query are dynamically selected from the larger set of data sources attached to the integration system depending on the query. The integration directives are then created the same way as with structure-dynamic integration.

The approach of dynamic data integration obviously implies several serious challenges. Most importantly, after the query has been posed, all the process steps must be performed automatically. Automatic integration of data sources in particular requires automatic schema matching, which has not yet been achieved. Existing approaches to automatic schema matching leave the resolution of conflicts and doubtful decisions to manual intervention by domain experts. Such a procedure is not feasible in dynamic environments so that ways for automatic conflict resolution need to be found. Tackling this challenge, however, does not only concern dynamic integration; achieving automatic integration will also benefit static and fixed integration. Especially with dynamic integration, the integration process also needs to be performed in a tolerable time frame since it takes place while the user is waiting for the results. A feasible time frame is thus in the order of seconds, not minutes or more.

The intensified challenge of automatic integration within a closely limited time foreseeably leads to a decreased result quality compared to careful integration with manual optimizations, i.e., matches between the participating data sources or details of the mapping of the query to the data sources may be incorrect. Dynamic integration therefore has a delimited field of application in scenarios where the requirements for flexible support of changing queries outweigh the requirements for precise results. Such scenarios typically have exploratory characteristics, e.g. the search for information (similar to amateur usage of Web search engines) or the initial analysis of data source content prior to static integration (as a tool for database professionals). Result quality and practical benefit can also be increased by limiting the content scope of the integration system to a specific domain, which leads to more uniform data source content and thus better match quality.

4   The DynaGrid Virtual Data Source

In order to investigate demand-oriented data provision through virtual data sources, we developed a prototype of a virtual data source in our *DynaGrid* project. Its architecture is shown in Figure 3. The DynaGrid virtual data source has been designed as a group of Grid services, which are currently implemented

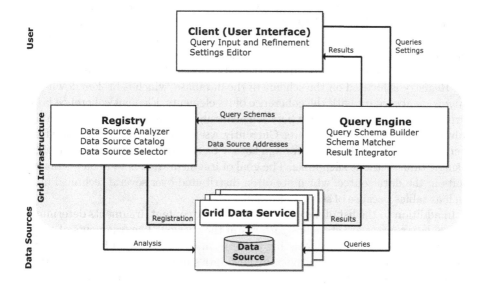

Fig. 3. Architecture of the DynaGrid virtual data source

with the Globus Toolkit [8]. It is intended to be used in Service Grids the same way as a conventional data source while in fact pooling the content of several original data sources. The actual virtual data source comprises two Grid services. They each contain several modules that could be deployed as external services as well in order to provide their respective functionality to other applications in the Grid or to enable load balancing for complex functionality such as schema matching.

Original data sources are autonomously run by data source operators under locally individual conditions. In order to be considered for the virtual data source, they need to be connected to the Grid via OGSA-DAI *Grid Data Services* which provide access to the data sources abstracting from technical aspects such as database drivers [9]. These services are typically run by the data source operators and relatively tightly coupled with the data sources; however, logically, they are located within the Grid service infrastructure. Plain data services simply offer access to data sources via XML *Perform Documents* without enhancing or modifying the structures and content of the data sources. Enhanced data services can act as wrappers which provide special views on their underlying data sources or host adaptive functionality such as data model transformations. The details of Grid Data Services are beyond the scope of this paper; for reasons of clarity, we only consider relational databases as data sources.

We investigate selection-dynamic integration since it offers a greater degree of dynamism than structure-dynamic integration while offering a more practical approach than discovery-dynamic integration. The Registry component thus maintains a *catalog* of original data sources known to the virtual data source. Data sources are explicitly registered through a *registration* interface. A newly registered data source is analyzed by the Registry with regard to its content and structures in order to be cataloged. OGSA-DAI Grid Data Services natively support querying basic metadata (mostly concerning the schema) from the underlying database; data source operators may implement extended *analysis* interfaces in order to provide more specific information about the data source. The analysis performed by the Registry is focused on the schema of the database, which is broken down into *fragments* accordant with the coherence of its elements. Element coherence is determined through relationships between elements such as hierarchies (e. g. table–column) or foreign key constraints. Currently, a set of tables are regarded as a fragment if they are interlinked by foreign keys, i. e., the smallest possible fragment is a single table without such links. The goal of fragmentation is to detect semantic units in the data source, which are often distributed over several technical units such as tables because of schema normalization.

In addition to the list of data sources with their content, fragments determined in the data sources are stored as *patterns* in the catalog. The fragments of a new data source are compared to existing patterns in the catalog. If a fragment corresponds to a pattern, a reference to the new data source is added to that pattern; if not, a new pattern with a reference to the data source is created from the fragment. After the registration of a number of data sources, the catalog thus holds a set of patterns, each referencing the original data sources which contain a fragment corresponding to the pattern. Consequently, given a fragment, a comparison to the patterns in the catalog provides data sources that contain equal or similar fragments and can thus contribute to answering queries containing this fragment. We call such lookups *content-based lookups* since data sources are not retrieved by identifying information such as names or URIs, but by their content. Content-based lookups are the decisive feature of the Registry and set it apart from common directory services such as the original OGSA-DAI Service Group Registry which only allow name-based lookups [10]. They enable the dynamic selection of data sources depending on a given query as described later on.

The Query Engine component comprises the functionality for the processing of user queries. It accepts conjunctive queries posed in a variant of SQL, i. e., typically Select-Where statements with an optional OrderBy clause. We chose to base our query language on SQL since it is a widely popular and easily learned, yet powerful and precise way to specify queries. A query specifies *result entities* and their attributes about which information is demanded. In SQL, this translates to table and column names in the Select clause. Constraints on the attribute values are defined in the Where clause. They may be based on literal values or entity attribute values. *Auxiliary entities*, i. e., entities which are not used in the Select clause, may be used in the Where clause to specify constraints or link result entities. In contrast to general SQL, attribute names must always be qualified with the respective entity names since without a predefined schema, attributes cannot be associated with entities automatically. Also, attribute data types should be specified where possible to facilitate matching the query to data sources and achieve higher match quality. Specifying UNKNOWN instructs the integration system to detect the data type automatically; if no specification is

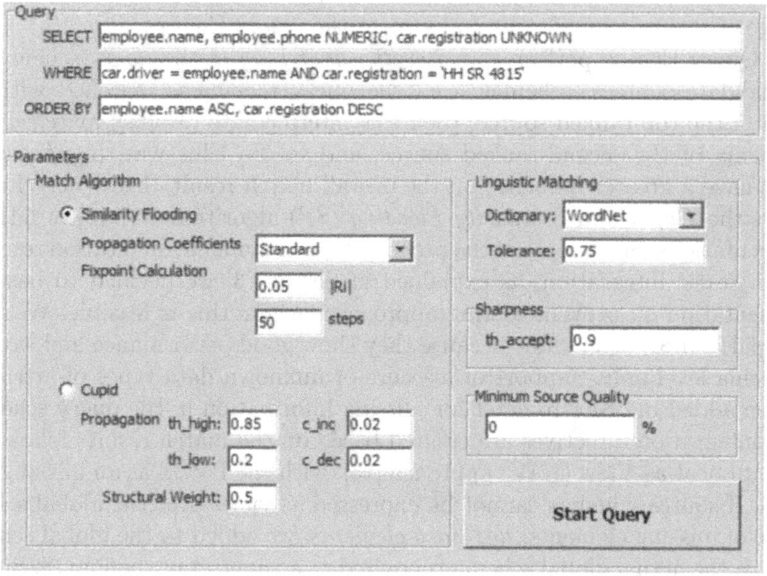

Fig. 4. Free query formulation and match parameter editor

given, any data type is regarded valid. As all the referenced entities (i. e., tables) are mentioned in the Select and Where clauses, the From clause can be omitted. In the OrderBy clause, a sort order for results may be defined based on result entity attributes. An example query can be seen in the upper part of Figure 4.

The query schema is built from the information on entities, their attributes, and their relationships contained in the query. In the example in Figure 4, the Query Engine can deduce an entity "employee" with the attributes "name" and "phone" as well as an entity "car" with the attributes "registration" and "driver". Also, the join between "driver" and "name" suggests a foreign key constraint between "car" and "employee", and the constraint on "registration" hints at an alphanumeric data type. Obviously, entities may possess more attributes than those mentioned in the query. We therefore refer to the query schema as the *partial virtual global schema* (PVGS). There are many potential *actual global schemas* that contain the section specified by the PVGS, which alleviates the creation of the integration directives.

The query schema is directly used as a *registry query* for suitable data sources. It is always regarded as one single fragment since it is feasible to assume that all the entities in the query are meant to be interlinked. The query fragment is compared to the patterns in the catalog, the similarity being calculated by the number of elements that can be regarded as equal. Currently, the determination of equality is based on a linguistic matching. In case of a similarity greater than zero, the data sources referenced by a pattern can contribute to answering the query and are selected as candidate sources for further processing. The list of candidate sources is sorted by the cohesion of their relevant fragments and their coverage of the query fragment and sent to the Query Engine.

The Query Engine performs an *iterative matching* of the query schema and the candidate sources' schemas, i.e., the query schema is matched with the schema of the top-ranked source, then this intermediate result is matched with the schema of the second-ranked source, and so on. This way, higher ranked sources have a greater influence on the overall match result. The Query Engine employs the *Cupid* and *Similarity Flooding* (SF) algorithms [11,12] in adapted implementations. Since some of the process steps in dynamic integration resemble those in static integration, as explained in Section 3, we decided to base our implementation on proven existing approaches where this is feasible. We chose the Cupid and SF algorithms because they show good performance and work on the schema level only. Support of insecure or unknown data types of attributes has been added in order to cater for missing information in the query schema.

The integration directives are created based on the match results following a modified Local-as-View (LAV) approach [13], with the PVGS as an initial global schema. If source schemas cannot be expressed as views over the global schema because of missing elements, *auxiliary elements* are added to the global schema. This way, the actual global schema is created as a superset of the PVGS. Similar to auxiliary entities in the query, auxiliary elements of the actual global schema provide information that will not be contained in the result, but is needed to link the schemas of the participating data sources. The query is then executed on the data sources using the MiniCon algorithm [14], and the results are delivered to the client. In order to decrease the complexity of query processing, *query sessions* are supported. If e.g. a query is refined by adjusting attribute value constraints and reissued, the refined query can directly be executed on the existing actual global schema of the original query.

As a client for the Query Engine, we developed a graphical user interface with special emphasis on supporting both amateur and experienced users in posing, evaluating and refining queries. Figure 4 shows a section of the user interface for experienced users, allowing free editing of queries and match algorithm settings. The user interface for amateur users provides a wizard to construct queries without knowledge of SQL syntax and predefined parameter profiles for the match algorithms. For both types of users, query results are displayed in tables, and additional information on result provenance and quality can be displayed. The details of the user interface and especially the handling of result quality are beyond the scope of this paper.

5   Conclusion and Future Work

In this paper, we proposed demand-oriented data provision services for Grids in order to implement the notion of resource virtualization and abstraction of location for data as a resource. We identified six requirements to such services, which existing approaches fulfill only partially. Comprehensive demand-oriented data provision services must adopt features of both search engines and direct data source access and add new functionality to implement virtual data sources that cater for user demands. We argued that such a virtual data source must integrate data from distributed sources and that existing integration approaches are not suitable for this application. We therefore introduced dynamic data integration as a new type of integration and elaborated on its characteristics and challenges. Finally, we gave an overview of our DynaGrid virtual data source as a prototype implementation of a demand-oriented data provision service.

Future work will be directed at enhancing the usability of the virtual data source by implementing a registry browser. We expect such a browser to facilitate query formulation by helping users to get an overview of the information stored in the data sources attached to the integration system. We will also perform evaluations regarding query processing performance and result quality in various application contexts.

References

1. Wiederhold, G.: Mediators in the Architecture of Future Information Systems. IEEE Computer 25(3), 38–49 (1992)
2. Do, H.H., Rahm, E.: Matching large schemas: Approaches and evaluation. Inf. Syst. 32(6), 857–885 (2007)
3. Rahm, E., Bernstein, P.A.: A survey of approaches to automatic schema matching. VLDB J. 10(4), 334–350 (2001)
4. Gounaris, A., Sakellariou, R., Comito, C., Talia, D.: Service Choreography for Data Integration on the Grid. In: Talia, D., Bilas, A., Dikaiakos, M.D. (eds.) Knowledge and Data Management in GRIDs, pp. 19–33. Springer, US (2007)
5. Gorton, I., Almquist, J., Dorow, K., et al.: An Architecture for Dynamic Data Source Integration. In: 38th Hawaii Int. Conf. on System Sciences (January 2005)
6. Chang, K.C.C., He, B., Zhang, Z.: Toward Large Scale Integration: Building a MetaQuerier over Databases on the Web. In: CIDR, January 2005, pp. 44–55 (2005)
7. Al-Hussaini, L., Viglas, S., Atkinson, M.: A Service-based Approach to Schema Federation of Distributed Databases. Technical Report EES-2006-01, University of Edinburgh (November 2005)
8. Foster, I.T.: Globus Toolkit Version 4: Software for Service-Oriented Systems. In: IFIP Int. Conf. on Network and Parallel Computing, November 2005, pp. 2–13 (2005)
9. Antonioletti, M., Atkinson, M.P., Baxter, R., et al.: The design and implementation of Grid database services in OGSA-DAI. Concurrency - Practice and Experience 17(2-4), 357–376 (2005)
10. Antonioletti, M., Atkinson, M., Baxter, R., et al.: OGSA-DAI: Two Years On. In: The Future of Grid Data Environments Workshop, GGF10 (March 2004)
11. Madhavan, J., Bernstein, P.A., Rahm, E.: Generic Schema Matching with Cupid. In: VLDB, September 2001, pp. 49–58 (2001)
12. Melnik, S., Garcia-Molina, H., Rahm, E.: Similarity Flooding: A Versatile Graph Matching Algorithm and Its Application to Schema Matching. In: ICDE, March 2002, pp. 117–128 (2002)
13. Lenzerini, M.: Data Integration: A Theoretical Perspective. In: PODS, June 2002, pp. 233–246 (2002)
14. Pottinger, R., Halevy, A.Y.: MiniCon: A scalable algorithm for answering queries using views. VLDB J. 10(2-3), 182–198 (2001)

Towards Parallel Processing of RDF Queries in DHTs

Björn Lohrmann[1], Dominic Battré[2], and Odej Kao[2]

Technische Universität Berlin, Complex and Distributed IT Systems
Secr. EN 59, Einsteinufer 17, 10587 Berlin, Germany
[1] bjoern@blohrmann.net
http://www.blohrmann.net
[2] {firstname.lastname}@tu-berlin.de

Abstract. Efficient RDF query evaluation is a requirement if the vision of a Semantic Web is to come true one day. Peer-to-peer (P2P) networks, specifically distributed hash tables (DHTs), could be one of the enabling technologies for the Semantic Web. Several DHT based RDF triple stores have been proposed but despite their differences they all process queries sequentially and hence leave an untapped potential for parallelism. This paper proposes and analyzes a scheme for parallel processing of RDF queries in DHTs. We describe a planning algorithm that attempts to reduce the response time of a query by considering parallel query plans prior to query execution. We provide an experimental evaluation of our approach and compare its results to an already existing scheme, i.e. the one of the BabelPeers project.

1   Introduction

A goal of the Semantic Web [1] initiative is to enable computers to combine information with well-defined meaning from many different sources in order to realize services that are infeasible in the current web. This requires us to enable computers to "understand" this information so that they are able to answer detailed queries. RDF/S is a knowledge-representation language of the Semantic Web and addresses this issue. However, we also require strategies to efficiently evaluate queries on RDF data. By definition, the Semantic Web can only be truly useful if it has the universal scope of the World Wide Web. That requires countless different sources to provide machine-processable information. Due to their scalability, fault-resilience and massive potential for storing and processing data, P2P networks, specifically DHTs, could be the enabling technology for the Semantic Web. Several systems that process RDF in a DHT have been proposed but despite their differences they all share the characteristic of processing queries sequentially. This paper proposes and analyzes a strategy for parallel processing of RDF queries in a DHT setting. Specifically, we describe a protocol, cost model and a query planning algorithm that attempts to reduce the estimated response time of a query by considering parallel query plans prior to processing the first

A. Hameurlain and A M. Tjoa (Eds.): Globe 2009, LNCS 5697, pp. 36–47, 2009.

join. The focus of our work is query optimization, hence other aspects such as reliability or security have not been taken into special consideration.

While existing RDF query engines provide good efficiency in many cases, we believe that there is still an untapped potential in P2P networks. Current P2P based RDF query processing schemes either sequentially fetch triple pattern matches to a single peer where the candidate sets are joined, or they successively move query processing from one peer to another and intersect the candidate sets in this way. We believe that due to its massive number of peers we can harness the parallelism inherent to any P2P network in order to reduce the response time of queries. Consequently, we perform RDF query optimization not with the goal of minimizing traffic but with the goal of reducing query response time. It should however be noted that a query plan with low response time implicitly generates little traffic since traffic is also very costly in terms of time, especially in a P2P network.

2   Related Work

Prior work in RDF query processing can roughly be divided into query processing in centralized and distributed systems. Centralized triple stores, such as Jena [2] and Sesame [3] were the first ones to properly support query processing. They provide a framework to build RDF based applications for the Semantic Web. ARQ, the SPARQL compliant query processor of Jena, implements optimization of basic graph patterns for in-memory RDF graphs by using selectivity estimation heuristics to optimize the join order of patterns. Our cost model is partly inspired by the *variable counting* heuristic of Jena. Jena also offers more sophisticated heuristics, e.g. the ones presented in [4]. Recent work [5] by Neumann an Weikum massively improves SPARQL query processing speed for large quantities of RDF data by a bottom-up redesign of data structures, intelligent use of indexes and query optimization that yields bushy join trees.

P2P networks have often been proposed as an alternative to centralized systems. Edutella [6] was one of the first systems of this type. As it is based on an unstructured network similar to Gnutella, it uses flooding for query processing, which does not scale very well to large numbers of peers. By using a DHT, other systems such as RDFPeers [7] address this issue. It indexes triples by their subject, predicate and object. It supports processing of atomic triple patterns but also of conjunctions of patterns limited to the same variable in the subject. The query processing algorithm intersects the candidate sets for the subject variable by routing it through the peers that hold the matches to each pattern. The GridVine [8] project applies the same indexing approach and a similar query processing scheme in a different P2P network.

Later systems were mostly able to process at least queries with complete basic graph patterns, e.g. the BabelPeers project [9,10,11,12]. It offers both strategies for exhaustive and top-k query evaluation and uses relational algebra to describe query processing. The general idea of the exhaustive approach is to use a heuristic that determines which set of pattern matches to fetch next to the peer that processes the query. The heuristics strive at minimizing network traffic. The limitation of joining the intermediate relations of the query on just a single host has been relaxed in [12] where query evaluation can be migrated to other peers. BabelPeers also speeds up joins by using Bloom filters [13], a technique that we apply as well. The authors of [14] also describe RDF query processing with relational algebra and propose two evaluation strategies. RDFCube [15] uses the hashing scheme of RDFPeers but adds a three-dimensional hash space that stores so-called *existence flags* for triples which are used to construct and combine filters that minimize the number of transferred triples during query evaluation.

For our query planning algorithm we adopted the approach in [16], Sec. 2 where Chen and Benn propose a recursive algorithm to create balanced bushy join trees in order to improve query response time. They start with a given left-deep join tree and apply simple tree transformations until a balanced bushy join tree is obtained.

3   System Architecture

This section briefly summarizes a selection of the architectural aspects fully described in [9]. We have limited ourselves to those that are most important for understanding our query processing algorithm. Due to space constraints we refrain from a thorough introduction to RDF and refer the reader to [17].

We assume a distributed system that consists of a set of peers connected by a DHT. Each peer stores knowledge in the form of RDF triples. Most importantly, every peer runs a *query server* that accepts connections from *query clients*. A *query client* is typically not part of the DHT but has a query that it wishes to be evaluated. The query server initiates query evaluation and returns the result to the client. In the algorithm presented later on in this paper, the query server will locally start a so-called *master agent* process that takes care of query evaluation. Furthermore each peer runs a triple disseminator process that distributes the peer's own RDF data. It stores each triple on the peers responsible for the hash value of the subject, predicate and object (the hash function is provided by the DHT). Other processes like RDF reasoning might also run on the peers but are outside of the scope of this paper.

4   RDF Query Processing

Query processing is split into two subsequent phases – the query planning and the query execution phase. First we will present the protocol that the peers use to interact during query processing. Then we will focus on the query planning phase, specifically on join tree optimization and the cost model used to estimate join tree response times.

4.1   Inter-peer Protocol

Initially, each peer in the overlay network is listening for incoming RDF queries. A peer that receives a query starts a so-called *master agent* process which marks the beginning of the planning phase. Let us assume that an exemplary query $Q = \{q_1, q_2, q_3\}$ has been submitted where each q_i is a triple pattern. The master agent first determines a DHT id $dhtId_i$ for each pattern q_i. To do so it applies the DHT's hash function to one of the constant pattern components. We heuristically choose subjects over objects over predicates since usually there are more distinct subjects and objects than predicates. Choosing the look-up key in this fashion achieves better query load distribution and also helps to keep the size of the candidate sets small. This approach has already been used by numerous other algorithms (see [14,10]). The master agent then requests information by sending a message $SReq$ for each pattern q_i from the peer responsible for $dhtId_i$. Reception of a request triggers a *slave agent* process, that can handle this and any following requests. It determines the matching triples for each pattern q_i and constructs the *pattern relation* $\sigma_i = (H_i, B_i)$ where H_i and B_i are the relation header and body: The header consists of the pattern's variables and the body contains all possible valuations of the variables as given by the pattern matches. The slave agent then replies $(SRep)$ with the exact number of elements in the pattern relation, its *value upload rate* and *hash operation rate*. The *value upload rate* quantifies the peer's upstream throughput in *values* per second. The term *value* refers to an URI or a literal. It is used in the cost model, when trying to estimate the delay that arises from transferring relations. The *hash operation rate* quantifies the number of hash operations of *values* the slave agent's peer can perform per second. The hash operation rate plays an important role when estimating how fast a peer can compute a join result.

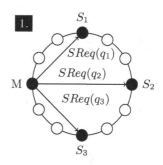

M : Master agent
S_i : Slave agents
$SReq(q_i)$: Statistics request for q_i
$SRep(q_i)$: Statistics reply for q_i
QEP_i : Query execution plan for S_i

After having received all replies, the master agent begins to plan the query. It will apply the algorithm described in Sec. 4.2 to find a parallel join order for the pattern relations. Finally it sends out a *slave-specific* query execution plan (QEP) to each slave agent. A QEP is a list of operations a slave agent has to perform during the execution phase. Possible operations include sending a relation or a Bloom filter to another peer, joining two local relations, etc. If possible, we use Bloom filters to minimize the size of transferred relations.

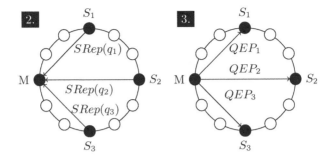

On the slave-side, reception of a QEP marks the beginning of the execution phase. After execution of the plans, the final relation(s) will be sent back to the master agent which returns them to the waiting query client and terminates. In our example, the master agent determined that the relations should be joined in the order $(\sigma_2, (\sigma_3, \sigma_1))$, that the join (σ_3, σ_1) shall be performed on S_1 and that the second join shall be computed on S_2, from where it is supposed to be sent to the master agent.

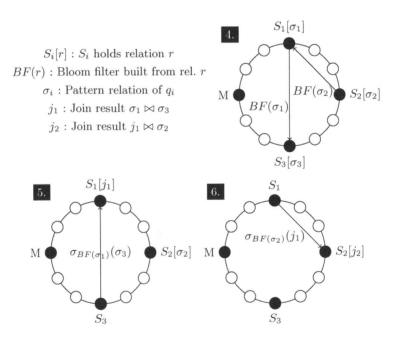

4.2   Join Tree Optimization

Based on the slaves' replies, the master agent is supposed to plan the query execution. The goal is to minimize the estimated query execution time. With the joins of pattern relations being the most costly operations, we have to (1) find an order in which to join the pattern relations and (2) assign a slave agent to each join. This section outlines the optimization procedures used to solve these two problems. Details are omitted as we rely on previous research from the area of parallel and multidatabase systems [18,16]. How to estimate response times will be covered in Sec. 4.3.

We model a solution as an annotated join tree where the leaves are pattern relations and the inner nodes are joins (intermediate relations). Each node is annotated with the DHT id of a peer that is supposed to hold the respective relation and has to perform the join in case of an intermediate relation. Naturally such a peer will always be one of those running a slave agent for this query. It is a well-established fact in the database community that optimizing the join order can yield substantial improvements in query execution time, e.g. by keeping the size of intermediate relations small [19,18]. For simplicity we use hash joins without pipelining and assume a join itself to be a non-parallel operation. Hence we need to create bushy join trees in order to exploit possible inter-operator parallelism.

We use a common two-phase approach for join tree optimization. First we determine independent subqueries of the original RDF query. The patterns from two independent subqueries do not have any variables in common. For each subquery we will then create a left-deep join tree, that contains all the subquery's pattern relations. The left-deep join tree does not contain any type of parallelism, it just describes an initial sequential solution. To create the tree, we use a simple greedy algorithm that works bottom-up and tries to find a local optimum in query execution time. This algorithm is very similar to S_{GD} discussed in [18]. Then, each left-deep tree will be transformed into a bushy one. The algorithm to transform left-deep trees is taken from [16], Sec. 2 and should give us a fairly balanced join tree with inter-operator parallelism. It is based on so-called *basic transformations* that make the tree "bushier". First we recursively descend to the bottom of the tree and then we start to check if there are transformations that lead to an improvement in estimated response time. If this is the case we choose the best one in terms of response time and apply it. Then we ascend to the parent node, search for and possibly apply a transformation and then ascend again etc. The procedure terminates if it has reached the root of the tree. For each (temporary) tree that evolves during these two phases, we assign a peer to each join based on a simple bottom-up procedure, thus problem (2) is solved "along the way". Peer assignment works as follows. The leaf nodes are assigned to the peers that have received the *statistics request* for the respective pattern. A join node is assigned to one of the two peers that hold the input relations. We choose the peer that gives the lowest response time estimation for the intermediate relation. From such a set of optimized join trees we can now easily derive slave-specific QEPs.

4.3   Cost Model

So far we have omitted the details of response time estimation which is one of the main contributions of our work. The cost model defines how we estimate the response time of a join tree or subtrees thereof. We chose to implement our cost model to meet the following goals. First, communication costs must dominate the total costs of a join tree, followed by computational costs but the exact ratio should depend on the peers involved. Second, response time estimations need to be fast and easy to compute, otherwise the planning overhead might be too large and outweigh the benefits.

What Does a Join Consist of? In a centralized RDBMS, a join is usually broken down into the disk IO and the actual computation. However, the P2P environment is distributed in nature and thus the steps necessary to perform a join differ:

1. Due to the way peer assignment works, the peer that computes the join result – we call it the *join peer* – has always at least one of the input relations locally available. If one of the input relations resides on a different peer, it needs to be transferred to the *join peer*. The time required for transfer shall be denoted as the *transport time*.
2. If the input relations have common attributes, the *join peer* builds an in-memory hash table of the smaller relation and probes it, using the tuples of the other relation. The time to perform this step will be referred to as the *join time*.
3. The *join peer* generates the resulting relation. This time span is called the *result generation time*.

Note that this is a simplified model of a join as it does not include the use of Bloom filters. Also, probing the hash table and generating the result relation are usually done at the same time. The distinction becomes important though, if the join is actually a Cartesian product. In this case we do not build a hash table.

Formal Cost Model Definition. Let us assume a join tree

$$JT = (rels, joins, left, right, peer)$$

where $rels = \{\sigma_1, \ldots, \sigma_t\}$ is the set of pattern relations (assuming there are t patterns in our subquery), a join is a tuple $(r_1, r_2) \in (joins \cup rels)^2$ of its two input relations r_1 and r_2, $joins$ is the set of all joins in the tree, *left* and *right* are injective functions that map each join to its left and right input relation and *peer* maps relations and joins in the tree to their peer. Furthermore for each involved peer p we have its *value upload rate* $vur(p) \in \mathbb{R}^+$ and its *hash operation rate* $hashops(p) \in \mathbb{R}^+$. To achieve dominance of communication costs, the value upload and hashing rates for a peer should be chosen such that $vur(p) \ll hashops(p)$. Now we can recursively define the response time function $rt(r)$ for a join tree node r as

$$rt(r) = \begin{cases} 0 & \text{if } r \in rels \\ max\{rt(r_1), rt(r_2)\} + tt(r) + jt(r) + gt(r) & \text{if } r = (r_1, r_2) \in joins \end{cases}$$

where the *transport time* $tt(r)$ shall be defined as

$$tt(r) = \begin{cases} 0 & \text{if } peer(r) = peer(r_1) = peer(r_2) \\ \frac{width(r_1) \cdot tup(r_1)}{vur(peer(r_1))} & \text{if } peer(r) = peer(r_2) \neq peer(r_1) \\ \frac{width(r_2) \cdot tup(r_2)}{vur(peer(r_2))} & \text{if } peer(r) = peer(r_1) \neq peer(r_2), \end{cases}$$

with $width(r_i)$ and $tup(r_i)$ being the number of attributes and tuples in relation r_i. The *join time* $jt(r)$ shall be defined as

$$jt(r) = \begin{cases} 0 & r \text{ is a Cartesian product} \\ \frac{tup(r_1)+tup(r_2)}{hashops(peer(r))} & \text{otherwise,} \end{cases}$$

and the *result generation time* $gt(r)$ shall be defined as

$$gt(r) = \frac{tup(r)}{hashops(r)}.$$

As we can see, the definition of the join's response time is based on an estimation of the input relation sizes, provided by a function tup. If the join $r = (r_1, r_2)$ is actually a Cartesian product (r_1 and r_2 have no common attributes), the size of r's relation shall be estimated as $tup(r) = tup(r_1) \cdot tup(r_2)$. If r is not a Cartesian product, a regular RDBMS would apply histogram based techniques. Instead we resort to so-called *variable-factors*, a concept inspired by the Jena *variable counting* heuristic (see [2]). For a pattern q_i with only a single variable $?v_1$, the *variable-factor* is $f_{?v_1}(q) = 1/2$. For a pattern q_i with two variables $?v_1$ and $?v_2$ and v being the set of join variables, we shall define $f_v(q_i)$ as

$$f_v(q_i) = \begin{cases} penalty(?v_2, q_i) & \text{if } v = \{?v_1\} \\ penalty(?v_1, q_i) & \text{if } v = \{?v_2\} \\ 1/2 & \text{if } v = \{?v_1, ?v_2\} \end{cases}$$

where

$$penalty(?v, q_i) = \begin{cases} 8 & \text{if } subj(q_i) = ?v \\ 2 & \text{if } pred(q_i) = ?v \\ 4 & \text{if } obj(q_i) = ?v \end{cases}$$

Intuitively speaking, such a factor approximates how much an arbitrary relation will shrink or grow if we join it with a pattern relation. The values have been chosen with the intent of rewarding joins that include all variables of a pattern and penalizing those joins that do not. If a join only includes one variable of a two-variable pattern, the height of the penalty should also depend on the unbound variable that is not part of the join. Under the assumptions that there are more distinct subjects than objects and more distinct objects than predicates, we should penalize non-join variables in subjects more than in objects more than in predicates. Although the absolute penalty values are certainly arguable, the general approach should be valid. Let again $r = (r_1, r_2)$ be a join tree node and v the set of join attributes between r_1 and r_2. Using *variable-factors* we can now distinguish the following three cases when estimating join result sizes.

Pattern – Pattern Join. If both r_1 and r_2 are pattern relations, we will use the *variable-factors* from the corresponding patterns q_1 and q_2:

$$tup(r) = \lceil min\{tup(r_1) \cdot f_v(q_2), tup(r_2) \cdot f_v(q_1)\}\rceil$$

Pattern – Intermediate Join. If only one of the input relations is a pattern relation, we will again use the corresponding pattern's *variable-factor*. Let r_1 be the pattern relation and q_1 the respective pattern then the estimated join result size is:

$$tup(r) = \lceil tup(r_2) \cdot f_v(q_1)\rceil$$

Intermediate – Intermediate Join. If both r_1 and r_2 are intermediate relations, we will temporarily reorder all pattern relations below r to form a left-deep tree and return the estimated number of tuples in that tree. In other words, this case is mapped back to the previous ones.

$$tup(r) = tup(toLDTree(r))$$

where $toLDTree(r)$ converts the tree rooted at r to a left-deep tree with the pattern relations ordered as they are visited by tree traversal.

5   Experimental Results

We have conducted an experimental evaluation of our approach in a computer pool with 120 desktop PCs connected via ethernet. All peers used 1500 as their *hash operation rate* and 1 as their *value upload rate*, with the intention of letting network communication dominate the response time estimations. We compared our parallelized approach to the sequential algorithm (SG4 heuristic with Bloom filters) described in [10]. We extended a software prototype provided by BabelPeers to support parallel query processing. Benchmarks were performed on a dataset with 271483 triples created by the LUBM generator (see [20]). We used a set of 15 custom queries, where each query had between four and eight patterns, with five patterns per query on average. The queries were designed such that intermediate relations can become quite large for bad join orders, hence the queryset honors good execution plans. The queries were submitted sequentially with only one query active at any time. Figure 1a shows the mean processing time (PT) of all 15 queries on a logarithmic scale with varying numbers of peers in the DHT. On average our parallelized approach performs a lot better than the sequential approach. The mean PT of our approach rises until fourty peers have been reached due to anomalies in the distribution of triples among the peers. Then the parallelization and superior query planning effects cause the mean PT to drop quickly. The PT of the sequential algorithm is almost unaffected by the DHT size as it does not affect the join order. Its high mean PT is mainly caused by query 9. Figure 1b sheds more light on this issue where the individual PT (average over four query runs) of each query has been plotted. The sequential algorithm chooses a bad join order for query 9 which causes huge intermediate

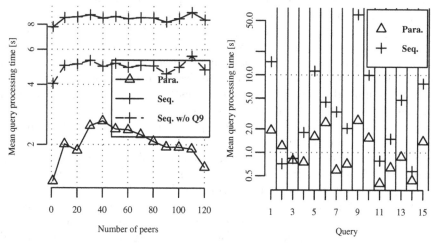

(a) Mean query processing time

(b) Mean query processing times by query (4 loops, 120 peers)

relations. Processing of this query had to be canceled after 60s in this case in order to preserve readability of the diagram. Even without query 9, our scheme outperforms the sequential approach consistently (with exception of query 2), mostly due to better query plans.

Other benchmarks were performed as well. First we compared how our approach scales when there is more than one active query. In this benchmark our approach performed worse due to a load imbalance. Specifically, a single peer was responsible for about 30% of all pattern relations among all queries. In consequence this peer was overloaded and delayed most queries. Second we measured the fraction of time spent on planning. On average only 6% of the PT is spent on gathering statistics, computing and delivering QEPs which is a reasonable planning overhead in our opinion.

6   Conclusions and Future Work

This paper presents and evaluates a novel approach for processing RDF basic graph patterns in DHTs. Our work is based on the system architecture presented in [9] and the query processing algorithm in [16], the latter of which treats query optimization in relational multidatabase systems. We believe to be the first to access the research done in the area of multidatabase systems and to harness the parallelism inherent to P2P networks. To compensate for the general lack of information about the relations involved in a query we designed a novel cost model based on a very simple rule of thumb.

We successfully benchmarked an adapted BabelPeers prototype in DHTs with up to 120 peers. Our findings are that in a network with no or low query load, a significant improvement in response time can be achieved over the sequential algorithm. In the setting of a network with query load however, we did not manage to outperform the sequential approach. This is due to the fact that we assign many costly operations like joins to other peers than the one that received the query. In networks with very uneven data and query load this leads to a hotspot problem. While in our experiments query processing time scaled well with the DHT size, it should be noted that the degree of parallelism during query processing is limited by the number of patterns in a query and the distribution of triples over the DHT. In other words, if each pattern of a query is already mapped to a different peer, adding more peers to the DHT will not improve query processing time any further.

We believe that our approach presents a viable alternative to the already existing ones. However, several issues will need to be addressed in future work to leverage more of its potential. We consider load balancing to be the most important focus for future work. Load balancing needs to be performed on two levels, i.e. in-query and between queries. Uneven load inside a query happens when a peer is involved in the processing of two sibling join trees. Uneven load between queries happens when a single peer is involved in processing two or more queries at the same time. Both problems could be addressed by the cost model. The former by considering the peers involved in sibling join trees of the current one, the latter by including the load of a peer incurred by other queries into the response time estimations. The *dynamic time table* data structure from [16] could provide a starting point as it addresses these problems for the purpose of query optimization in MDBSs. Other possible solutions include load balancing on the data side, maybe in combination with redundancy so that the query load can be spread more evenly. Further optimizations could include a caching strategy to improve or speed up the gathering relation statistics. Further improvements could also include calibration of the cost model parameters, i.e. the the *value upload rate* and the *hash operation rate*.

References

1. Berners-Lee, T., Hendler, J., Lassila, O.: The Semantic Web. Scientific American (2001)
2. Wilkinson, K., Sayers, C., Kuno, H., Reynolds, D.: Efficient RDF storage and retrieval in Jena2. In: Proceedings of SWDB 2003, The first International Workshop on Semantic Web and Databases, pp. 131–150 (2003)
3. Broekstra, J., Kampman, A., van Harmelen, F.: Sesame: A generic architecture for storing and querying RDF and RDF schema. In: Horrocks, I., Hendler, J. (eds.) ISWC 2002. LNCS, vol. 2342, pp. 54–68. Springer, Heidelberg (2002)
4. Stocker, M., Seaborne, A., Bernstein, A., Kiefer, C., Reynolds, D.: SPARQL basic graph pattern optimization using selectivity estimation. In: WWW 2008: Proceeding of the 17th international conference on World Wide Web, pp. 595–604. ACM Press, New York (2008)
5. Neumann, T., Weikum, G.: RDF-3X: a RISC-style engine for RDF. Proceedings of the VLDB Endowment archive 1(1), 647–659 (2008)
6. Nejdl, W., Wolf, B., Qu, C., Decker, S., Sintek, M., Naeve, A., Nilsson, M., Palmér, M., Risch, T.: EDUTELLA: A P2P networking infrastructure based on RDF. In:

WWW 2002: Proceedings of the 11th international conference on World Wide Web, pp. 604–615. ACM Press, New York (2002)

7. Cai, M., Frank, M.R.: RDFPeers: A scalable distributed RDF repository based on a structured peer-to-peer network. In: Proceedings of the 13th international conference on World Wide Web, WWW 2004, May 17-20, pp. 650–657. ACM Press, New York (2004)

8. Aberer, K., Cudré-Mauroux, P., Hauswirth, M., Pelt, T.V.: GridVine: Building internet-scale semantic overlay networks. In: McIlraith, S.A., Plexousakis, D., van Harmelen, F. (eds.) ISWC 2004. LNCS, vol. 3298, pp. 107–121. Springer, Heidelberg (2004)

9. Heine, F.: P2P based RDF querying and reasoning for grid resource description and matching. PhD thesis, Universität Paderborn, Germany (2006)

10. Heine, F.: Scalable P2P based RDF querying. In: InfoScale 2006: Proceedings of the 1st international conference on Scalable information systems, p. 17. ACM Press, New York (2006)

11. Battré, D., Heine, F., Kao, O.: Top k RDF query evaluation in structured P2P networks. In: Nagel, W.E., Walter, W.V., Lehner, W. (eds.) Euro-Par 2006. LNCS, vol. 4128, pp. 995–1004. Springer, Heidelberg (2006)

12. Battré, D.: Query Planning in DHT Based RDF Stores. In: IEEE International Conference on Signal Image Technology and Internet Based Systems, 2008. SITIS 2008, pp. 187–194 (2008)

13. Bloom, B.H.: Space/time trade-offs in hash coding with allowable errors. Communications of the ACM 13(7), 422–426 (1970)

14. Liarou, E., Idreos, S., Koubarakis, M.: Evaluating conjunctive triple pattern queries over large structured overlay networks. In: Cruz, I., Decker, S., Allemang, D., Preist, C., Schwabe, D., Mika, P., Uschold, M., Aroyo, L.M. (eds.) ISWC 2006. LNCS, vol. 4273, pp. 399–413. Springer, Heidelberg (2006)

15. Matono, A., Pahlevi, S.M., Kojima, I.: RDFCube: A P2P-based three-dimensional index for structural joins on distributed triple stores. In: Moro, G., Bergamaschi, S., Joseph, S., Morin, J.-H., Ouksel, A.M. (eds.) DBISP2P 2005 and DBISP2P 2006. LNCS, vol. 4125, pp. 323–330. Springer, Heidelberg (2007)

16. Chen, Y., Benn, W.: Query evaluation for distributed heterogeneous relational databases. In: COOPIS 1998: Proceedings of the 3rd IFCIS International Conference on Cooperative Information Systems, Washington, DC, USA, pp. 44–53. IEEE Computer Society Press, Los Alamitos (1998)

17. Manola, F., Miller, E.: RDF Primer (February 2004), http://www.w3.org/TR/rdf-primer/

18. Chen, M.S., Yu, P.S., Wu, K.L.: Optimization of parallel execution for multi-join queries. IEEE Transactions on Knowledge and Data Engineering 8, 416–428 (1996)

19. Selinger, P.G., Astrahan, M.M., Chamberlin, D.D., Lorie, R.A., Price, T.G.: Access path selection in a relational database management system. In: SIGMOD 1979: Proceedings of the 1979 ACM SIGMOD international conference on Management of data, pp. 23–34. ACM Press, New York (1979)

20. Guo, Y., Pan, Z., Heflin, J.: LUBM: A benchmark for OWL knowledge base systems. Web Semantics: Science, Services and Agents on the World Wide Web 3(2-3), 158–182 (2005)

DHTCache: A Distributed Service to Improve the Selection of Cache Configurations within a Highly-Distributed Context

Carlos E. Gómez[1], María del Pilar Villamil[2], Harold E. Castro[2],
and Laurent d'Orazio[3]

[1] University of Quindio - Republic of Colombia
[2] University of Los Andes - Republic of Colombia
[3] University Blaise Pascal - France
carloseg@uniquindio.edu.co, mavillam,hcastro@uniandes.edu.co,
laurent.dorazio@isima.fr

Abstract. Peer-to-peer (P2P) systems based on distributed hash tables allow the construction of applications with high scalability and high availability. These kinds of applications are more sophisticated and demanding on data volume to be handled as well as their location. A cache is quite interesting within these applications since a cache reduces the latency experienced by users. Nevertheless, configuring a suitable cache is not a trivial issue due to the quantity of parameters, especially within distributed and dynamic environments. This is the motivation for proposing the DHTCache, a cache service that allows developers to experiment with different cache configurations to provide information to make better decisions on the type of cache suitable for P2P applications.

1 Introduction

Peer-to-peer systems [1] (P2P Systems) are distributed systems composed of a large number of dynamic nodes. These systems are very interesting due to the possibility of being conformed in an ad-hoc manner without the aid of central servers or services. New distributed applications have appeared over the last few years for exploiting the good characteristics of P2P systems. Some examples of these are distributed games [3] and P2P databases [4].

Distributed Hash Table (DHT) systems are scalable and efficient data structures for object storage and location. These systems place objects over a very large set of nodes using different algorithms to uniformly distribute objects among nodes. Nodes form a DHT-based P2P overlay network that is decoupled from physical network topology using a hash function. This function is applied on nodes to determine their location, and, in the same manner, is used to identify objects within the system as well as for deciding which node is responsible for an object.

Caching is crucial for improving performance in distributed systems. However, a cache is efficient only if well configured and in accordance with its

A. Hameurlain and A M. Tjoa (Eds.): Globe 2009, LNCS 5697, pp. 48–59, 2009.

environment. Therefore, a cache is usually built from scratch for a given context. Such an approach is not affordable within P2P systems, where many heterogeneous caches may be required.

The present paper proposes the DHTCache[1] which is a sophisticated cache service for P2P systems that is placed on top of DHT Systems. The DHTCache allows developers to finely tune caches according to a specific context while making the selection of the appropriate cache strategies possible such as: Replacement Policies or Resolution Protocols. On the one hand, the DHTCache helps in reducing development costs, while supplying a cache framework and a library of components. On the other hand, the DHTCache enables greatly enhancing the performance of DHT systems as well as taking into account advanced caching techniques, particularly cooperative caching [7,2].

The rest of this paper is organized as follows: Section 2 presents an overview of P2P DHT systems and the manner in which caches, within these systems, can improve performance. Then, Section 3 describes work related to cache services. Section 4 presents the DHTCache, a cache service which validation and evaluation are shown in Sections 5 and 6, respectively. Finally, Section 7 provides conclusions and future work.

2   Key Elements for P2P Caching

Over the last few years, P2P systems have allowed for the creation of large-scale, highly available distributed applications, in particular, applications related to content sharing. The use of caches for enhancing their performance is interesting in this kind of systems. This section provides a description of DHT P2P systems and the use of caches in these systems in subsections 2.1 and 2.2.

2.1   DHT P2P Systems

P2P systems based on Distributed Hash Tables (DHT) are a major class of P2P systems. In these systems, objects are associated with a key (for instance produced by hashing the object name) and each node within the system is responsible for storing a certain range of keys. The hash function must guarantee the uniform distribution of keys, improving data retrieval and reducing issues related to high churn rates [1].

Typical DHT applications, called **DHTApplications** in the rest of this paper, merge node-management functions with data-management functions. A layer decomposition proposed in PinS [21] is used to facilitate the comparison of related works and to have a better understanding of DHTCache proposals. Three layers are identified: Distributed Lookup Service (DLS), Distributed Storage Service (DSS), and Distributed Data Service (DDS) as shown in Figure 1.

---

[1] Action ECOS C07M02.

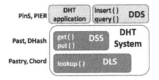

Fig. 1. DHT P2P functional layers

The first layer in a bottom-to-top description is the **DLS** layer. This manages the overlay network topology, the lookup of peers (identified by keys), and routing of the messages using routing information and stabilization protocols. Chord [20] and Pastry [16] are examples of DLS. The main function in this layer is: `lookup(key)` which returns the identity (e.g. the IP address) of the node storing the object with that *key*. The lookup() operation is a distributed function allowing nodes to put and get files based on their keys. Each node maintains a routing table consisting of a small subset of nodes within the system (typically *log N* entries). When a node receives a query for a key for which it is not responsible, the node routes the query to the neighbor node which is closest (according to specific semantics) to the node that is capable of solving the query. In the worst case, this process contacts *log N* nodes.

The second layer, the **DSS** layer, manages object storage and retrieval, assuring their durability, their reliability and efficient insertion and querying processes. The DSS layer then supplies the set of objects answering a query demand from the DDS layer or any DHTApplication.

This particular layer uses DLS functionality and offers load balancing and caching strategies. The main functionalities of the DSS layer are: `get(key)` which returns the object(s) identified by the *key*; and `put(key, object)` which inserts an *object* identified by its *key* into the system.

Examples of systems within the DSS layer are Past [17] and DHash [5]. Both, get() and put(), are distributed functions. They use the DLS layer to identify the node responsible for a key.

The last layer is the **DDS** layer. This layer manages data storage and declarative queries. Such queries have more semantics (i.e. SQL sentences). They enable multi-attribute, keyword, joins, and range queries. This layer translates declarative queries into the basic operations (i.e. get(), put(), lookup()) provided by the DSS and DLS layers. The DLS and DSS are jointly called the **DHTSystem** in the rest of this paper. Examples of systems within the DDS layer are PIER [9], PinS [21] and KSS [8].

2.2 Cache in DHT P2P Systems

Caching is crucial for enhancing performance within distributed systems. However, a cache is only efficient if it is suitably configured in accordance with its environment. Consequently, a cache is usually built from scratch for a given environment.

It is possible to identify minimal and optional functions within a cache, as proposed in ACS [6]. Minimal functionalities include the Content Management (in particular the data structure used for storing elements in the cache), the Replacement Policy (used for removing elements to add new ones), and the Resolution Protocol (used to retrieve an element absent from the cache). Examples of optional functionalities are Admission Strategy (which enables determining if an element is cacheable), or analyzing and assessing capabilities for building semantic caches.

Within a layered distributed system, such as a P2P system, other elements, related to distribution and dynamicity of nodes, are present. The cache itself is distributed over several nodes and is present across all layers. Cache distribution is aimed at making the path for retrieval of a shorter object.

Different kinds of information can be cached depending on the layer implementing it within a DHTSystem. For example, the DLS is able to cache (key-node) resolutions and the DSS is able to cache (key-object) resolutions. Consequently, the idea of having a cooperative cache between distinct layers of the DHTSystem as well as between caches located at different nodes emerges.

The use of a cache in a DHTSystem means that the get process, which involves following a chain of links to discover the real owner of an object can be improved. Thus, the node looks in its local cache for a copy of the requested object before following a new link. This is the way DHTsystems currently work. Nevertheless, the DLS layer would also benefit from such an approach. If instead of following the links we could find the direct link to the node responsible for the requested object, the path would then be shortened.

A distributed cache can be organized in different ways; for example, in a ring or in a hierarchical structure. Regarding the ring structure, the next node to visit, after a miss in the cache of the node n_i is produced, (i.e. the unsuccessful retrieval from the cache of the requested object), is the successor node of n_i. This option enables a spectrum of possibilities for configuring cache topologies to improve DHTSystem performance.

In despite of the accepted benefits of using caches in DHTApplications, it is very difficult to determine the appropriate strategy for a given context. Issues such as the ideal topology, resolution protocols, and replacement policies are very complex to fine tune.

3   Related Work on Cache Within Distributed Systems

Diverse proposals are directed at a cache in DHT P2P systems [10,12,18] and others are directed at adaptable caches [6] or at cache-context management services [11]. However, these do not respond to the issues regarding cache configuration or cooperation between heterogeneous caches.

Several works have been proposed regarding distributed caches. These works can be analyzed according to the services they provide. Three groups are identified: the first two groups are related to P2P systems, whereas the third group considers adaptable cache services. In the first group, DHTSystems used as caches of other P2P systems are analyzed, whereas in the second group, P2P systems that are implemented inside a cache are considered.

In the first group works such as Squirrel [10] and PierSearch [12] use the DHT as a cache. Squirrel attempts to reduce the use of network resources, and PierSearch improves the answer recall. Still, it is difficult to generalize the proposed solutions because they are coupled to the core of their proposals and there are certain important issues such as object placement, replacement policy, and coherence models that are not described. DHTCache tackles these issues.

In the second group, proposals are submitted according to the functional layer. There are works such as DHash [5] and Past [17] at the DSS level which propose a cache to ameliorate popular object queries. The load distribution on peers in these works is enhanced with regard to a reduction in response times. There are works such as DCT [18] and PinS [21] in the DDS layer, which improve response time by reducing the processing cost of previously executed queries. These proposals improve the traffic consumption and enable the use of cache semantics regarding queries comprised of equality and inequality terms. Although there are cache proposals within both DSS and DDS layers, it is difficult to reuse these solutions in new proposals as it is not clear how to provide cooperation between heterogeneous caches since these do not provide information on the context where they are used. An analysis of these problems is included in the DHTCache.

The third group is related to adaptable cache services such as: Cache4j [19], Ehcache [13], Perseus [14] and CaLi [22]. The last two are the most relevant. CaLi is a framework for building local or distributed caches. Perseus is a framework for building persistent object managers, supplying a dynamically adaptable cache service. Although the concept of a cache is very clear and exact in these works, Perseus does not incorporate the cooperative cache concept and the caches in CaLi cannot be dynamically adapted.

4   DHTCache

DHTCache is a sophisticated cache service placed on top of DHTSystems and is independent of the underlying DHTSystem. First, the DHTCache is a distributed cache that distinguishes different types of caches, according to the different layers of DHTSystems. This will then supports decisions on the type of cache suitable for developing in a particular DHTApplication. A detailed description of the DHTCache is given in this section.

4.1   Overview

The DHTCache can be enabled or disabled without modifications to the application under consideration. This allows DHTApplications to experiment with different cache configurations at both local and distributed levels. The DHTCache intercepts `get` and `put` messages sent to a DHTApplication. When a cache miss occurs, the DHTCache forwards the `get` message to the underlying DHTSystem. Figure 2 shows the manner in which the DHTCache works. Under

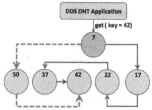

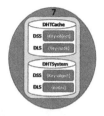

Fig. 2. Operation of DHTCache   **Fig. 3.** Typical node

normal conditions, the DHTApplications have only one path for object retrieval (following the DLS's `lookup` operation, represented by a thin continuous line). The DHTCache allows implementing a second path, representing a specific cache strategy. Thus, developers can test different cache strategies for their applications at a low cost. This second path follows a specific topology dictated by the cache strategy (represented by a thick non-continuous line). A zoom of the node which id is **7** is shown in the figure 3.

Each node used in deploying the DHTCache has two kinds of repositories. The first one is related to the DHTSystem and stores a subset of objects, those for which it is responsible as well as those within its DSS cache. The second one is related to the DHTCache and its caches at the DLS and DSS layers. Thus, the DHTCache implements a new level of cache to store objects according to a high level cache policy specified by the application developer. The DHTCache is based on two different types of caches: DSS caches and DLS caches, as illustrated in figure 3. The DSS caches aim at reducing data transfers. In DSS caches (at the DHTSystem and DHTCache levels), an entry is a pair (`key, object`) where *key* is the identifier of the *object* and object is the object itself. The objective of the DLS cache is to improve communications while retrieving nodes associated to a key within the DLS layer. An entry in a DLS layer of the DHTCache is a pair (`key, node`) where *key* is the identifier of the object and *node* is the node responsible for storing this particular object. It is important to remember that the DLS layer in the DHTSystem has only routing information for finding a node associated to a key and the same does not provide a cache.

4.2   Internal Functions

The DHTCache is a DHTApplication and so takes advantage of the cache. The cache is intended for improving applications performance, allowing developers to experiment with different cache configurations as well as for providing information for better decision making regarding the type of cache suitable for developer application. Figure 4 shows the different components making part of a DHT service and the manner in which the get function works within the DHTCache.

A `get` is described using the steps illustrated in figure 4. Operations ending in 1 such as `get1` are used to reference local functions related to a DHTSystem, whereas those ending in 2 are related to local functions within the DHTCache. Finally, those ending in 3 represent distributed operations within the DHTCache.

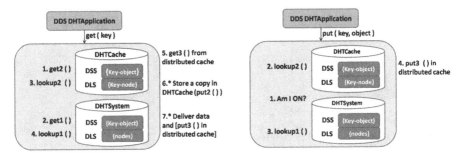

Fig. 4. Get function   **Fig. 5.** Put function

To illustrate the process, let's say a node (called the **Access Node** in the rest of this paper) looks for an object (i.e. executes a `get` operation). The process starts by the DHTCache intercepting this `get` in an attempt to solve the query directly from the cache. As the cache is distributed, it gathers all of the local information before moving to the next node in the cache path. The next node visited in a cache path is identified according to the cache topology defined by the DHTApplication developer. The `get` works as follows:

1. Attempts to get the object from the local DSS-DHTCache (cache implemented by DHTCache in the DSS layer). If the requested object is found, it is delivered.
2. Attempts to get the object from the DSS-DHTSystem layer (remember the DSS has all the objects administered by the local node as well as those formerly retrieved by the node, which are stored in the small DSS cache). The DHTCache makes a local `get` represented as `get1` in figure 4. This `get` is responsible for searching for the object within its local cache. The DHTCache is benefited from this cache although it does not have control over it.
3. If the object is not there, before going to the next node within the cache path, the DHTCache verifies the information this node has on the owner node of the object, referenced as the **Owner Node** in the rest of the present article. If a link to the Owner Node exists, then follow this link. Thus, in step 3, the DHTCache looks within its DLS cache for searching the Owner Node (i.e. IP address) of the requested object.
4. Then, the DHTCache gathers information on the next node to be visited. This information is used to determine the best next node to visit after exhausting the distributed cache search. In this step, it looks within the DLS-DHTSystem for a link to the Owner Node. But even if the node does not have a direct link, here the node will have a link to a closer node. The information on the closer node should be stored in an attempt to find the closest node known by all of the nodes within the cache path.
5. If the object is not in this local node and there is not any information on the IP address of the node responsible for the object, the DHTCache then

uses its topology to identify the next node to contact. Then the DHTCache goes to the next node within the cache path.

Steps 6 and 7 are only executed by the Access Node (Figure 4 represents this using an'*'), once the requested object reaches it.

6. The DHTCache stores a copy within the DSS-DHTCache along with the key-node association in the DLS- DHTCache.
7. As an option (depending on the cache policy), the Access Node places a copy of the object into the distributed cache.

Finally, when there is a cache miss, the search continues using the information gathered regarding the best link to go through to the node responsible for the requested object. It is important to note that the cache search only wastes time if the DHTCache was not able to find a better link than the one already known by the Access Node.

According to the cache policies defined by the DHTApplication developer, a put process will be executed when a put service is demanded by a DHTApplication. This last case occurs for example, when a prefetch cache policy was chosen. In this last case, the put follows the process illustrated in figure 5.

The put process is based on discovering the Owner Node for the key associated with the object to be stored. The DHTCache put process is essentially the same as in any DHTSystem: 1. The DHTCache verifies if the Access Node is the Owner Node, but then, before looking within the DLS layer (step 3 according to Figure 5), 2. The DHTCache, using a lookup2, consults the DLS-DHTCache to verify if the Owner Node for the object's key is already known.

Finally, and as an option, as in the get function (depending on the cache policy), the DHTCache executes step 4. The Access Node places a copy of the object into the distributed cache.

4.3   External Functions

The DHTCache allows DHTApplication developers to configure the most important parameters of a cache configuration: the type of cache, the amount of space that should be reserved for storing items within the cache, the Replacement Policy, and the Resolution Protocol, for one specific application. With regard to the Resolution Protocol, the DHTCache provides the option to define a cache topology. It is possible to create, for example, a ring, a hierarchical structure of one or more levels, or a completely irregular structure on top of the overlay network. These parameters are used to create and to deploy a customized cache configuration for the DHTApplication to be analyzed by the DHTApplication developer.

The DHTCache records events related to put and get functions and misses and hits (i.e. the successful retrieval of requested object from the cache) frequencies in log files. These logs are consolidated by the Analyzer component to obtain metrics of application performances. Logs are not only used by users but also for automatic caching adaptation, without human administration. The metrics are related to time and frequency of the hits, object insertions, and object lookups using a specific configuration of the cache (e.g., replacement policy, space for storing items). Then, the developer can use these metrics to compare and to decide the better configurations of the cache to implement.

5   Implementation

A DHTCache prototype was built to validate our proposal as well as to provide a cache framework and a library of components. In addition to implementing the get and put operations, our prototype focuses on the cache configuration and evaluation aspects. The prototype was implemented in *java*1.5 using ACS [6] as a framework for building the cache and FreePastry [15] as a DHT system providing Past [17] and Pastry [16] as DSS and DLS layers, respectively. ACS and FreePastry were selected because they match most of our requirements: Freepastry is a widely accepted implementation of a DHTSystem whereas ACS is a good environment for easily implementing different cache configurations.

The prototype includes the cache in DSS layer, the configuration of some parameters such as size, and the Replacement Policy, distinct topologies for applying the Resolution Protocol, management of the cycles that can be produced within distributed cache topologies, the interception of get and put messages from DHTApplications, the logs on cache events as well as those related to the underlying DHTSystem and the Analyzer component.

ACS was used to create the DSS-DHTCache. ACS implements a framework for cache systems development and allows configuring parameters such as the cache size and the Replacement Policy (LRU or FIFO).

New kinds of topologies for the Resolution Protocol were included in ACS. A cache topology can be created by assigning links among nodes belonging to a distributed cache. For example, a link between the caches on nodes a and b indicates that the cache in b will be used to find an object when a cache miss occurs on node a. It is important to note that several nodes can be assigned to support the Resolution Protocol within a specific node. The order for assigning the links determines the priority to be applied in the Resolution Protocol. A distributed cache topology can have redundant link which generate cycles when applying the Resolution Protocol. We controlled those cycles (to avoid searching the same object twice within the same node during the same search process) using a recursive algorithm which searches in the distributed cache according to the predefined order.

FreePastry was modified to include a cache implemented with ACS for each node for these caches to use all ACS current features. However, in this version of the DHTCache the Resolution Protocol was not integrated with FreePastry.

New methods were included at the level of Past [17] to integrate the processes associated to get and put operations, described in subsection 4.2 However, all object storage associated with the DHTCache is implemented using the ACS repository.

Logs related to cache events were implemented using the logger feature of ACS whereas logs for DHTSystems were implemented using the Freepastry logger.

With the DHTCache logger, several events such as hit rates, insert, and lookup operations are recorded.

The Analyzer component gathers all the logs for each node within the system to create a summary after the execution of a test finish. Each node generates two different logs related to DHTCache and DHTSystem events. These two logs are used by the Analyzer to generate a new log containing summaries on average times and frequencies of the events associated with each object used in the test. These results are delivered to the developer in a plain file. Developers can then use these results to compare different cache configurations for a particular application.

6   Evaluation

Before explaining the strategy to evaluate the DHTCache, several non-functional features of the DHTCache are going to be highlighted. The DHTCache is flexible due to the use of input/output plain files. Thus, the developer can store the file properties along with the results to analyze these later. Regarding usability, the DHTCache is used in the same manner FreePastry is used. However, the log-files-gathering process needs to be automated. The DHTCache has other features inherited from FreePastry such as portability and scalability.

Evaluation of the DHTCache is a twofold issue. To evaluate the DHTCache, the proposed functionality and the capability of a developer to make decisions based on the information provided by this tool requires validating.

Several experiments were performed to compare the obtained results in terms of hit rate (percent between the number of requests satisfied by the cache of the DHTCache over the number of requests performed). A third-party DHTApplication was used, which was originally conceived for running on FreePastry while using Past as a repository to store objects within the DHTSystem. The application performs queries on metadata to retrieve objects shared within the system.

Scenarios including distinct number of nodes and cache configurations were proposed for validating scalability. These scenarios contain three diferent network configurations using 400, 600 and 800 nodes sharing up to 1000 objects, three cache sizes of 200, 400 and 600 objects and two Replacement Policy FIFO and LRU. Cache size was computed to fit a fixed fraction of the objects within the system.

Figure 6 shows the hit rate metric calculated using the DHTCache with one specific DHTApplication using different scenarios. In these cases we can observe the relationship between the cache size and the Replacement Policy. A DHT developer responsible for DHTSystems with a number of nodes up to 600 can use these results for deciding to implement only LRU policy and to configure the cache size in 200. It is important to note that (1) DHTApplication developers are responsible for analyzing metrics and deciding the cache configuration to be implemented and (2) the results obtained are highly dependent on the DHTApplication used to test the DHTCache, thus, the results obtained do not apply within a different context.

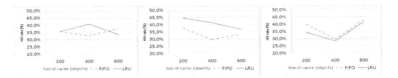

Fig. 6. Evaluation of the DHTCache with 400, 600 and 800 nodes

7   Conclusions

The present article presents the DHTCache, a DHTApplication to provide information on the impact of different types of caches associated with a DHTApplication for supporting making decisions about the more appropriated cache configuration for one specific application. The DHTCache aids in reducing development costs, facilitating the identification of one appropriate cache configuration before its implementation in one DHTApplication, and enables enhancing the performance of DHTApplications by taking into account advanced caching techniques as cooperative caching.

The DHTCache provides a set of metrics that can be used by a DHTApplication developer to identify how the use of one cache configuration can improve the query execution time as well as how a local configuration can affect a global performance.

A first prototype of the DHTCache is functional and allows validating the ideas of this proposal. This prototype was used to evaluate functionality as well as the use of the DHTCache as a decision-making tool. A first performance evaluation using up to 800 nodes with 1000 objects yields interesting results that can be used to continue this work specifically with topics on cooperative, adaptable, and semantic caches for DHTP2P Systems.

Other elements, related to DHTCache implementation and evaluation, are considered for future work. First, the development of cache within the DLS layer and its interaction with caching within the DSS layer have been included, which is an easier way to specify the distributed cache topology and a mechanism for automatically defining new metrics and collecting the log files. Second, the evaluation of scenarios with more peers interacting and with concurrent execution of divers DHTApplications will be included in order to identify the impact of local configurations in global behavior as well as to identify types of DHTApplications where a group of cache configurations will be of particular interest.

References

1. Androutsellis-Theotokis, S., Spinellis, D.: A survey of peer-to-peer content distribution technologies. ACM Computing Surveys 36(4), 335–371 (2004)
2. Barish, G., Obraczka, K.: World wide web caching: Trends and techniques. IEEE Communications Magazine 38(5), 178–184 (2000)
3. Bharambe, A.R., Agrawal, M., Seshan, S.: Mercury: Supporting Scalable Multi-Attribute Range Queries. In: Proc. of ACM SIGCOMM (2004)

4. Bonifati, A., Khrysanthis, P., Ouksel, A.M., Sattler, K.U.: Distributed Databases and Peer to peer databases: past and present. In: Proc. of ACM SIGCOMM (2008)

5. Cates, J.: Robust and efficient data management for a distributed hash table. Master's thesis, Massachusetts Institute of Technology (May 2003)

6. d'Orazio, L., Jouanot, F., Labbé, C., Roncancio, C.: Building adaptable cache services. In: Proc. of the intl ws on Middleware for grid computing, pp. 1–6 (2005)

7. Dahlin, M., Wang, R.Y., Anderson, T.E., Patterson, D.A.: Cooperative caching: Using remote client memory to improve file system performance. In: Proc. 1st Symposium on Operating Systems Design and Implementation, pp. 267–280 (1994)

8. Gnawali, O.: A Keyword-Set Search System for Peer-to-Peer Networks. Master thesis, Massachusetts Institute of Technology (2002)

9. Huebsch, R., Chun, B.N., Hellerstein, J.M., Loo, B.T., Maniatis, P., Roscoe, T., Shenker, S., Stoica, I., Yumerefendi, A.R.: The architecture of pier: an internet-scale query processor. In: Proc. of the Conf on Innovative Data Systems Research, pp. 28–43 (2005)

10. Iyer, S., Rowstron, A.I.T., Druschel, P.: Squirrel: a decentralized peer-to-peer web cache. In: Proc. of the ACM Symposium on Principles of Distributed Computing, pp. 213–222 (2002)

11. Jouanot, F., d'Orazio, L., Roncancio, C.: Context-aware cache management in grid middleware. In: Hameurlain, A. (ed.) Globe 2008. LNCS, vol. 5187, pp. 34–45. Springer, Heidelberg (2008)

12. Loo, B.T., Hellerstein, J.M., Huebsch, R., Shenker, S., Stoica, I.: Enhancing p2p file-sharing with an internet-scale query processor. In: Proc. of the Intl. Conf. on Very Large Data Bases, pp. 432–443 (2004)

13. Luck, G.: Ehcache, http://ehcache.sourceforge.net/

14. Object Web. Perseus, http://perseus.objectweb.org/

15. Rice University Houston USA (2002), http://freepastry.rice.edu/FreePastry/

16. Rowstron, A., Druschel, P.: Pastry: Scalable, decentralized object location, and routing for large-scale peer-to-peer systems. In: Guerraoui, R. (ed.) Middleware 2001, vol. 2218, pp. 329–350. Springer, Heidelberg (2001)

17. Rowstron, A.I.T., Druschel, P.: Storage management and caching in past, a large-scale, persistent peer-to-peer storage utility. In: Proc. of the Symposium on Operating System Principles, pp. 188–201 (2001)

18. Skobeltsyn, G., Aberer, K.: Distributed cache table: efficient query-driven processing of multi-term queries in p2p networks. In: Proc. of the intl ws on Information retrieval in peer-to-peer networks, pp. 33–40 (2006)

19. Stepovoy, Y.: Cache4j, http://cache4j.sourceforge.net/

20. Stoica, I., Morris, R., Liben-Nowell, D., Karger, D.R., Kaashoek, M.F., Dabek, F., Balakrishnan, H.: Chord: a scalable peer-to-peer lookup protocol for internet applications. IEEE/ACM Transactions on Networking 11(1), 17–32 (2003)

21. Villamil, M.-D.-P., Roncancio, C., Labbé, C.: Pins: Peer-to-peer interrogation and indexing system. In: Proc. of the Intl Database Engineering and Applications Symposium, pp. 236–245 (2004)

22. Zola, J.: Cali, efficient library for cache implementation. In: Proc. of the Mexican Intl. Conf. on Computer Science, pp. 415–420 (2004)

Proactive Uniform Data Replication by Density Estimation in Apollonian P2P Networks

Nicolas Bonnel, Gildas Ménier, and Pierre-François Marteau

Valoria, European University of Brittany, 56000 Vannes, France

Abstract. We propose a data replication scheme on a random apollonian P2P overlay that benefits from the small world and scale free properties. The proposed algorithm features a replica density estimation and a space filling mechanism designed to avoid redundant messages. Not only it provides uniform replication of the data stored into the network but it also improves on classical flooding approaches by removing any redundancy. This last property is obtained at the cost of maintaining a random apollonian overlay. Thanks to the small world and scale free properties of the random apollonian P2P overlay, the search efficiency of the space filling tree algorithm we propose has comparable performances with the classical flooding algorithm on a random network.

1 Introduction

Although costly (bandwidth wise and/or memory side), data replication remains a crucial operation for distributed systems to ensure scalability and fault toler-ance. Optimizing the data replication is needed to harness the expensive cost of creating replicas : there must be as few replicas as possible and these replicates should be wisely chosen and distributed. In unstructured P2P network [5,9,16], most of the search strategies involves a blind query propagation leading to a cost proportional to the number of random nodes to visit, called the Expected Search Size (ESS) [6].

In uniform replication, since data are evenly replicated, the ESS is minimized for high quantity of unsolvable queries [6]. This strategy can be achieved as follows: each time a new piece of data is inserted into the network, a fixed number of replicas is created and spread accross the network. This strategy is efficient in structured P2P networks [11,15,10,7] because routing protocols allow to easily query for the presence of the data into the network. On the other hand, this approach is very costly to implement in unstructured P2P network since data presence can be answered only by querying the whole network, which is very costly.

A replication strategy that is lineary proportional to popularity is used in most unstructured or centralized P2P architecture designed to exchange files as it lowers the access cost to popular data. For low number of unsolvable queries, the best performance is reached when using the square root of popularity [6]. It is defined as follows: given two pieces of data A and B in the network, the

A. Hameurlain and A M. Tjoa (Eds.): Globe 2009, LNCS 5697, pp. 60–71, 2009.

ratio between the number of copy R_A and R_B of these data is the square root of the ratio of their popularity P_A and P_B : $\frac{R_A}{R_B} = \sqrt{\frac{P_A}{P_B}}$. Freenet [4] achieves this replication mechanism thru path replication as stated in [6].

In most P2P structured architectures, data can be replicated when a node leaves the network : the missing data is detected because of the direct relationship used to bind data to a node-location. This reactive replication only uses bandwidth when necessary thus leading to accidental surges of bandwidth use that can be a problem for overlying applications.

Proactive replication scheme anticipates this problem by wisely replicating data to balance the load over time [14] however at a cost of a slightly higher network traffic that can be tuned to a bandwidth budget (see also path replication scheme in Freenet [4]).

We present in this paper a uniform replication strategy that uses a local replica density estimation. Because performances of the algorithm are linked to the exploration strategy, we also present an unstructured random apollonian P2P overlay that features non redondant exploration scheme. Next section introduces data replication by density estimation, section 3 presents random apollonian P2P networks, section 4 shows and discusses experiments and section 5 concludes this papers with suggestions for future work.

2   Data Replication by Density Estimation

Since the relationship between data position and node position in unstructured network is not defined as in structured P2P, the query language capabilities are not limited or constrained by any assumptions. In this study, we focus on languages with XPath-like [12] or XQuery-like [3] features. The more specific queries are, the least answers are returned: this also increases the number of unsolvable queries. As stated previously, uniform replication seems to be one of the best approaches when the number of unsolvable queries is high because it minimizes the expected search size. Because it may be difficult to detect missing data after a node departure, we focus here on proactive replication.

In this paper, we propose a uniform proactive replication scheme based on a local estimation of replica density for unstructured P2P networks where the average number of replica remains proportional to the (unknown) network size. This proactive strategy can be tuned to the amount of available network resources: nodes with higher bandwidth can replicate data more often than the ones featuring low bandwidth.

2.1   Principle

Our architecture is designed as follows: each user (node) n has two storage spaces. The first one is its home space E_n in which all data explicitly downloaded by n or shared with other users are stored. The second storage space is a cache C_n whose size is controlled by the users. C_n is used by our architecture to store data replicas. In order to distributively maintain the correct amount of replica, a score is periodically computed for each replica. According to their score, data are then replicated, kept or removed.

2.2   Replica Management

Let each piece of data have a unique identifier d. Each node n in the network maintains a list L_n containing all pieces of data that are candidates for replication. Elements in L_n are submited by other peers in the network. More precisely, L_n contains pairs (d, A_m), with d a data identifier and A_m the address of the node m that submitted the data to n and owns a local copy of this data. We make no assumption on the size of L_n.

Score Measurement. Let S_d be the measure of the score for a piece of data d. S_d is related to the density estimation of the replicas for d. This estimation is made by exploring the neighborhood of the node and counting the number of replicas of d encountered during this exploration. Therefore, most replicated data should have the highest scores.

Proactive Uniform Replication. In the following part of the paper, we do not take into account heterogeneity in data size. The replication algorithm features several stages that are performed periodically (and asynchronously) on every node of the network. For each node n, a data candidate d is selected for replication/removal according to a score S_d. As described below, S_d is related to the local replica density which is estimated by a local exploration of the neighbourhood of the node n. This exploration quantifies the number of d on each node n.

For each piece of data d that could be potentially replicated, if its score S_d is lower than the average score of all data in the cache of node n, then the piece of data with the highest score in C_n is deleted and d is dowloaded into C_n. When this is finished, L_n is cleared.

The node n then selects k pieces of data in $C_n \cup E_n$ having the lowest scores, contacts k nodes selected at random (with a random walk) and submits to each node a piece of data for replication. The algorithm 1 describes the whole replication process. The frequency of the execution of this algorithm can be tuned for each node, for instance according to the resources available at the node.

3   Apollonian P2P Networks

3.1   Apollonian Networks

2-dimensional Apollonian Networks (ANs) [1] can be produced as illustrated on figure 1: the initial network is reduced to a triangle and at each generation step, a node is added into each triangle and connected to the 3 nodes that compose the triangle. More precisely, we call these networks Deterministic ANs (DANs)

Algorithm 1. Replication algorithm performed periodically on each node n.

Data: k : number of data submitted per node for replication
while *true* **do**

    `// Performs local exploration for computating the score`
    `// ` S_d ` for all data ` d ` in ` $C_n \cup E_n \cup L_n$

    $\overline{S} \leftarrow \frac{\sum_{d \in C_n} S_d}{|C_n|}$

    forall $d \in L_n$ **do**
        if $S_d < \overline{S}$ **then**
            $C_n \leftarrow C_n \cup \{d\}$
            $C_n \leftarrow C_n \setminus \{d_{max} \in C_n / \forall d_x \in C_n, S_{d_{max}} \geq S_{d_x}\}$

    end
    $L_n \leftarrow \emptyset$
    $[d_1..d_k] \leftarrow k$ pieces of data that have the lowest score in $C_n \cup E_n$
    $[m_1..m_k] \leftarrow k$ nodes in the network randomly contacted
    forall $i \in [1..k]$ **do**
        $L_{m_i} \leftarrow L_{m_i} \cup (d_i, A_n)$
    end
    `// Waits for the next iteration`
end

---

because of their building algorithm. Random Apollonian Networks (RANs) have the same properties that DANs (scale-free, small-world, Euclidean and space filling) [19] but are slightly different in their construction. 2-dimensional RANs are incrementaly built by inserting at each step a node in a triangle chosen at random. This node is then connected to the three other nodes of the triangle, an example of such network obtained is shown on figure 1(d). Both deterministic and random ANs have also been studied in higher dimension [17,18] by replacing triangles with simplexes.

In a fully distributed P2P environment, peers do not have a global knowledge, it is therefore impossible to distributively build a DAN. However it is possible in such environment to build a RAN by contacting a random node and obtaining a random simplex from this node, that is why we focus our study on RANs.

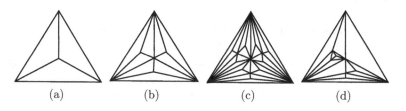

(a)   (b)   (c)   (d)

Fig. 1. Three 2D DANs with one (a), two (b) and three (c) generations of nodes, and a 2D RAN (d)

3.2   Efficient Exploration in Apollonian P2P Networks

We propose an efficient way to perform not redundant exploration in P2P RANs [2]. While our approach needs a few more hops than flooding or Lightflood for the same coverage, it does not generate redundant messages, and do not use cache on nodes to avoid the redundancy. Furthermore, it guarantees completeness as long as the overlay contains only one connected component. Contrary to flooding (or LightFlood [8]) filling trees on RANs are exhaustive and do not need a cache on nodes to store previous seen queries, as there is no discarding process.

Principle. We assume the network is stable during the flooding process. We design walkers able to incrementally build a spanning tree to explore a network area. They keep the sequence of the visited nodes, recording a kind-of Ariadne sequence composed with successive visited nodes. This sequence ensures that a node is visited once and only once. On a planar graph, this sequence builds incrementally an uncrossable fence for the walker. When encountering this limit, the walker splits, and each new walker inherits the previously recorded path. The sequences of paths taken by the walkers is a tree that fills the neighborhood of the source node P_s, ensuring that all nodes are scanned at least and at most one time.

When the request carried out by the walker is fulfilled, it returns to the initial node using the inverse path it has recorded. The walker terminates if all neighbors have already been visited or if its TTL (Time To Live) reaches 0.

Cloning Mechanism. Let $N(n)$ be the 1-hop neighborhood of node n. When a walker visits n, it clusters the unvisited nodes of $N(n)$. Thanks to the triangular mesh, all nodes in $N(n)$ describe a ring. By removing from this ring already visited nodes and their connections, there are between 0 and $x = \lfloor \frac{|N(n)|}{2} \rfloor$ remaining connected components. A clone of the walker is spawned inside each of these remaining connected component to fullfill the exploration.

A node is selected for propagation in each connected component according to different heuristics, for instance the node with the highest or smallest neighborhood, a random node, etc.

4   Experiments

We evaluate in this section several exploration strategies for estimating the density of replica: flooding, biased random walk (walkers cannot visit twice the same node) and filling trees. For this last exploration strategy, we study different heuristics for propagation. All simulated networks contains 10000 nodes. Flooding and biased random-walk are performed on a random graph while filling trees are used on a random apollonian network.

In order to deal with heterogeneity among node resources [13], we attribute to each node a capacity level according to the empirical distribution given in figure 2. This capacity level is used to compute the maximum degree and amount

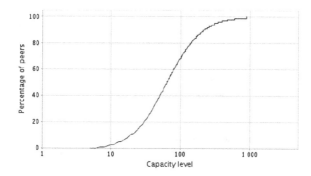

Fig. 2. Cumulative distribution of peers capacity

of data nodes can store. In order to simulate heterogeneity among data popularity, we give each piece of data a popularity level according to a uniform distribution. Nodes then receive an amount of data proportionnal to their capacity level,
data pieces being chosen with a biased probability proportional to its popularity.

Each time a node enters the network, its cache is freed. The size of the node
cache is equal to the amount of data the node received at the begining of the
experiment. We can then tune the average number of replica for each data by
altering data diversity.

We use the standard deviation estimation to measure the uniformity of the
replication. More precisely, we use a relative standard deviation in order to
compare the different approaches we evaluate.

4.1   Static Network

In this experiment, the starting average replication rate is 0.6% (the target
replication rate is 1.2%). We set the TTL for the different approaches so that we
obtain approximatively the same network coverage, near 20%. Results are shown
in the table 1. At each step, nodes submit $k = 2$ pieces of data having the lowest
score for replication. This allows the algorithm to converge faster than when k
is set to 1, while preventing nodes copying many pieces of data simultaneously.

Figure 3 shows the evolution of relative standard deviation for replica quantity.
Random walk and filling trees with either a random or smaller degree neighbor

Table 1. Network coverage for different exploration strategies

Strategy	TTL	Network coverage
Flooding	4	19, 65%
Random walk	2000	19.98%
FT-2hopNeighboor	13	18.07%
FT-random	120	19.86%
FT-smallestNeighborhood	290	20.67%

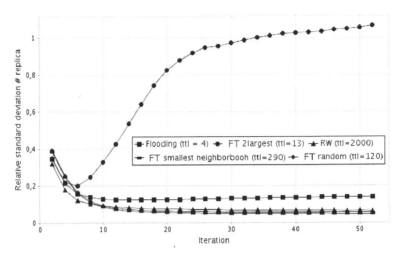

Fig. 3. Evolution of relative standard deviation for replica quantity

selection ffer the best performances. Results obtained with flooding are accept-able while filling trees with the selection of the neighbor that has the highest degree offers very poor performances: while the relative standard deviation de-creases in the few first steps, it then highly increases. We believe this phenomenon is because nodes with the lowest degree are never visited and some data may have a lot of replicas located on these nodes.

Figure 4 shows the average number of replicas created on each node at each step. We can see that the algorithm converges on a static network with a flood-ing exploration while there is no convergence at all with random walk. Results obtained with filling trees are between random walk and flooding. We believe these results are due to the randomness of the exploration strategy chosen: filing trees with the selection of the higest degree neighbor features less randomness that the selection of the smallest degree neighbor.

It seems that it is very important to visit the same nodes during each explo-ration for the algorithm to converge on a static network, and performances could be improved for filling trees. However we demonstrate in the next experiment this criterion is not as important in a dynamic environment.

4.2   Impact of the Density Estimation

We can see on Figure 4 that the amount of created replica becomes steady within 20 steps. We measure the efficiency of uniform replication by estimating replica density while running our replication algorithm for 20 steps. Each 20 run, the average amount of data replica is updated so that we can evaluate the average number of replicas seen per exploration. We compare in this study flooding (best convergence on a static network) and filling trees with the selection of the smallest degree neighbor (most uniform replication on a static network).

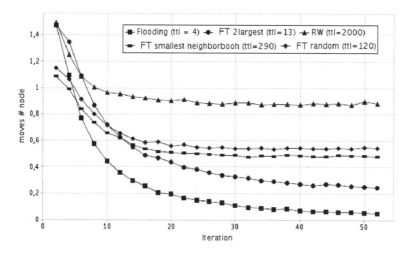

Fig. 4. Number of replicas created per nodes each step

Figure 5 shows the relative standard deviation obtained after 20 iterations. When the number of visited node is too small or when the data is loosely replicated, the number of replicas encountered during the exploration is too small and the algorithm does not converge, and even worse, it diverges (the initial relative standard deviation is bound between 0.3 and 0.4 as illustrated on figure 3).

Using flooding exploration, at least 7 replicas are needed to obtain a relative standard deviation bellow 0.2 whereas an exploration with filling tree with the

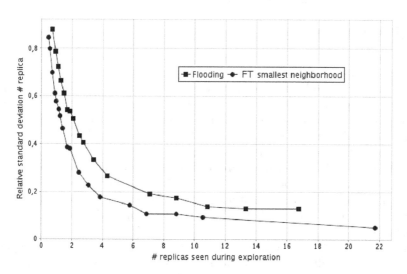

Fig. 5. Relative statard deviation within 20 steps of replication algorithm according to the average number of node having a replica seen during exploration

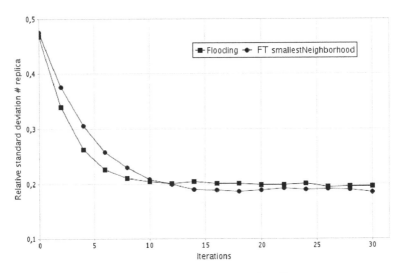

Fig. 6. Relative standard deviation of replicas amount

choice of the lowest degree neighbor for propagation requires only 4 replicas. Two hypothesis could explain this difference. The first one being the partial randomness of filling tree exploration whereas flooding is fully deterministic. The second one could be the heterogeneity of the size of the 4-hop neighborhood in a random topology: a more homogoneous exploration space size could lead to better performances.

Moreover, this experiment shows that uniform replication with density estimation is adpated to environment featuring high replication rates.

4.3   Dynamic Network

We have simulated a dynamic network by removing and adding new nodes at each iteration step, so that the size of the network remains on average constant in time. When new nodes are added, they receive an amount of data proportional to their capacity, data being taken at random as described at the begining of this section. Caches of newly added nodes are empty and their sizes are equal to the number of data the node has. The replication algorithm is performed when 10% of nodes have been renewed.

Parameters in this experiment are as follows: the initial replication rate is 0.6% (the target replication rate is 1.2%). Each node submits only one ($k = 1$) piece of data for replication to another node at each replication step: this reduces the number of replicas created at each step but the algorithm takes more time to converge.

Figure 6 shows the evolution of the relative standard deviation of replicas amount. At the begining the amount of data adapts to the network, and then there is a steady state with an average number of replica that remains nearly constant. An exploration with flooding allows to go a little bit faster to the steady

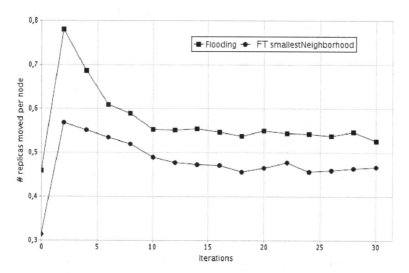

Fig. 7. Average number of replicas created per node each iteration step

state and both exploration schemes produce a replication similarly uniform. The relative standard deviation is higher comparatively to a static network mainly because new added nodes have empty caches.

Figure 7 shows the average number of replicas created per node at each iteration step. We can see that the copy rate is lower with an exploration strategy using filling trees comparatively to flooding. Performing the replication algorithm when 10% of nodes have been renewed could seem to be important but for the record, half of the nodes are renewed within one hours in operationnal P2P networks [13]. We have not tried a configuration for which the algorithm is performed when 50% of nodes have been renewed, since we believe that high delay between two replication steps could lead to data loss.

5   Conclusion and Future Work

We have presented a uniform replication strategy based on a local density estimation scheme. This approach is mainly designed for unstructured P2P architectures supporting complex query languages with high rejection capability (ie many requests cannot be fulfilled).

The local replica density estimation is performed by an efficient local exploration: we proposed a random apollonian P2P small world and scale free architecture that pairs with a non redundant exploration scheme and that does not use any cache on nodes. This architecture manages the heterogeneity among peers capacities and deals very well in transient or dynamic environments.

We have shown that random walk is not well suited for density estimation, while flooding produces quite good results - but also introduces a lot of redundant messages. We deduced from our experiments that two exploration strategies are best adapted to the replication scheme: LightFlood on Random P2P networks and filling trees on random apollonian networks: experimental results show similar performances with both approaches.

While apollonian networks do not use node caching to eliminate redundancy, the LightFlood overlay is less costly to maintain. Filling trees offer several heuristics for query propagation. The smallest neighbourhood heuristic helps the exploration space size remain constant given a fixed TTL : this seems to reduce significantly network traffic in dynamic environment.

This study is still preliminary: data size is uniform and the replica coherency problem remains to be addressed. Moreover, candidate nodes to the reception of data replica are randomly chosen, which could be improved by the use of heuristics.

References

1. Andrade, J., Herrmann, J.H., Andrade, R.F.S., da Silva, L.R.: Apollonian networks: Simultaneously scale-free, small world, euclidean, space filling, and with matching graphs. Phys. Rev. Lett. 94(1), 018702 (2005)
2. Bonnel, N., Ménier, G., Marteau, P.-F.: Search in p2p triangular mesh by space filling trees. In: 16th IEEE Int. Conf. on Networks (ICON 2008), New Delhi, India, December 2008. IEEE, Los Alamitos (2008)
3. Chamberlin, D.: Xquery: An xml query language. IBM Syst. J. 41(4), 597–615 (2002)
4. Clarke, I., Sandberg, O., Wiley, B., Hong, T.W.: Freenet: A distributed anonymous information storage and retrieval system. In: Federrath, H. (ed.) Designing Privacy Enhancing Technologies. LNCS, vol. 2009, pp. 46–66. Springer, Heidelberg (2001)
5. Clip2. The gnutella protocol specification v0.4 (2002)
6. Cohen, E., Shenker, S.: Replication strategies in unstructured peer-to-peer networks (August 2002)
7. Jagadish, H.V., Ooi, B.C., Vu, Q.H.: Baton: A balanced tree structure for peer-to-peer networks. In: VLDB, pp. 661–672 (2005)
8. Jiang, S., Guo, L., Zhang, X., Wang, H.: Lightflood: Minimizing redundant messages and maximizing scope of peer-to-peer search. IEEE Transactions on Parallel and Distributed Systems 19(5), 601–614 (2008)
9. Liang, J., Kumar, R., Ross, K.: The kazaa overlay: A measurement study (2004)
10. Maymounkov, P., Mazieres, D.: Kademlia: A peer-to-peer information system based on the xor metric (2002)
11. Ratnasamy, S., Francis, P., Handley, M., Karp, R., Shenker, S.: A scalable content addressable network. Technical Report TR-00-010, Berkeley, CA (2000)
12. Robie, J., Fernández, M.F., Boag, S., Chamberlin, D., Berglund, A., Kay, M., Siméon, J.: XML path language (XPath) 2.0. W3C proposed reccommendation, W3C (November 2006), http://www.w3.org/TR/2006/PR-xpath20-20061121/
13. Saroiu, S., Gummadi, K., Gribble, S.: Measuring and analyzing the characteristics of napster and gnutella hosts (2003)
14. Sit, E., Haeberlen, A., Dabek, F., Chun, B., Weatherspoon, H., Morris, R., Kaashoek, M., Kubiatowicz, J.: Proactive replication for data durability (2006)

15. Stoica, I., Morris, R., Karger, D., Kaashoek, M.F., Balakrishnan, H.: Chord: A scalable peer-to-peer lookup service for internet applications. In: SIGCOMM 2001: Proceedings of the 2001 conference on Applications, technologies, architectures, and protocols for computer communications, pp. 149–160. ACM, New York (2001)
16. Terpstra, W.W., Kangasharju, J., Leng, C., Buchmann, A.P.: Bubblestorm: resilient, probabilistic, and exhaustive peer-to-peer search. In: SIGCOMM 2007: Proceedings of the 2007 conference on Applications, technologies, architectures, and protocols for computer communications, pp. 49–60. ACM, New York (2007)
17. Zhang, Z., Comellas, F., Fertin, G., Rong, L.: High dimensional apollonian networks (2005)
18. Zhang, Z., Rong, L., Comellas, F.: High dimensional random apollonian networks (2005)
19. Zhou, T., Yan, G., Zhou, P.-L., Fu, Z.-Q., Wang, B.-H.: Random apollonian networks (2004)

Designing, Specifying and Querying Metadata for Virtual Data Integration Systems

Leopoldo Bertossi[1] and Gayathri Jayaraman[2]

[1] School of Computer Science,
Carleton University, Ottawa, Canada
and
University of Concepcion, Chile
bertossi@scs.carleton.ca
[2] Dept. Systems and Computer Engineering
Carleton University, Ottawa, Canada
gayatri_jraman@yahoo.com

Abstract. We show how to specify and use the metadata for a virtual and relational data integration system under the local-as-view (LAV) approach. We use XML and RuleML for representing metadata, like the global and local schemas, the mappings between the former and the latter, and global integrity constraints. XQuery is used to retrieve relevant information for query planning. The system uses an extended inverse rules algorithm for computing certain answers that is provably correct for monotone relational global queries. For query answering, evaluation engines for answer set programs on relational databases are used. The programs declaratively specify the legal instances of the integration system.

1 Introduction

Current day computer applications have a need to access, process, and report, and specially integrate data from various and disparate sources. Those data integration systems aim to provide a single unified interface for combining data in various formats from those multiple sources [5]. Virtually integrating heterogeneous data for query answering is still an ongoing research challenge.

A common approach uses a mediation system [18] that offers a query interface over a *single global schema*. This global schema consists of relational predicates, in terms of which the user can pose queries. However, there is no actual data contained in them. When the mediator receives a query, it produces a *query plan* that identifies the relevant data sources and the relevant data in them, and specifies how the data obtained from them has to be combined to build the final answer. To produce such a plan, the mediator stores and processes certain *mappings* that associate the predicates in the global schema with those in the local sources.

Some of the challenges in designing a mediator system are: (a) Using standard and expressive enough languages, and formats, for representing all the metadata contained in the mediator; (b) Using a standard way to query the metadata to extract the relevant information; (c) Developing a general query planning mechanism that uses the relevant metadata; and (d) Developing a methodology for executing those plans.

A. Hameurlain and A M. Tjoa (Eds.): Globe 2009, LNCS 5697, pp. 72–84, 2009.

There are different approaches to virtual data integration, depending on how the mappings are represented. The *local-as-view* (LAV) approach, which we follow in this paper, consists in defining the local relations as views over the global schema [12, 4]. In this way, each relevant source relation can be defined independently from other source relations. By doing so, it is easier for any source to join or leave the system, without affecting other source definitions.

Example 1. Consider a relational data source, ***animalkingdom***, containing data about animals. It contains the relation **V1** with attributes *Name, Class, Food*. Another data source, ***animalhabitat***, contains data about animals and their natural habitat. This data is available in the relation **V2** with attributes *Name, Habitat*.

V1	Name	Class	Food
	dolphin	mammal	fish
	camel	mammal	plant
	shark	fish	fish
	frog	amphibian	insect
	nightingale	bird	insect

V2	Name	Habitat
	dolphin	ocean
	camel	desert
	frog	wetlands

An information system designer interested in providing information on animals defines the following global schema $\mathcal{G}$: *Animal(Name, Class, Food), Vertebrate(Name), Habitat(Name, Habitat)*. This can be done even before the data sources **animalkingdom** and **animalhabitat** (and possibly others) are available to the system. The global relations *Animal* and *Vertebrate* are associated with the local relation **V1** via a Datalog query which defines **V1** as a view over $\mathcal{G}$, as containing animals that are vertebrates:

$$\mathbf{V1}(Name, Class, Food) \leftarrow Animal(Name, Class, Food), Vertebrate(Name). \tag{1}$$

Another mapping describes **V2** as containing animals and their habitat:

$$\mathbf{V2}(Name, Habitat) \leftarrow Animal(Name, Class, Food), Habitat(Name, Habitat). \tag{2}$$

Now consider a Datalog query, $\Pi(\mathcal{Q})$, posed to the mediator, to get all animals with their names and habitat:

$$Ans(Name, Habitat) \leftarrow Animal(Name, Class, Food), Habitat(Name, Habitat). \tag{3}$$

This is a conjunctive Datalog query whose answers cannot be computed by a simple direct computation of the rule body, because the data is not stored as material relations over the global schema. Instead, the mappings that describe the source relations have to be used; to produce a query plan that eventually queries the local sources, where the data is stored.   □

In this paper we describe the methodology that is followed in the design of a general system, the *Virtual Integration Support System (VISS)*, that can be used to specify and use specific mediator-based data integration systems under LAV. The system can be used to integrate multiple relational data sources (or sources wrapped as relational). It uses a standard format, based on XML and RuleML, for representing metadata. More specifically, data about the schemas is represented in and stored as native

XML: (a) The access parameters for the data sources (userid, password, etc.); (b) The structure of the relations at the sources; and (c) The structure of relations in the global schema. The mappings between the global schema and the local schemas are represented in *VISS* using RuleML [7], which is an XML-based markup language for the representation and storage of rules that are expressed as formulas of predicate logic. In order to gather the information needed to compute a query plan, the system uses XQuery, to query the metadata. *VISS* also supports the creation of query plans and their evaluation.

For query planning, *VISS* uses the EIRA algorithm, which is an extended version, introduced in [3, 4], of the *inverse-rules algorithm* (IRA) [9]. EIRA inherits the advantages of the IRA algorithm, but it can handle all the monotone queries, including those with built-ins. We assume that view definitions, i.e. of the source relations, are given by conjunctive queries. A resulting query plan is expressed as an extended Datalog program with stable model semantics [10]. The information gathered from the metadata is used to build this program. In the rest of this paper we illustrate the complete process using our previous and running example.

This paper is structured as follows. Section 2 introduces basic definitions related to virtual data integration, and the Extended Inverse Rules Algorithm. Section3 describes the architecture of *VISS*. Section 4 shows how to use XML and RuleML to specify schemas and mappings. Section 5 describes how XQuery is used to extract the relevant information from the metadata. Section 6 provides a detailed explanation of the query answering mechanism in *VISS*. Section 7 presents some conclusions and ongoing work.

2   Preliminaries

In general terms, a virtual data integration system has three main components: (a) A collection of local data sources with a (union) schema $\mathcal{S}$; (b) A global schema $\mathcal{G}$; and (c) A set of mappings $\mathcal{M}$ between the global and source schemas. A data source is an autonomous database that adheres to its own set of integrity constraints (ICs). In Example 1, **V1**, **V2** are predicates in the source schema $\mathcal{S}$. Those predicates offered by the global schema $\mathcal{G}$ do not have corresponding material instances. In Example 1, *Animal*, *Vertebrate* and *Habitat* are elements of the global schema. In the following we will also denote the integration system with $\mathcal{G}$.

Example 1 shows that it is possible to define other sources contributing with information about animals, such as invertebrates. In this sense, the information in the sources **animalkingdom** and **animalhabitat** can be considered as incomplete with respect to what $\mathcal{G}$ might potentially contain. More precisely, consider that we have a definition $V(\bar{x}) \leftarrow \varphi_i^{\mathcal{G}}(\bar{x}')$, with $\bar{x} \subseteq \bar{x}'$, of a source relation V as a view of $\mathcal{G}$, and a material extension, say v for V. If we have an instance D for $\mathcal{G}$, the view V gets an extension $V[D]$ over D. This instance D is considered to be a *legal instance* of the integration system if $V[D] \supseteq v$, for each view V. This reflects the openness assumption about the sources. *Legal*$(\mathcal{G})$ denotes the class of legal instances.[1]

---

[1]   In order to simplify the presentation, we will assume that sources are all open. However, we could easily deal with closed and exact sources [4].

Example 2. Consider the extensions for the source predicates: $v_1 = \{(dolphin,$
$mammal, fish), (camel, mammal, plant),$ $(shark, fish, fish),$ $(frog, amphibian,$
$insect), (nightingale, bird, insect)\}$; and $v_2 = \{(dolphin, ocean), (camel, desert),$
$(frog, wetlands)\}$. And the global instance D_0: $Animal = \{(dolphin, mammal, fish),$
$(camel, mammal, plant), (shark, fish, fish), (frog, amphibian, insect), (nightingale,$
$bird, insect), (snake, \quad reptile, frog)\}$; $Vertebrate = \{dolphin, camel, shark, frog,$
$nightingale, snake\}$; $Habitat=\{(dolphin, ocean), (camel, desert), (frog, wetlands)\}$.

The evaluation of the views on D_0 gives:

$\mathbf{V1}[D_0]=\{(dolphin, mammal, fish), (camel, mammal, plant), (shark, fish, fish),$
$(frog, amphibian, insect), (nightingale, bird, insect), (snake, reptile, frog)\}$;
$\mathbf{V2}[D_0] = \{(dolphin, ocean), (camel, desert), (frog, wetlands)\}$.

In this case, $v_1 \subseteq \mathbf{V1}[D_0]$ and $v_2 = \mathbf{V2}[D_0]$. Hence, D_0 is a legal global instance;
and all its supersets are also legal instances.   □

Now, given a global query $Q(\bar{x})$, i.e. expressed in terms of the global predicates, a tuple
$\bar{t}$ is a *certain answer* to Q if for every $D \in Legal(\mathcal{G})$, it holds $D \models Q[\bar{t}]$, i.e. the query
becomes true in D with the tuple $\bar{t}$. $Certain_{\mathcal{G}}(Q)$ denotes the set of certain answers [1]
to Q.

The Extended Inverse Rules Algorithm for obtaining certain answers from the integration system is based on a specification as a logic program $\Pi(\mathcal{G})$ with stable model
semantics of the legal instances of the system: The stable models of the program $\Pi(\mathcal{G})$
are (in correspondence with) the legal instances of $\mathcal{G}$. The specification is inspired by
the IRA algorithm [9], which introduces Skolem functions to invert the view definitions. In our case, instead of functions, we use auxiliary predicates whose functionality is enforced in the specification by means of the *choice operator* [11]. Actually,
what the program specifies is the collection of *minimal legal instances*, those that do
not contain a proper legal instance. This is because these instances are used to restore
consistency of the system for doing consistent query answering (CQA) [3, 4]. (Cf. [2]
for a survey of CQA). For monotone queries, using all the legal instances or only the
minimal ones does not make a difference. The program $\Pi(\mathcal{G})$ contains the following
rules:

1. The facts: $dom(a)$, for every constant $a \in U$; and $V(\bar{a})$ whenever $V(\bar{a}) \in v$, for
some source extension $v \in \mathcal{G}$.
2. For every view (source) predicate V in the system with definition $V(\bar{X}) \leftarrow P_1(\bar{X}_1),$
$..., P_n(\bar{X}_n)$, the rules: $P_j(\bar{X}_j) \leftarrow V(\bar{X}), \bigwedge_{X_i \in (\bar{X}_j \setminus \bar{X})} F_i(\bar{X}, X_i), \quad j = 1, ...n.$
3. For every auxiliary predicate $F_i(\bar{X}, X_i)$ introduced in 2., the rule that makes it func-
tional wrt the dependency of the last argument upon the first arguments:

$$F_i(\bar{X}, X_i) \leftarrow V(\bar{X}), dom(X_i), choice(\bar{X}, X_i).$$

The choice operator picks up only one value for X_i for every combination of values
for $\bar{X}$. This operator can be eliminated as such, or equivalently, defined using standard
rules. This point and the whole program is illustrated at the light of Example 3.[2]

---

[2] These specifications programs can be modified in order to capture also closed and exact
sources [4].

Example 3. Program $\Pi(\mathcal{G})$ contains the facts: $dom(dolphin)$, $dom(mammal), \ldots,$ $\mathbf{V}1(dolphin, mammal, fish), \ldots, \mathbf{V}2(dolphin, ocean), \ldots.$ And the rules:

$Animal(Name, Class, Food) \leftarrow \mathbf{V}1(Name, Class, Food).$

$Vertebrate(Name) \leftarrow \mathbf{V}1(Name, Class, Food).$

$Animal(Name, Class, Food) \leftarrow \mathbf{V}2(Name, Habitat), F_1(Name, Habitat, Class),$
$$F_2(Name, Habitat, Food).$$

$F_1(Name, Habitat, Class) \leftarrow \mathbf{V}2(Name, Habitat), dom(Class),$
$$chosen_1(Name, Habitat, Class).$$

$chosen_1(Name, Habitat, Class) \leftarrow \mathbf{V}2(Name, Habitat), dom(Class),$
$$not\ diffchoice_1(Name, Habitat, Class).$$

$diffchoice_1(Name, Habitat, Class) \leftarrow chosen_1(Name, Habitat, U),$
$$dom(Class), U! = Class.$$

$F_2(Name, Habitat, Food) \leftarrow \mathbf{V}2(Name, Habitat), dom(Food),$
$$chosen_2(Name, Habitat, Food).$$

$chosen_2(Name, Habitat, Food) \leftarrow \mathbf{V}2(Name, Habitat), dom(Food),$
$$not\ diffchoice_2(Name, Habitat, Food).$$

$diffchoice_2(Name, Habitat, Food) \leftarrow chosen_2(Name, Habitat, U),$
$$dom(Food), U! = Food.$$

$Habitat(Name, Habitat) \leftarrow V2(Name, Habitat). \qquad \square$

Specification programs like these can be evaluated with the *DLV* system [14], for example. It computes certain answers wrt the skeptical (or cautious) stable model semantics of disjuntive logic programs with weak negation and program contraints.

3   Overview of *VISS* ' Architecture

The *VISS* system is implemented in C++. It uses Oracle's Berkeley DB XML [16], an open source XML database, for storing all the XML documents related to a global schema. All XML documents, including the RuleML mappings, are stored in a container which can be queried using XQuery. The intermediate XML results can be stored in the same container.

When a Datalog query is posed to the mediator supported by *VISS*, the latter analyzes the query, to determine the source relations required to answer it. After that, using XQuery to query the metadata, the access information for those relations and their corresponding databases is obtained. Next, import commands are produced, to read tuples from the chosen source relations and store them as facts. These facts form the extensional database used by the program obtained with EIRA, which becomes the query plan. The program is run as in *DLV* (or *DLVDB* [13]). DLV allows for the evaluation of disjunctive Datalog^{not} programs [10], and provides an easy interface to external databases using ODBC drivers. The result of this program evaluation is the set of certain answers to the global query.

We assume in the rest of this paper that all the schemas are relational. However, the system can also be used to integrate XML data through the use of ODBC XML drivers, which represent native XML documents as relational tables. The virtual data integration system described in [15] also uses RuleML. However, it follows the *global-as-view* approach, according to which global relations are defined as views over the union of the local schemas [12].

The rest of this section explains some of the components of *VISS* as shown in Figure 1. Other components are explained in more detail in subsequent sections.

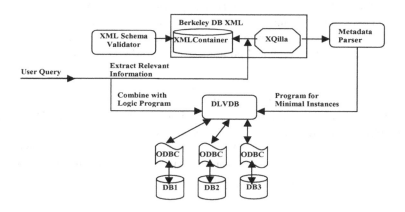

Fig. 1. Architecture of *VISS*

User Queries: *VISS* gives certain answers to monotone queries with built-ins that are expressed in Datalog. Queries in SQL3 format can be translated to Datalog using the SQL3 front end of *DLV*, which is invoked by *VISS*. The query is posed in terms of the predicates in the global schema. The query program is stored in a file named *query*, in the same directory where *VISS* is invoked. (Cf. Section 6 for details.)

XMLSchema Validator: In *VISS* the metadata about the global and source schemas is stored in an XML document; and the mappings are stored in RuleML format. This is described in Section 4. All this metadata is tested using the W3C XML Schema Validator, *XSV*, against the Datalog XML Schema Definition Document and its related submodules (they can be obtained from the RuleML web site). In spite of its name, its has extensions to first-order predicate logic.

Berkeley DB XML: *VISS* uses Oracle Berkeley DB XML 2.4.16 (BDBXML) [16], which is an open source, embeddable XML database/container for storing the XML metadata document. BDBXML includes an XQuery engine. The main BDBXML C++ objects used in *VISS* are *XMLManager*, a high-level class for managing containers; and *XMLContainer*, a file containing XML document. BDBXML uses XQilla 2.0, an open source XQuery, XSLT and XPath implementation that conforms to the XQuery 2.0 W3C recommendations [16]. *VISS* uses generic XQuery to extract the relevant information from the XML and RuleML metadata documents, to build the logic program specification. The results of the query in XQuery are obtained in the form of an *XMLResults* object.

Metadata Parser and Program Builder: The XML output obtained from the execution of XQuery against the XML metadata is parsed (using the Xerces C++ SAX Parser API calls), and the heads and bodies of the mappings are obtained. It next builds the file containing the program specification for the legal instances.

DLV: The generated logic program, $\Pi(\mathcal{G})$, specifies the minimal legal instances, and is combined with the query program in Datalog, $\Pi(\mathcal{Q})$, and with the *import commands* which load data (the program facts) that are *relevant* to a user query from the source relations. The latter are stored in relational DBMSs, with which *DLV* is able to interact (cf. next item). This combined program is run in *DLV* [13], which is invoked by *VISS*.

Wrappers and Data Sources: *DLV* provides interoperation with relational databases using ODBC connections. The ODBC connection is created as a ODBC Data Source Name (DSN) when a data source is registered with *VISS*. The ODBC connection uses a suitable ODBC driver for the DBMS at a data source. The name and connection parameters for each ODBC connection are also stored in the XML metadata document in *VISS*. Currently *VISS* supports integration of relational data sources.

4   XML and RuleML for the System's Metadata

This section first explains how XML is used in *VISS* for describing the metadata about each of the sources and global schema. For the sources, it stores the type and connection parameters, and the structure of the relations.

   All this information is stored using descriptive labels in XML, because it offers the flexibility for defining database schemas that vary from source to source, and also within each of them. All XML documents describing metadata in *VISS* start with a root node **VirInt**. The parameters for connecting to a particular data source are defined by labels such as **Userid, Password** and **Databasename**. Relation names in a data source are described using the labels **Rel**, and their attributes are represented using **Var**, as siblings for that **Rel**. The **Source** label is used to list all the data sources participating in the system and their details. The **Global** label is used to list all the details of the global schema, such as its relation names. Listing 1 shows the XML representation of the local and global schema for Example 1.

Example 4. The XML metadata about the data sources **animalkingdom** and **animalhabitat**, and the structure of the local relations **V1** and **V2**, and the global schema consisting of *Animal, Habitat* and *Vertebrate* in *VISS* are shown in Listing 1.   □

VISS also contains the mappings between the schemas. They are represented and stored in RuleML format, which is a markup language for representing logical rules. Apart

Listing 1. Sample XML describing the Local and Global Schema in *VISS*

```
<VirInt xmlns:xs="http://www.w3.org/2001/XMLSchema">
<Schema>
    <Local>
        <Source name="animalkingdom">
            <Type>sqlexpress</Type>
            <Hostname>animalkingdom</Hostname>
            <Databasename>animalkingdom</Databasename>
            <Userid>test</Userid>
            <Password>test</Password>
            <Atom>
                <Rel>V1</Rel> <Var>Name</Var> <Var>Class</Var> <Var>Food</Var>
            </Atom>
        </Source>
        <Source name="animalhabitat">
            <Type>mysql</Type>
            <Hostname>animalhabitat</Hostname>
            <Databasename>animalhabitat</Databasename>
            <Userid>test1</Userid>
            <Password>test1</Password>
            <Atom>
                <Rel>V2</Rel> <Var>Name</Var> <Var>Habitat</Var>
            </Atom>
        </Source>
    </Local>
    <Global>
        <Atom>
            <Rel>Animal</Rel> <Var>Name</Var> <Var>Class</Var> <Var>Food</Var>
        </Atom>
        <Atom>
            <Rel>Habitat</Rel> <Var>Name</Var> <Var>Habitat</Var>
        </Atom>
        <Atom>
            <Rel>Vertebrate</Rel> <Var>Name</Var>
        </Atom>
    </Global>
</Schema>
</VirInt>
```

from being similar to and based on XML for representing data, RuleML is also streamlined for storing rules using standard labels, according to the XML Schema Definition
for Datalog Rules in the RuleML 0.91 specification [7].

As in the preceding section, the database predicates are represented using **Rel**, and
their attributes, using **Var**. Built-ins are represented using **Ind**. **And** indicates that the
body of the rule is a conjunction of predicates. **Assert** opens and closes the list of
Datalog rules. **Implies** describes the rule is an implication, and hence contains **head**
and **body** labels.

Example 5. (example 1 continued) The mappings that are given as view definitions of
local relations, **V1** and **V2**, as views of the global schema consisting of *Animal, Habitat*
and *Vertebrate* are represented in RuleML format in Listing 2.   □

Currently, the metadata that *VISS* uses, as XML documents, has to be created manually,
and made available to *VISS*. However, *POSL* could be used to convert Datalog rules to
RuleML [6].

5   Using XQuery to Build the Specification

In order to compute the certain answers to a query, the XML metadata and RuleML
mappings have to be queried. After extracting the relevant information, the logic program $\Pi(\mathcal{G})$ that specifies of the legal instances can be generated. It will have the form
shown in Example 3. The extraction of the relevant information from the XML and

Listing 2. Sample RuleML describing the mappings in *VISS*

```
<RuleML xmlns:rule="http://www.ruleml.org/0.91/xsd"
xmlns:xsi="http://www.w3.org/2001/XMLSchema-instance"
xsi:schemaLocation="http://www.ruleml.org/0.91/xsd
file:///C:/thesis/VDI/datalog.xsd">
<Assert>
  <Implies>
    <head>
      <Atom>
        <Rel>V1</Rel> <Var>Name</Var> <Var>Class</Var> <Var>Food</Var>
      </Atom>
    </head>
    <body>
      <And>
      <Atom>
        <Rel>Animal</Rel> <Var>Name</Var> <Var>Class</Var> <Var>Food</Var>
      </Atom>
      <Atom>
        <Rel>Vertebrate</Rel> <Var>Name</Var>
      </Atom>
      </And>
    </body>
  </Implies>
  <Implies>
    <head>
      <Atom>
        <Rel>V2</Rel> <Var>Name</Var> <Var>Habitat</Var>
      </Atom>
    </head>
    <body>
      <And>
      <Atom>
        <Rel>Animal</Rel> <Var>Name</Var> <Var>Class</Var> <Var>Food</Var>
      </Atom>
      <Atom>
        <Rel>Habitat</Rel> <Var>Name</Var> <Var>Habitat</Var>
      </Atom>
      </And>
    </body>
  </Implies>
</Assert>
</RuleML>
```

RuleML metadata is done using XQuery, an SQL-type query language for XML documents. We use a reduced class of queries expressed in XQuery, the *FLWOR* expressions, which are of the form:

```
FOR <var> IN <expr>
LET <var> := <expr>
WHERE <expr>
ORDER BY <expr>
RETURN <expr>
```

FOR and LET clauses select all the tuples and bind the expressions. The WHERE clause specifies the condition for filtering the tuples. The ORDER BY clause gives the sorting order.

The RETURN clause specifies the projected attributes for the result. A generic query in XQuery is presented in Listing 3. It is used to extract, from the Listings 1 and 2, the heads and bodies, including built-ins, that are required to build the relevant view definitions, as Datalog rules.

Example 6. Using the query in XQuery shown in Listing 3, the XML metadata in Listings 1 and 2 can be queried. The rules are obtained in XML format as shown in Figure 2.   □

The intermediate information in XML thus obtained in Example 6 is then parsed using a C++ program called *minInstance*. In this way, the program specifying the legal instances shown in Example 3 is constructed. *minInstance* is implemented in C++, to read in an XML file that contains details of each LAV mapping, such as the head and body of each

Listing 3. Querying XML and RuleML metadata with XQuery

```
<!--First navigate to the node using the container in Berkeley DB XML 2.4.16-->
for $n in collection('mappingAlias')/VirInt return
<rules>                              <!--List all rules-->
    {for $x in $n/RuleML/Assert/Implies
    where distinct-values($x/body/And/Atom/Rel) =
    ("Animal", "Habitat")
    return
    <rule>                           <!--Describe the rule-->
    {for $d in $x return
        <head rl='{$d/head/Atom/Rel}'>    <!--Describe the rule-->
        { for $v in $x/head
        where $v/Atom/Rel=$d/head/Atom/Rel
        return
            concat($d/head/Atom/Rel,'(',
            string-join($v/Atom/Var,','),')')
        }
        </head>
    }
    {for $b in distinct-values($x/body/And/Atom/Rel)
    return
        <body rl='{$b}'>             <!--Describe the body of the rule-->
        { for $m in $n/Schema/Global/Atom
        where $m/Rel=$b
        return concat($b,'(',
        string-join($m/Rel/following-sibling::Var,','),')')
        }
        </body>
    }
    <body rl=''>                      <!--Describe built-ins in the rule-->
{ for $q in distinct-values($x/body/And/Atom/Ind)
let $l as xs:integer := index-of($x/body/And/Atom/*,$q)-1
let $r := $x/body/And/Atom/Ind/preceding-sibling::Rel/text()
let $s := $n/Schema/Global/Atom/Rel[text()=$r]/../Var[$l]
return
if ($q != '') then
(concat('(',$s,'=',$q,')',','))
else ()
}
    </body>
    </rule>
    }
</rules>
```

```
<rules xmlns:xsi='http://www.w3.org/2001/XMLSchema-instance'
xsi:noNamespaceSchemaLocation='mappingrule.xsd'>
    <rule>
        <head rl="V1">V1(Name, Class, Food)</head>
        <body rl="Animal">Animal(Name, Class, Food)</body>
        <body rl="Vertebrate">Vertebrate(Name)</body>
    </rule>
    <rule>
        <head rl="V2">V2(Name, Habitat)</head>
        <body rl="Animal">Animal(Name, Class, Food)</body>
        <body rl="Habitat">Habitat(Name, Habitat)</body>
    </rule>
</rules>
```

Fig. 2. Rules obtained with XQuery

rule, as shown in Example 6. It then outputs the specification logic program, but without the ground facts. *minInstance* first parses the XML file using the Xerces C++ SAX Parser API calls, and stores the content of each rule in a simple internal data structure. After reading in all the atoms of a rule (one head and the bodies of the rules defining it), each rule atom is parsed into the predicate and attributes. The strings are then manipulated in C++ using the STL String class functionality, to output the legal instances specification.

6 Query Answering

The current implementation of *VISS* supports the computation of the certain answers to queries. The program $\Pi(\mathcal{G})$, illustrated in Example 3, is combined with a program that generates the facts from the relevant relations using *#import* commands. This combined program is run in *DLV* with the query program $\Pi(\mathcal{Q})$. For monotone queries, the certain answers can be computed in this way [4].

However, for a given query $\Pi(\mathcal{Q})$, only a relevant portion of $\Pi(\mathcal{G})$ is required, the one containing rules that define global predicates that appear in $\Pi(\mathcal{Q})$.[3] Accordingly, first the relevant source relations are identified using a simple C++ module called *relExtract*. It is used to identify the global relations in $\Pi(\mathcal{Q})$. Next, the source relations defined in terms of the latter are derived, using XQuery as shown in Example 7.

Example 7. Consider query (3). Using *relExtract*, we get the predicates *Ans, Animal, Habitat*. XQuery is used against the intermediate XML result obtained in Example 6, to get the relevant source relations:

```
for $a in /rules/rule
where $a/body/@r1 = ("Ans", "Animal", "Habitat")
return data($a/head/@r1)
```

We obtain **V1** and **V2** as the relevant source relations for this query.   □

Once the relevant source relations have been detected, the system extracts from the Listing 1 the connection information for those sources, i.e. *hostname, databasename, userid*. Import commands are generated to extract from the data sources the facts needed by the specification program. They are of the form *#import(databasename, "username", "password", "query", predname, typeConv)*, where *databasename, username, password* are read from the XML metadata. *query* is an SQL statement that constructs the table that will be imported, *predname* defines the name of the predicate that will be used, and *typeConv* specifies the conversion for mapping DBMS data types to Datalog data types for each column. XQuery is used to simultaneously obtain relevant information and construct the import commands around the former.

Example 8. Running a query in XQuery against the XML metadata in Listing 1, we generate the import commands for the relevant source relations obtained in Example 7:

```
#import(animalkingdom,"test","test","SELECT * FROM V1",
V1, type : Q_CONST, Q_CONST, Q_CONST).
#import(animalhabitat,"test1","test1","SELECT * FROM V2",
V2, type : Q_CONST, Q_CONST).
```

Here, Q_CONST is a conversion type specifying that the column is converted to a string with quotes. It can be used in general for all data types. These import commands are combined with the program for the legal instances shown in Example 3. The rules specifying the global relations, plus the import commands, are combined with the query program $\Pi(\mathcal{Q})$ at hand. To obtain the certain answers to query $\mathcal{Q}$, this combined program is run with *DLV*, that provides an interface to the databases at the sources. For the query in (3), we obtain:

---

[3] We are not considering global ICs. Cf. Section 7.

```
dl.exe -silent -cautious test2.dlv
dolphin, ocean
camel, desert
frog, wetlands                                                    □
```

7 Conclusions

The *VISS* system provides an infrastructure for virtually integrating multiple data sources according to the LAV approach. Concrete integration systems are specified in terms of metadata using a standard XML/RuleML representation. This design allows data sources to be added or removed from the system without affecting other data sources. XQuery is used to extract the relevant information that is needed to create plans for evaluation of global queries. In their turn, these plans are expressed as logic programs with stable model semantics; and they involve a specification of the legal instances of the integration system.

Currently the system does not provide support for global integrity constraints (GICs). Enforcing them on the system is not possible due to the autonomy of the local sources. In consequence, GICs have to be handled as in *consistent query answering* [2]. In our running example, we might have the functional dependency (FD) $Name \rightarrow Class$ satisfied by relations **V1** and an additional **V3**, which is defined by $V3(Name, Class, Food)$ $\leftarrow Animal(Name, Class, Food), Vertebrate(Name)$. However, there is no guarantee that the same (now global) FD will be satisfied by (the legal instances of) the global relation $Animal(Name, Class, Food)$. In cases like this, it becomes necessary to retrieve those answers that are consistent wrt these GICs, at query time. A characterization of- and mechanisms for this form of consistent query answering in virtual data integration have been introduced in [4].

This addition of support for consistent query answering in *VISS* corresponds to work in progress. Global ICs (and also local if desired) can be easily specified in *VISS* using RuleML 0.91. Admitting global ICs would enhance the functionality of *VISS*, providing support for computation of consistent answers, similar to the approach used in the *Consistency Extractor System* [8], which works on single and possibly inconsistent databases.

References

[1] Abiteboul, A., Duschka, O.: Complexity of Answering Queries Using Materialized Views. In: Proc. ACM Symposium on Principles of Database Systems (PODS 1998), pp. 254–263 (1998)

[2] Bertossi, L.: Consistent Query Answering in Databases. ACM Sigmod Record 35(2), 68–76 (2006)

[3] Bravo, L., Bertossi, L.: Logic Programs for Consistently Querying Data Integration Systems. In: Proc. International Joint Conference on Artificial Intelligence (IJCAI 2003), pp. 10–15. Morgan Kaufmann, San Francisco (2003)

[4] Bertossi, L., Bravo, L.: Consistent Query Answers in Virtual Data Integration Systems. In: Bertossi, L., Hunter, A., Schaub, T. (eds.) Inconsistency Tolerance. LNCS, vol. 3300, pp. 42–83. Springer, Heidelberg (2005)

[5] Bernstein, P., Haas, L.: Information Integration in the Enterprise. Communications of the ACM 51(9), 72–79 (2008)

[6] Boley, H.: Integrating Positional and Slotted Knowledge on the Semantic Web (2005), http://www.ruleml.org/posl/poslintweb-talk.pdf

[7] Boley, H., Tabet, S., Wagner, G.: Design Rationale for RuleML: A Markup Language for Semantic Web Rules. In: Proc. Semantic Web and Web Services (SWWS 2001), pp. 381–401 (2001)

[8] Caniupan, M., Bertossi, L.: The Consistency Extractor System: Querying Inconsistent Databases using Answer Set Programs. In: Prade, H., Subrahmanian, V.S. (eds.) SUM 2007. LNCS, vol. 4772, pp. 74–88. Springer, Heidelberg (2007)

[9] Duschka, O., Genesereth, M., Levy, A.: Recursive Query Plans for Data Integration. Journal of Logic Programming 43(1), 49–73 (2000)

[10] Eiter, T., Gottlob, G., Mannila, H.: Disjunctive Datalog. ACM Transactions on Database Systems 22(3), 364–418 (1997)

[11] Giannotti, F., Pedreschi, D., Sacca, D., Zaniolo, C.: Non-Determinism in Deductive Databases. In: Delobel, C., Masunaga, Y., Kifer, M. (eds.) DOOD 1991. LNCS, vol. 566, pp. 129–146. Springer, Heidelberg (1991)

[12] Lenzerini, M.: Data Integration: A Theoretical Perspective. In: Proc. ACM Symposium on Principles of Database Systems (PODS 2002), pp. 233–246 (2002)

[13] Leone, N., Lio, V., Terracina, G.: DLV^{DB}: Adding Efficient Data Management Features to ASP. In: Lifschitz, V., Niemelä, I. (eds.) LPNMR 2004. LNCS (LNAI), vol. 2923, pp. 341–345. Springer, Heidelberg (2003)

[14] Leone, N., Pfeifer, G., Faber, W., Eiter, T., Gottlob, G., Perri, S., Scarcello, F.: The DLV System for Knowledge Representation and Reasoning. ACM Transactions on Computational Logic 7(3), 499–562 (2006)

[15] Maclachlan, A., Boley, H.: Semantic Web Rules for Business Information. In: Proc. IASTED International Conference on Web Technologies, Applications and Services, pp. 146–153 (2005)

[16] Anatomy of an XML Database: Oracle Berkeley DB XML. An Oracle white paper (2006), http://www.oracle.com/technology/products/berkeley-db/xml/index.html

[17] Ullman, J.: Information Integration Using Logical Views. Theoretical Computer Science 239(2), 189–210 (2000)

[18] Wiederhold, G.: Mediators in the Architecture of Future Information Systems. IEEE Computer 25(3), 38–49 (1992)

Protecting Data Privacy in Structured P2P Networks

Mohamed Jawad[1], Patricia Serrano-Alvarado[1], and Patrick Valduriez[2]

[1] LINA, University of Nantes
[2] INRIA and LINA, University of Nantes

Abstract. P2P systems are increasingly used for efficient, scalable data sharing. Popular applications focus on massive file sharing. However, advanced applications such as online communities (e.g., medical or research communities) need to share private or sensitive data. Currently, in P2P systems, untrusted peers can easily violate data privacy by using data for malicious purposes (e.g., fraudulence, profiling). To prevent such behavior, the well accepted Hippocratic database principle states that data owners should specify the purpose for which their data will be collected. In this paper, we apply such principles as well as reputation techniques to support purpose and trust in structured P2P systems. Hippocratic databases enforce purpose-based privacy while reputation techniques guarantee trust. We propose a P2P data privacy model which combines the Hippocratic principles and the trust notions. We also present the algorithms of PriServ, a DHT-based P2P privacy service which supports this model and prevents data privacy violation. We show, in a performance evaluation, that PriServ introduces a small overhead.

1 Introduction

Peer-to-Peer (P2P) systems provide efficient solutions for distributed data sharing which can scale up to very large amounts of data and numbers of users. Online peer-to-peer (P2P) communities such as professional ones (e.g., medical or research) are becoming popular due to increasing needs on data sharing. In such communities, P2P environments offer valuable characteristics (e.g., scalability, distribution, autonomy) but limited guarantees concerning data privacy. They can be considered as hostile because data, that can be sensitive or confidential, can be accessed by everyone (by potentially untrustworthy peers) and used for everything (e.g., for marketing, profiling, fraudulence or for activities against the owners preferences or ethics).

Data privacy is the right of individuals to determine for themselves *when, how* and *to what* extent information about them is communicated to others [14]. It has been treated by many organizations and legislations which have defined well accepted principles. According to OECD[1], data privacy should consider: collec-

---

[1] Organization for Economic Co-operation and Development. One of the world's largest and most reliable source of comparable statistics, on economic and social data. http://www.oecd.org/

A. Hameurlain and A M. Tjoa (Eds.): Globe 2009, LNCS 5697, pp. 85–98, 2009.

tion limitation, purpose specification, use limitation, data quality, security safeguards, openness, individual participation, and accountability. From these principles we underline *purpose* specification which states that data owners should be able to specify the purpose (data access objective) for which their data will be collected and used. Several solutions that follow the OECD guidelines have been proposed. A major solution is Hippocratic databases [2,9] where purpose-based access control is enforced by using privacy metadata, i.e. privacy policies and privacy authorizations stored in tables. A privacy policy defines for each attribute, tuple or table the access purpose, the potential users and retention period while privacy authorization defines which purposes each user is authorized to use.

In addition to purpose-based data privacy, to prevent data misuse, it is necessary to trust users. Reputation techniques verify the trustworthiness of peers by assigning them *trust levels* [7,10,13]. A trust level is an assessment of the probability that a peer will not cheat.

Motivations. In the context of P2P systems, few solutions for data privacy have been proposed. They focus on a small part of the general problem of data privacy, e.g. *anonymity* of uploaders/downloaders, *linkability* (correlation between uploaders and downloaders), *content deniability*, data encryption and authenticity [3,8]. However, the problem of data privacy violation due to data disclosure to malicious peers is not addressed.

As a motivating example, consider a collaborative application where a community of researchers, doctors, students and patients focus on the evolution of cardiovascular diseases (e.g. heart attacks, atherosclerosis, etc.). In such application, doctors share selected patients' records, researchers share last research results and this information is considered as sensitive. In order to control disclosure without violating privacy, data access should respect the privacy preferences defined by concerned users, for instance:

- A researcher may allow reading access on her research results to doctors for *diagnosing* and to students for *analyzing*.
- A doctor may allow writing access on her diagnosis to researchers for *adding comments*.

In this P2P application, sharing data (i.e., medical records, research results) based on privacy preferences is a challenge. Purposes defined by users (e.g. diagnosing, analyzing, etc.) should be respected. In addition, data should not be shared equally by all users. It is necessary to consider the concept of trust among users. For instance, doctors need to trust researchers to share their private data with them. Currently, P2P systems do not take into account privacy preferences. In this context, an efficient P2P purpose-based privacy service with trust control is needed.

Contributions. This paper has two main contributions.

- We propose a P2P data privacy model in which we combine several concepts related to P2P data privacy. We use this model as a basis to enforce users privacy preferences.

– We propose PriServ[2], a DHT privacy service which, based on the proposed model, prevents privacy violation by limiting malicious data access. For that, we use purpose-based access control and trust techniques. In PriServ, we consider that private data are stored and managed by their owners. The system manages only data references. To our knowledge, PriServ is the first proposition that introduces data access based on purposes in P2P systems. The performance evaluation of our approach through simulation shows that the overhead introduced by PriServ is small.

Next, Section 2 discusses related work. Section 3 presents our P2P data privacy model. Section 4 presents PriServ our privacy service. Section 5 describes performance evaluation. Section 6 shows current work. Section 7 concludes.

2   Related Work

The first work that uses purposes in data access is Hippocratic databases [2]. Inspired by the Hippocratic Oath and guided by privacy regulations, authors propose ten principles that should be preserved, namely, purpose specification, consent of the donor, limited collection, limited use, limited disclosure, limited retention, accuracy, safety, openness and compliance. Subsequent works have proposed solutions for Hippocratic databases. In [9], the goal is to enforce privacy policies within existing applications. In [1], the authors address the problem of how current relational DBMS can be transformed into their privacy-preserving equivalents. In this paper, compared to those works which enforce purpose-based disclosure control in a centralized relational datastore, we apply the Hippocratic database principles to P2P networks.

Many P2P systems propose access control services. OceanStore [8] provides efficient location of data. Protected data are encrypted and access control is based on two types of restrictions: *reader* and *writer* restrictions. Compared to OceanStore, our work improves private data access by adding the notion of purpose. Freenet [3] is a distributed storage system which focuses on privacy and security issues. It uses anonymous communications. Messages are not send directly from sender to recipient, thus, uploader and downloader anonymity is preserved. Besides, all stored files are encrypted so that a node can deny the knowledge of the content. In this work, we deal with data privacy protection and we do not address peer anonymity nor content deniability.

Other works propose trust-based management systems [7,10,13]. In [13], a considerable number of trust models and algorithms have been presented to tackle the problem of decentralized trust management. In [7], authors employ a shared global history of peer interactions to identify potential malicious owners. In [10], a peer A asks for trust levels to a limited number of peers called friends. Friends are trustworthy peers from the point of view of A. A calculates a mean value from collected trust levels. PriServ uses [10] because it generates a low

---

[2] In [6], our first ideas were proposed.

trust level searching cost. Unlike [10] where the trustworthiness of data owners is verified, in our work the trustworthiness of data requesters is verified.

Our privacy service marries reputation-based trust and purpose-based access control. Trust-based systems do not take into account the notion of purpose. This makes PriServ different from the existent trust management systems.

3   P2P Data Privacy Model

This section presents our P2P data privacy model.

Peer Types. In our model, we can have three distinguished types of peers:

- **Requester.** A peer that requests data in the system.
- **Owner.** A peer that provides data to the system. It owns the data it shares.
- **Reference manager.** A peer that stores meta-information as data references, owner identifiers, etc.

Privacy Policy. Each data owner can have its own privacy preferences which are reflected in privacy policies. A privacy policy can include:

- **Users.** Peers who have the right to access data. A user can be an individual or a group.
- **Access rights.** Authorizations that determine what a peer can do with data. We use three basic types of access: read, write and disclose (delegate).
- **Access purposes.** Objectives for which peers can access data.
- **Conditions.** Conditions under which data can be accessed. This may concern data values, for example age>10.
- **Obligations.** Obligations which a user must accomplish after the data access, for example a researcher Ri should return research results after using the record of patient x.
- **Retention time.** A time to limit the retention of the data, for example, a researcher should destroy the record of patient x after 6 months.
- **Minimal trust levels.** Minimal trust levels[3] which requester peers should have in order to gain access to data.

Trust. It is a fuzzy concept where trusted peers are supposed to respect privacy policies defined by data owners. Trust control uses many concepts:

- **Trust levels.** They reflect a peer reputation with respect to other peers. A peer can have different trust levels at different peers. Trust levels vary in a range of [0,1]. For instance, an *honest peer* can have a trust level in a range of [0.5, 1] and a *malicious peer* in a range of [0, 0.5]. Peers can locally register the trust levels of some peers which have interacted with them.
- **Reputation.** A peer reputation is an overall estimation of the peer behavior generally calculated from its trust levels given by peers who know it.
- **Friends.** A friend of a peer P is a peer with a high trust level from P's point of view. The number of friends held by a peer can vary from one peer to another.

---

[3] These levels' definition depends on the used trust model and the owner's opinion [13].

Operations. A peer can publish data, request data, or search for a trust level.

publishing(dataID, purpose). An owner uses this function to publish its data references created from its private data (*dataID*) and the corresponding access purpose (*purpose*). Publishing references allow to share private data without violating their privacy. These references allow requesters to find owners and ask them for data access. An owner has complete control of its private data which guarantees data privacy.

requesting(dataID, purpose). A requester uses this function to request data (*dataID*) for a specific purpose (*purpose*). Including the access purpose in data requests represents a contract between requesters and owners. At the same time, that makes requesters aware of their responsibilities on the data usage.

searchTrustLevel(peerID1, peerID2, nestL). A peer (*peerID1*) uses this function[4] to search the trust level of another peer (*peerID2*). The parameter *nestL* defines the nested level of searching.

Data Model. In order to respect privacy policies, we define a specific data model where privacy policies are associated with data[5].

Data Table. Each owner stores locally the data it wants to share in *data tables*. Tables 1 and 2 show two data tables. Table 1 contains the research result of researcher Ri and Table 2 contains medical records of doctor Dj.

Table 1. Data table of researcher Ri

Data table DTi			
Age	Gender	Smoker	Risk of heart attack
18 - 35	Female	No	7 % (rated 1)
35 - 50	Male	Yes	50 % (rated 4)
50 - 80	Female	Yes	80 % (rated 5)

Table 2. Data table of doctor Dj

Data table DTj						
PatientID (PK)	Name	Country	Birthdate	Gender	Smoker	Diagnosis
Pat1	Alex	France	1990	Male	Yes	No cardiovascular disease
Pat2	Chris	France	1973	Male	No	Cardiovascular disease (rated 2)
Pat3	Elena	Russia	1968	Female	Yes	Cardiovascular disease (rated 4)

Purpose Table. It contains information about the available purposes: purpose identifier, purpose name, purpose description, etc.

Privacy Policies Table. Each owner stores data contained in privacy policies in a table named *privacy policies table*. In this table, each line corresponds to a privacy policy which contains an id, data subject to privacy (table, column or line), access rights (read, write, disclose), allowed users, access purposes, conditions, and the required minimal trust level of allowed users. Table 3 shows the privacy policies table of doctor Dj.

---

[4] The use of the trust function is optional.

[5] In this paper, we use relational tables. However our model supports any type of data (XML documents, multimedia files, etc.).

Table 3. Privacy policies table of doctor Dj

	Privacy policies table PPTj						
ID	Data			Access	User	Purpose	Condition	Minimal
	Table	Column	PK	right				trust level
PP1	DTj	—	Pat3	r/w	Di	Updating	—	0.65
PP2	DTj	Diagnosis	Pat2	r	Pat2	Seeing diagnosis	—	0.5
PP3	DTj	—	—	r/w/d	Dj	Monitoring	—	0.9
PP4	DTj	Birthdate	—	r	Researchers	Research on cardiovascular disease	Birthdate < 2000	0.6

4 PriServ

In this section, we present PriServ, a service which, based on the privacy model of the previous section, prevents privacy violation in DHT-based systems.

4.1 Design Choices

In this section, we present PriServ main design choices.

DHT. All DHT systems (e.g. Chord [12], Pastry [11], etc.) support a distributed lookup protocol that efficiently locates the peer that stores a particular data item. Data location is based on associating a *key* with each data item, and storing the key/data item pair at the peer to which the key maps. A DHT maps a key k to a peer P called *responsible for k with respect to a hash function h.* Every peer has the IP address of log N peers in its finger table. DHT provides two basic operations, each incurring $O(logN)$ messages.

- $put(k, data)$ stores a key k and its associated data in the DHT.
- $get(k)$ retrieves the data associated with k in the DHT.

All DHT systems can be used in PriServ. We choose *Chord* for its efficiency and simplicity.

Data keys. In PriServ, peer identifiers are chosen by hashing the peer IP address and data keys are calculated by hashing the pair (*dataID, purpose*). *dataID* is a unique data identifier and *purpose* is the data access purpose[6]. *dataID* should not contain private data (e.g. patient name, country, etc.) but only meta-information (table name, column, etc.) (see Table 4). Because keys include access purposes, requesting data is always made for a defined purpose. This allows to enhance purpose-based access control.

Required Tables. In PriServ, each reference manager maintains locally a *reference table* which contains keys and corresponding owner identifiers. Each owner maintains locally a *trust table* and a *private table*. A trust table contains the trust level of some peers in the system. A private table shows the mapping of the requested keys with corresponding privacy policies.

---

[6] [4] has analyzed how to manage schemas and process simple queries efficiently in a flexible P2P environment. Thus, we consider that all peers accessing the same data are capable of schema mapping and that peers allowed to access particular data are informed of their allowed purposes. Thus, requester peers are able to produce keys.

Table 4. Private table of the doctor Dj

Private table			
DataID	**Purpose**	**Key**	**Privacy policy**
DTj.Pat3	Updating	21	PP1
DTj	Monitoring	71	PP3
DTj.Birthdate	Researching on cardiovascular disease	83	PP4
DTj.Pat3	Having second diagnosis	96	PP5

4.2   PriServ Algorithms

PriServ implements the P2P data privacy model proposed in Section 3. In particular, it focuses on the publishing, requesting and searchTrustLevel operations.

Publishing algorithm. In PriServ, when a peer enters the system, it uses the *put(key, ownerID)* function to publish the key/ownerID pair of the data it shares. The owner hashes the data identifier and the access purpose parameters of the *publishing(dataID, purpose)* function to produce the data key. This allows to avoid requesting data for invalid purposes because keys corresponding to invalid access purposes will not be available in the system. Unlike the traditional DHT *put(key, data)* function, instead of publishing shared data *(data)*, the data provider identifier is published. Thus data are not published in the system. Only data providers control their data sharing.

Requesting algorithm. (Figure 1). Data requesting is done in two steps. First, the requester hashes the data identifier and the access purpose parameters of the *requesting(dataID, purpose)* function to produce the data key. It searches for the reference manager in order to get the owner identifier bu using the *get(key)* function. Second, the requester contacts the owner to retrieve data. The owner verifies locally the privacy policy corresponding to the data key. In particular, the owner verifies the trustworthiness of the requester.

Trust level searching algorithm. If a peer *(ID)* has the trust level of the requester *(requesterID)* in its trust table, this level is returned directly and the peer *(ID)* does not have to contact other peers. If a peer does not have the requester trust level, PriServ defines three methods for searching the requester trust level in the system:

  - *With-friends algorithm* (Figure 2). Each peer has at least one friend, the owner asks its friends for the trust level of the requester. Each received trust level *(RTL)* is weighted with the trust level *(FTL)* of the sending friend. The final trust level is computed from the received trust levels. Searching for the requester trust level is recursive[7]. If a friend does not have the requested

---

[7] In order to assure that a peer will not be contacted twice, we consider the trust level searching as a tree in which the owner is the root and the depth is equal to the maximum depth of searching. Contacted peers form the tree nodes. If a peer already exists in the branch where it should be added, it will not be contacted a second time.

```
0: requesting(dataID,purpose)
1: begin
2:   ownerID is initialized to null;
3:   requestedData is initialized to null;
4:   key = hashFunction(dataID,purpose);
5:   ownerID = DHT.get(key);
6:   if (ownerID not null) do
7:     requestedData = retrieve(requesterID,
                      ownerID, key);
8:   return requestedData
9: end;

10: retrieve(requesterID, ownerID, key)
11: begin
12:   requestedData is initialized to null;
13:   nestL is intitialized to 0;
14:   if(requesterID has the rigth to
       access data correspondant to key) do
15:     requesterTrustL = searchTrustLevel
          (ownerID,requesterID,nestL);
16:   if(requesterTrustL is higher than
        minTrustL)
17:     requestedData = data correspondant
                       to key;
18:   return requestedData
19: end;
```

```
0: searchTrustLevel(ID,requesterID,nestL)
1: begin
2:   requesterTrustLevel is initialized to 0;
3:   if(nestL has reached MaxDepth)
4:     if(trustL of requesterID in trustTable)
5:       requesterTrustL=trustL of requesterID;
6:     else
7:       return -1;
8:   else
9:     if(trustL of requesterID in trustTable)
10:      requesterTrustL=trustL of requesterID;
11:  else
12:     nestL is incremented;
13:     NbPeersContacted is initialized to 0;
14:     for each friend
15:       FTL = trustL of friendID;
16:       RTL = searchTrustLevel(friendID,
                         requesterID,nestL);
17:       if (RTL != -1)
18:         FTL*RTL is added to requesterTrustL;
19:         NbPeersContacted is incremented;
20:     requesterTrustL = requesterTrustL /
                          NbPeerscontacted;
21: return requesterTrustL
22:end;
```

Fig. 1. Requesting algorithm   **Fig. 2.** SearchTrustLevel: with-friends

trust level it asks for it to its friends and the number of nested levels (*nestL*) is incremented. Recursion is limited by a predefined number of iterations (MaxDepth). The maximum number of contacted friends can also be limited to a predefined number.

- *Without-friends algorithm.* Each peer does not have friends. The algorithm will proceed in the same way as the with-friends algorithm. However, instead of contacting friends, an owner will contact the peers in its finger table ($O(LogN)$ peers).
- *With-or-without-friends algorithm.* Each peer may have friends or not. In this case, if an owner has some friends, it uses the with-friends algorithm, otherwise it uses the without-friends algorithm.

Figure 3 illustrates the data requesting algorithm and the with-friends algorithm to search for trust levels. P18 requests data corresponding to key 21 from P25. P25 returns P36 which is the owner peer of 21. Then P18 contacts P36. P36 contacts its friends (P54) to find the trust level of P18. P54 does not have the trust level of P18 in its trust table so it contacts also its friends (P25). P25 has the trust level and sends it to P54. P54 updates its trust table and sends the trust level of P18 to P36. As it is higher than the level required in PP1 (i.e., 0.65) the access is granted.

To summarize, PriServ allows to prevent malicious access based on privacy policies and requester trust levels. A contract between requesters and owners is established by including access purposes to data requests. Owners control the

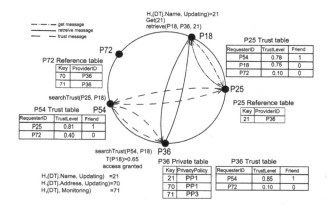

Fig. 3. Data requesting: with-friends algorithm

access to their private data and requesters are aware of their responsibilities on the data usage.

4.3 Cost Analysis

In this section, we analyze the costs of the previous algorithms in terms of number of messages. We do not analyze the join/leave cost which is the same of Chord with the advantage that data transfer of a leaving/joining peer is lighter in PriServ because only data references are stored in the system.

Publishing, data requesting and retrieving costs are in $O(logN)$ as explained in [6]. However trust level searching cost (C_{STL}) is different in function of the trust searching algorithm:

- *With-friends algorithm.* This cost depends on the number of friends (NF) and the maximum depth of the nested search (MaxDepth).

$$C_{STL_{WF}} = \sum_{i=1}^{MaxDepth} NF^i = O(NF^{MaxDepth})$$

- *Without-friends algorithm.* This cost depends on the number of fingers which is log N and the maximum depth of the nested search (MaxDepth).

$$C_{STL_{WOF}} = \sum_{i=1}^{MaxDepth} (logN)^i = O((logN)^{MaxDepth})$$

- *With-or-without-friends algorithm.* This cost depends on the number of friends (NF), the number of fingers which is log N and the maximum depth of the nested search (MaxDepth).

$$C_{STL_{WWF}} = O((max(logN, NF))^{MaxDepth})$$

The trust level searching cost C_{STL} can be one of the three costs $C_{STL_{WF}}$, $C_{STL_{WOF}}$ or $C_{STL_{WWF}}$. Note that if NF > log N, $C_{STL_{WWF}}$ is equal to $C_{STL_{WF}}$, else it is equal to $C_{STL_{WOF}}$. In all cases $C_{STL_{WWF}}$ can be used for C_{STL}:

$$C_{STL} = O((max(logN, NF))^{MaxDepth})$$

To summarize,

$$C_{publishing} = O(nbData * nbPurpose * logN)$$
$$C_{Requesting} = C_{Request} + C_{Retrieve} + C_{STL}$$
$$= 2O(logN) + O((max(logN, NF))^{MaxDepth}) = O((max(logN, NF))^{MaxDepth})$$

Compared to the traditional DHT functions, $C_{request}$ and $C_{retrieve}$ costs do not introduce communication overhead in term of number of messages. However, C_{STL} increases the data requesting cost due to the nested search. Next section shows how this cost can be reduced and stabilized to a minimum cost.

5   Performance Evaluation

In [6], we have shown by simulation that publishing and data requesting costs are in $O(logN)$ and that having ten access purposes per datum (which is realistic) PriServ is scalable. This section evaluates the performance of the trust level searching cost and the stabilization of the trust level searching cost.

For the simulation, we use SimJava [5]. We simulate the Chord protocol with some modifications in the $put()$ and $get()$ functions. The parameters of the simulation are shown in Table 5. In our tests, we consider N peers with a number of data keys equal to the number of data multiplied by the number of purposes. Data and peer keys are selected randomly between 0 and 2^n. In our simulation, we set n to 11 which corresponds to 2^{11} peers. This number of users is largely sufficient for collaborative applications like medical research.

Trust Level Searching Cost. We measure the trust level searching cost (in number of messages) versus the number of peers for the three algorithms.

With-friends algorithm. We consider that peers have the same number of friends (*NF*) and the maximum depth (*MaxDepth*) is set to 11 (the highest maximum depth we allow in the simulation). Figure 4.a illustrates 3 measures where we consider 1, 4 and 10 friends. Those measures are slightly different of the cost model where the cost is $O(NF^{MaxDepth})$ thanks to our tree-based optimization and because the probability to contact twice a peer in a system of 100 peers is higher than in a system of 1000 peers. That is why in Figure 4.a, the trust level searching cost increases with the number of peers. We observe that for a small number of friends the trust level searching costs depends only on the number of friends as predicted by our cost model.

Without-friends algorithm. Figure 4.b illustrates 4 measures where the maximum depth of searching varies between 1, 2, 3 and 11. We recall that the number of contacted peers is $log(N)$. Thus, the trust level searching costs is logarithmic for small values of depth. This cost increases with the maximum depth of searching as predicted by our cost model.

With-or-without-friends algorithm. We consider that the probability that a peer has friends in our simulation is 0.9. Figure 4.c illustrates 3 measures where the maximum depth of searching varies between 5, 8 and 11. We observe that the

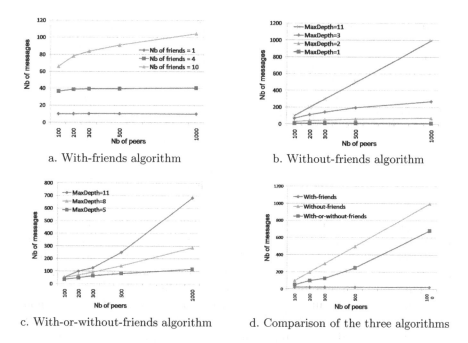

a. With-friends algorithm

b. Without-friends algorithm

c. With-or-without-friends algorithm

d. Comparison of the three algorithms

Fig. 4. Trust level searching costs

trust level searching cost is rather logarithmic for small values of depth. This cost increases with the maximum depth as predicted by our cost model[8].

Comparison. Figure 4.d compares the three algorithms seen above. We consider a number of friends equal to 2 and a maximum depth equal to 11. As predicted before, the with-friends case introduces the smallest cost while the without-friends case introduces the highest. However, intuitively, the probability to find the trust level is higher in the without-friends algorithm than in the with-friends algorithm. This is due to the fact that the number of contacted peers is higher in the without-friends algorithm, which increases the probability to find the trust level. We estimate that the with-or-without-friends algorithm is the most optimized because it is a tradeoff between the probability to find the requester trust level and the trust level searching cost.

Stabilization of the Trust Level Searching Cost. We now focus on the number of messages used to search the trust level of a requesting peer versus the number of its requests. Here we consider the three algorithms of trust (see Figure 5). We observe that the number of messages decreases and stabilizes after a number of searches. This is due to the fact that the more a peer requests for data, the more it gets known by the peers in the system.

---

[8] We do not measure in this case the trust level searching cost versus the number of friends which will be the same as the with-friends case.

Table 5. Table of parameters

Simulation parameters		
Variable	Description	default
n	Number of bits in the key/peer	11
N	Number of peers	2^{11}
FC	Number of friends	2
MaxDepth	Maximum depth of trust searching	11

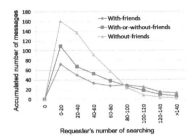

Fig. 5. Stabilization of the trust level searching cost

When peers ask for a trust level, answers are returned in the requesting order and the trust tables are updated with the missing trust level. Thus, the trust tables evolve with the number of searches. After a while, these tables stabilize. Thus, the number of messages for searching trust levels is reduced to a stable value. This value is not null because of the dynamicity of peers[9].

We also observe in Figure 5, that the trust level searching cost in the without-friends algorithm stabilizes first. This is due to the fact that a larger number of peers are contacted in this algorithm. The with-or-without-friends algorithm comes in second place, and the with-friends algorithm comes last. As we have seen in the comparison of the three algorithms, we find again that the with-or-without-friends algorithm is the most optimized because it is a tradeoff between the time to stabilization and the trust level searching cost.

6   Current Work

Storing data on owner peers gives a maximal guaranty of privacy protection. However, this hypothesis may affect availability if the owner peer fails or leaves.

To improve availability, we are working on extending PriServ functionalities where owners will choose to store locally their data or to distribute them on the system. Because distribution depends on the DHT, owners could see their private data stored on untrusted peers. To overcome this problem, before distribution, data will be encrypted and decryption keys will be stored and duplicated by owners. This will guarantee that a) private data are protected from malicious server peers, and b) an owner is able to control the access to its data since a requester peer should contact him to obtain decryption keys. In addition, owners will be able to recover their data from local storage failures.

Another extension of PriServ focuses on verification to detect misbehaviors of malicious peers. The idea is to be able of auditing the storage space dedicated to PriServ by monitoring data distribution and data access.

---

[9] In our simulation, we consider that the number of peers joining the system is equal to those leaving the system. Thus, there are always new peers which do not know the requester trust level.

7 Conclusion

In this paper, we addressed the problem of protecting data privacy in structured P2P systems. We apply the Hippocratic database principle to enforce purpose-based privacy. We also use reputation-based trust management in order to verify the trustworthiness of requester peers. Our solution is a P2P data privacy model which combines Hippocratic principles and trust notions. We also proposed the algorithms of PriServ, a DHT-based P2P privacy service which supports this model and prevents data privacy violation. The performance evaluation of our solution through simulation shows that the overhead introduced by PriServ is small.

References

1. Agrawal, R., Bird, P., Grandison, T., Kiernan, J., Logan, S., Rjaibi, W.: Extending Relational Database Systems to Automatically Enforce Privacy Policies. In: IEEE Conference on Data Engineering, ICDE (2005)
2. Agrawal, R., Kiernan, J., Srikant, R., Xu, Y.: Hippocratic Databases. In: Very Large Databases, VLDB (2002)
3. Clarke, I., Miller, S.G., Hong, T.W., Sandberg, O., Wiley, B.: Protecting Free Expression Online with Freenet. IEEE Internet Computing 6(1) (2002)
4. Furtado, P.: Schemas and Queries over P2P. In: Andersen, K.V., Debenham, J., Wagner, R. (eds.) DEXA 2005. LNCS, vol. 3588, pp. 808–817. Springer, Heidelberg (2005)
5. Howell, F., McNab, R.: Simjava: a Discrete Event Simulation Library for Java. In: Society for Computer Simulation, SCS (1998)
6. Jawad, M., Serrano-Alvarado, P., Valduriez, P.: Design of PriServ, A Privacy Service for DHTs. In: International Workshop on Privacy and Anonymity in the Information Society (PAIS), collocated with EDBT (2008)
7. Kamvar, S.D., Schlosser, M.T., Garcia-Molina, H.: The Eigentrust Algorithm for Reputation Management in P2P networks. In: ACM World Wide Web Conference, WWW (2003)
8. Kubiatowicz, J., Bindel, D., Chen, Y., Czerwinski, S.E., Eaton, P.R., Geels, D., Gummadi, R., Rhea, S.C., Weatherspoon, H., Weimer, W., Wells, C., Zhao, B.Y.: OceanStore: An Architecture for Global-Scale Persistent Storage. In: Conference on Architectural Support for Programming Languages and Operating Systems (ASP-LOS) (2000)
9. LeFevre, K., Agrawal, R., Ercegovac, V., Ramakrishnan, R., Xu, Y., DeWitt, D.J.: Limiting Disclosure in Hippocratic Databases. In: Very Large Databases, VLDB (2004)
10. Marti, S., Garcia-Molina, H.: Limited Reputation Sharing in P2P Systems. In: ACM Conference on Electronic Commerce, EC (2004)
11. Rowstron, A., Druschel, P.: Pastry: Scalable, decentralized object location, and routing for large-scale peer-to-peer systems. In: Guerraoui, R. (ed.) Middleware 2001. LNCS, vol. 2218, pp. 329–350. Springer, Heidelberg (2001)

12. Stoica, I., Morris, R., Karger, D.R., Kaashoek, M.F., Balakrishnan, H.: Chord: A Scalable Peer-to-Peer Lookup Service for Internet Applications. In: ACM Conference on Applications, Technologies, Architectures, and Protocols for Computer Communication, SIGCOMM (2001)
13. Suryanarayana, G., Taylor, R.N.: A Survey of Trust Management and Resource Discovery Technologies in Peer-to-Peer Applications. Technical report, UCI Institute for Software Research, university of California, Irvine (2004)
14. Westin, A.: Privacy and Freedom. Atheneum, New York (1967)

Pace: Privacy-Protection for Access Control Enforcement in P2P Networks*

Marc Sánchez-Artigas and Pedro García-López

Department of Computer Engineering and Mathematics
Universitat Rovira i Virgili, Catalonia, Spain
{marc.sanchez,pedro.garcia}@urv.cat

Abstract. In open environments such as peer-to-peer (P2P) systems, the decision to collaborate with multiple users — e.g., by granting access to a resource — is hard to achieve in practice due to extreme decentralization and the lack of trusted third parties. The literature contains a plethora of applications in which a scalable solution for distributed access control is crucial. This fact motivates us to propose a protocol to enforce access control, applicable to networks consisting entirely of untrusted nodes. The main feature of our protocol is that it protects both sensitive permissions and sensitive policies, and does not rely on any centralized authority. We analyze the efficiency (computational effort and communication overhead) as well as the security of our protocol.

1 Introduction

Peer-to-Peer (P2P) networks offer the chance of global data sharing and collaboration. To take this opportunity, P2P networks share data access via file sharing, using remote file access in decentralized filesystems. Representative examples include Plutus [1] and SiRiUS [2]. However, most of those decentralized filesystems suffer from inappropriate assumptions, weak security and trust in a (possibly centralized) authority. For instance, Plutus assume that users authenticate each other on-demand: if a user wishes to access a file, Plutus requires the user to contact the file owner to obtain the relevant key to decrypt it. This dependence restricts file availability to the lifetime period of file owners. In pure P2P networks, population is highly dynamic. Thereby, an offline-tolerant way to control access through key material must be found and yet is missing.

To guarantee availability of files at all times, file owners could transfer the ability of enforcing access control to a group of peers. As a group, these peers would act as the delegate of the file owner, enforcing access control on his behalf. Although theoretically sound, the problem of delegation is that delegate peers might be subverted, weakening the security of the system in (at least) two important ways:

- *Insider attacks.* Delegate peers must be unable to change permissions or gain access to the protected objects; and
- *Disclosure of permissions and/or access policies.* If permissions or access policies are sensitive, delegation can lead to substantial problems. Since delegate peers need

---

* This research was partially funded through project P2PGRID, TIN2007-68050-C03-03, of the Ministry of Education and Science, Spain.

A. Hameurlain and A M. Tjoa (Eds.): Globe 2009, LNCS 5697, pp. 99–111, 2009.

to know the access policies to protect access to resources, they might change their behavior based on their knowledge of the policies, for example, to block access to legitimate users. This is particularly critical for policies that conceal a commercial secret — e.g., a researcher has devised an innovative way of securely encoding data and knowledge of the policy could compromise its commercial strategy.

To remedy this problem, we propose Pace, an access control enforcement protocol for decentralized systems that provides privacy-protection for both access policies and permissions. Essentially, Pace makes novel use of cryptographic primitives and features highly scalable key management while allowing file owners to securely delegate control over who gets access to their files. As Plutus, we assume that all data is stored encrypted. However, the key to access a given content is handled in a decentralized and a privacy-preserving manner. Principally, we want requesters to get an object only if they satisfy the policy, delegate peers do not learn anything about requesters' permissions (not even whether they got access), and requesters learn nothing about the policy. This aspect is what makes Pace unique among existing access control protocols for P2P networks.

One fundamental issue of access control is authentication. In pure P2P systems, one cannot generally assume the existence of any fixed infrastructure, such as a public key infrastructure (PKI). PKIs utilize a trusted third party (TTP), or a collection of TTPs acting as the certification authority, to perform public key authentication. The result is that scalability is poor along with the introduction of a single point of failure. Moreover, the existence of TTP(s) contradicts the extremely decentralized nature of P2P systems.

To address this issue, Pace adopts the Pathak and Iftode's public-key authentication protocol described in [3]. Concretely, this protocol offers decentralized authentication through an honest majority. Each user dynamically maintains a trusted group (TG) of users which perform distributed challenge-response authentication on his behalf.

1.1 Problem Definition

The goal of this work is to develop an access control enforcement protocol that permits decentralized administration of permissions and guarantees privacy-protection for both access control policies and permissions. The entities that participate in our protocol are the following:

- *Object owner.* The owner is responsible for granting permission to those users who are authorized to access their objects.
- *Policy holders.* Since owners can be offline, each owner transfers its access policy to a group of policy holders in order to preserve service availability. Policy holders are normal peers that might be subverted or leave the system anytime, and that need to be contacted by legal requesters to gain access to a particular object. *The use of multiple policy holders is for protection against insider attacks.*
- *Storage nodes.* Objects and their replicas are kept on storage nodes. An object and all its replicas are encrypted with a unique symmetric key (e.g., a DES key) to retain direct control over who gets access to that object.

The framework for our problem can then be described as follows: *a requester n_A has multiple authorization certificates issued by the owner of a data object O. A set of policy* holders have a policy $\mathcal{P}$ for controlling access to object O, and a set of storage nodes keep replicas of O. For simplicity, we assume that at the time of requesting access to O, n_A has already finished a searching process and got a list of storage peers. When n_A wants to access O, he engages in a protocol with a policy holder h. n_A provides the protocol with a subset of his authorization certificates (n_A should provide only legal certificates), whereas h provides the policy $\mathcal{P}$. If at least one of the certificates that n_A inputs into the protocol meets $\mathcal{P}$, he gets a cryptographic key, K, to decrypt the contents of a replica and access O; otherwise, he gets nothing. Specifically, we want n_A to learn as little information as possible about $\mathcal{P}$ and h to learn as little information as possible about n_A's certificates. We formally state the problem below.

Definition 1 (Privacy-Protection Enforcement). *Let n_A be a requester and denote by C_A a valid certificate that is in his possession and grants access to an object O. Let h be an arbitrary policy holder that stores the access control policy $\mathcal{P}$ for object O. Then privacy-preserving enforcement can be described in terms of a function F as follows:*

$$F_{n_A}(C_A) = \begin{cases} K & \text{if } C_A \text{ satisfies } \mathcal{P} \\ \bot & \text{otherwise} \end{cases} \quad ; \qquad F_h(\mathcal{P}) = \bot.$$

where F_{n_A} represents the output of the requester, F_h represents the output of the policy holder and $\bot$ denotes nothing is learned.

In other words, our goal is for the policy holder h to learn nothing from F, and for the requester to learn $F_{n_A}(C_A)$ without learning anything else, i.e., he learns key K iff C_A satisfies the policy and nothing otherwise. Ideally, this definition means that policy holders should not learn anything about which and how many authorization certificates satisfy the policy, whereas requesters should not learn anything about the policy. Thus, *our objective will be to devise a protocol that implements F when the ability to enforce access control is transferred to a set of untrusted and transient users.*

Notation. Finally, we summarize the notation used throughout this paper:

Symbols	Descriptions
n_i	i^{th} node in the system
K_i	Public key of node n_i
K_i^{-1}	Private key of node n_i
S	Symmetric key used to encrypt and decrypt an object
$[x]\, K_i^{-1}$	Digest of string x appended to x and signed by node n_i
"$||$"	String concatenation operator
q	A large prime from which a finite field F_q is formed
f	A cryptographic hash function, i.e., $f : \{0,1\}^* \longrightarrow \{0,1\}^q$

2   Related Work

So far, security concerns for P2P networks has received much attention. It covers a wide range of aspects such as anonymity, content protection, rights management and privacy. However, access control has been principally investigated in the context of distributed storage systems such as Plutus [1] and SiRiUS [2], to name a few. These systems make use of cryptographic tools to sustain access control but either fail to address revocation (SiRiUS) or to abandon dedicated authorities (Plutus).

P-Hera [4] proposes a scalable infrastructure for secure content hosting. To do this, P-Hera allows the users and content providers to dynamically establish trust using fine-grained access control, which is enforced by a network of superpeers. Concretely, any request for an object is dropped by the superpeers before reaching the content providers. However, P-Hera assumes that superpeers are trustworthy, an assumption far from reality: sharing of objects and access should be granted between users who are unknown to each other.

DAAL [5] is an access control mechanism for P2P networks. It requires neither an online authentication server nor uses a centralized reference monitor. Users' identities are built using Identity Based Encryption which allows users to interact without needing to look up public keys online. However, the binding between an identity and the public key used is effectuated through the attestation provided by a mutually trusted authority. This process can be carried out either offline or by using an out-of-band channel, which reduces the applicability of the system.

Finally, it must be mentioned the work of Palomar *et. al.* [6]. To solve the problem of decentralized authentication, Palomar et al. integrated Pathak and Iftode's scheme [3] into their certificate-based access control protocol for P2P networks. Our work is based on the same lines of [6]. However, we have distributed the task of access control among several entities and addressed the problem of privacy protection for access policies, two issues not addressed by Palomar *et. al.*

3   Background and Assumptions

We first overview some essential concepts used throughout this paper and discuss a few working assumptions.

3.1   Review of Access Control Polynomial

The concept of Access Control Polynomial (ACP) was proposed by X. Zou et. al. [7] to distribute secret information so that only the intended recipients can recover the secret. Specifically, an ACP is a *polynomial* over $F_q[x]$, which is defined as follows:

$$A(x) = \prod_{i \in \psi} (x - f(SID_i || z)), \tag{1}$$

where ψ denotes the group of recipients under consideration and SID_i is the Personal Permanent Portable Secret of recipient i in ψ. z is random integer from F_q and is made public. Also, z is changed every time $A(x)$ is computed. It is readily obvious that $A(x)$ is equated to 0 when x is substituted with $f(SID_i || z)$ by a legal user; $A(x)$ is a random value otherwise. In order to broadcast a secret value such as K to the users in group ψ, the following polynomial is computed by a trusted server:

$$P(x) = A(x) + K. \tag{2}$$

Then $\langle z, P(x) \rangle$ is publicized (broadcast) and K is hidden, mixed with the constant of $A(x)$. More specifically, the constant term of $P(x)$ is $c_0 = (K + V) \ (mod \ q)$, where

$V = v_1 \cdot v_2 \cdot ... \cdot v_n$ and $v_i = f(SID_i||z)$. Since there are many other pairs $\langle K', V' \rangle$ such that $c_0 = K + V$, an attacker cannot uniquely determine K from c_0. Hence, the security of the ACP scheme lies in the *infeasibility* to determine key K from c_0.

From $\langle z, P(x) \rangle$, any recipient with a valid SID_i can finally obtain K by:

$$K = P(f(SID_i||z)). \tag{3}$$

In Pace, the ACP scheme is used to implement the enforcement function. Because of its properties, the ACP mechanism provides an elegant solution to protect privacy in decentralized access control: the polynomial hides the group of permissions that satisfy a policy. A legal user cannot learn the SIDs of other users. However, he can easily get K by just plugging his SID into the polynomial. Even the owner can hide the number of permissions available to access a particular object of those he shares. Concretely, the ACP scheme can be easily extended for this purpose by simply appending some random pseudo terms in the polynomial:

$$A(x) = \prod_{i \in \psi}(x - f(SID_i||z)) \prod_{j \in \varphi}(x - VID_j), \tag{4}$$

where φ is the set of pseudo access rules and VID_j are random numbers in F_q, i.e., the pseudo terms. As a result, the degree of $P(x)$ does not reveal the number of permissions that grant access to the object.

3.2 Assumptions

Throughout this work, we will assume the following working hypotheses:

1. *Cryptographic material.* We assume that digital signatures cannot be forged unless the attacker gets access to the private keys. Any user can verify the authenticity of a signature by applying the Pathak and Iftode's Byzantine fault-tolerant public-key authentication protocol described in [3]. Concretely, we assume that the adversary is a probabilistic polynomial-time algorithm. Hence, the security of our problem is defined in a "computationally infeasible" sense.
2. *Reliable networking.* We assume that protocols both at the overlay level and the IP level provide secure and reliable communication among peers. At the overlay layer, secure routing is achieved using algorithms such as [8,9].

4 Access Control Model

Implementing access control protection requires means to specify what legitimate users can perform. For this reason, the way access policies represent the access rules exert an enormous effect on the flexibility and the cost of managing permissions. This has raised the question of which access control models are adequate for P2P networks. We do not wish to involve ourselves in this question here; rather, we want to introduce an access enforcement protocol that minimizes disclosure of permissions and access policies.

Literature identifies three models: discretionary and mandatory access control (DAC and MAC, respectively), and role-based access control (RBAC). However, in this paper,

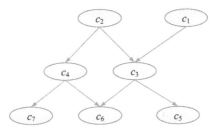

Fig. 1. A typical access control hierarchy

we adopt hierarchical access control (HAC) to minimize the number of keys that object owners need to manage, policy holders need to distribute and requesters receive.

In typical collaborative systems, many objects are equivalent in the sense of access rights that requesters need to present in order to gain access to them. These equivalent classes of objects naturally form a hierarchical structure, usually known as the resource hierarchy. To facilitate the task of specifying and maintaining access control definitions, we only consider hierarchies on objects, and not on users and permissions, though there exists a handful of hierarchical models that integrate and/or unify the three hierarchies. This means that file owners can categorize their shared objects into security classes, but there are no user groups such as "scientific staff", which does not contradict the general philosophy of P2P applications.

Informally, the general model is that there is a partially ordered relation on a set of classes. The most generic format can be represented as a directed acyclic graph (DAG) (Figure 1), where nodes correspond to classes and arrows indicate their ordering. Then, a user who is entitled to have access to a certain class obtains access to that class and all its descendants in the hierarchy.

More formally, there is a directed acyclic graph $G = (\mathcal{C}, E, \mathcal{O})$ such that $\mathcal{C}$ is a set of vertices $\mathcal{C} = \{c_1, c_2, ..., c_m\}$ of cardinality $|\mathcal{C}| = m$, E is a set of edges, and $\mathcal{O}$ is a set of objects. Each vertex c_j represents a class in the access hierarchy and has a set of objects associated with it. Function $o : \mathcal{C} \longrightarrow 2^{\mathcal{O}}$ maps a class to a unique set of objects such that $|o(c_j)| \geq 0$ and $\forall j, k, o(c_j) \cap o(c_k) = \emptyset$ iff $j \neq k$.

In the access hierarchy, a path from class c_j to class c_k means that any subject that have access permissions at class c_j is also permitted to access any object from class c_k. This property can be defined as follows:

Definition 2. *In an access hierarchy* $G = (\mathcal{C}, E, \mathcal{O})$, *let* '$\preceq$' *be the partially ordered relation on* $\mathcal{C} = \{c_1, c_2, ..., c_m\}$, *where* '$\preceq$' *is a reflexive, anti-symmetric and transitive relation on the set of classes* $\mathcal{C}$. *Then, we define ancestry function* $a_G(c_j)$ *as:*

$$a_G(c_j) = \{c_k \in \mathcal{C} : c_j \prec c_k\}, \tag{5}$$

where $c_j \prec c_k$ *means that* c_k *is an ancestor of* c_j, *i.e., there exists a path from* c_k *to* c_j *directed downwards in* G.

Thus $(\mathcal{C}, \preceq)$ is a partially ordered set (POSet), which reflects the hierarchical access relations among users. Specifically, given two classes c_j and c_k, $k \neq j$, if $c_k \in a_G(c_j)$ implies that any object assigned at class c_j is *accessible* by a user at class c_k.

With this representation in hand, any data owner can implement access control by assigning a symmetric key S_j to each class c_j, for example, as in Plutus [1]. Thereby, S_j can be used to encrypt the objects in class c_j and guard their access from unauthorized users. The fact of grouping objects into classes is to prevent the number of cryptographic keys that a user manages from growing proportional to the number of objects.

Implementation. As discussed above, we use the ACP scheme to implement access control in Pace. The power of this scheme is that each user can establish access policies for each object very easily. Given an access hierarchy $G = (\mathcal{C}, E, \mathcal{O})$, the representation of G in form of access policy can be done as follows:

- For each class c_j in G, the owner selects a random integer, $\mathtt{CID}_j$, less than q. $\mathtt{CID}_j$ can be viewed as the authorization certificate used in the the evaluation function F.
- Then it constructs a polynomial $A_j(x)$ for that class using $\mathtt{CID}_j$ and the CIDs of all its ancestors as:

$$A_j(x) = (x - f(\mathtt{CID}_j||z)) \prod_{c_k \in a_G(c_j)} (x - f(\mathtt{CID}_k||z)), \qquad (6)$$

  where the first term corresponds to c_j itself and the next terms are associated with all the ancestors of c_j.
- Finally, the owner constructs $P_j(x) = A_j(x) + S_j$.

As a result, a user belonging to class c_j can get S_j by $S_j = P_j(f(\mathtt{CID}_j, z))$. Further, any user in an ancestor class, c_k, of c_j can also derive S_j by computing $P_j(f(\mathtt{CID}_k, z))$. However, c_j cannot reversely get key S_k. Consequently, hierarchical access control is *securely* enforced.

One important benefit of this policy representation is that users do not need to know the exact hierarchy: all users of a specific class receive an authorization certificate that contains the $\mathtt{CID}$ of that class. Each user can then plug its $\mathtt{CID}$ into $P(x)$ to get the secret key. Further, the users that are assigned to an ancestor class will also obtain the correct secret when substituting their CIDs into $P(x)$, but the others will not.

Dynamics. There are three types of dynamics related to the access policy: addition and deletion of a class, and the movement of a class from one place to another — dynamics that are expected to occur less frequently. Due to space constraints, we restrict ourselves to the deletion of a security class, since deletion is generally more difficult to achieve.

Let c_j be the class to be deleted from the hierarchy. There are two cases to consider:

- c_j *is a leaf class.* In this case, nothing needs to be done except discarding the key and the $\mathtt{CID}$ related to this class.
- c_j *is an internal class.* First, a location for all the descendant classes of c_j needs to be chosen. Relocation is a responsibility of the owner and it is not considered here. Since the users from class c_j know the keys of all the descendant classes of c_j, new keys need to be generated, which is easy. In addition, for each descendant class, the owner needs to recompute its $A(x)$ to include the CIDs of all the new ancestors and exclude $\mathtt{CID}_j$.

It is worth to note here that the new polynomials must be redistributed to the policy holders to preserve *forward secrecy* — i.e., users in class c_j must not have access to the objects of descendant classes.

5 Our Protocols

Pace consists of four main subprotocols. Subsequently, we will describe in detail each building block of our proposal: *setup* subprotocol, *join* subprotocol, *access* subprotocol and *revocation* subprotocol.

5.1 SETUP Subprotocol

In the boostrapping phase, the owner represents his access control policy in form of an ACP (as shown in Section 4), and delegates to a set of policy holders, $\{h_1, h_2, ..., h_d\}$, the ability to enforce access control. For simplicity, we assume that policy holders are automatically assigned, although they could be manually selected by the owner. Since policy holders can be malicious and launch an inside attack, we have incorporated *secret sharing* [10] in our scheme. The idea of secret sharing is to divide a secret K into pieces or shares which are distributed amongst users such that pooled shares of certain subsets of users allow reconstruction of the secret K. Albeit the ACP mechanism is resistant to both external and internal attacks, and collusion (see [7]), the use of secret sharing was motivated by the following fact:

Suppose that a single polynomial, $P(x) = A(x) + K$, is given to all policy holders, where $A(x) = \prod_{i \in \psi}(x - f(\text{CID}_i||z))$, ψ is the set of access rules and K is a class key. Each policy holder can attempt three things to obtain K: (1) to guess K directly; (2) to guess an $v_i = f(\text{CID}_i||z)$ and then compute K; and (3) to guess CID_i and then compute v_i to obtain K. Assuming that the degree of $P(x)$ is n, we have that:

The probability that a random guess hits K is $\frac{1}{q}$, that hits any v_i is $\frac{n}{q}$ and another $\frac{n}{q}$ to hit any CID_i. So, the overall probability for a random trial to succeed is $\frac{2n+1}{q}$. This means that the ACP scheme increases the success chance attack by a factor of $2n$. With $t < d$ malicious policy holders this probability increases by a factor of $t \cdot 2n$. Albeit q can be selected to be reasonably large (e.g., 128 bits), key K might be compromised in the long term.

To constrain the attack probability to $\frac{2n+t}{q}$, we divide key K into two shares s_1 and s_2 using a $(2, 2)$-threshold secret sharing scheme. Then, a (c, d)-threshold secret sharing method is used to split s_2 into d shares $ss_{2,1}, ss_{2,2}, \ldots, ss_{2,d}$. Share s_2 is erased and s_1 is distributed by the owner to authorized users (see Section 5.2). Furthermore, the ith share-share, $ss_{2,i}$, is assigned to the ith policy holder. Consequently, K can only be recovered with the participation of a legal user as well as of at least c policy holders. It is evident that to make this approach useful, each policy holder must receive a distinct polynomial $P_i(x)$, with its own set of valid CIDs; otherwise, guessing a single CID will suffice to obtain the shares of all polynomials. Henceforward, we will refer to $P_i(x)$ as the ith *polynomial share*.

In this paper, we use Shamir's secret sharing [11] to implement the above scheme. Shamir's scheme is based on polynomial interpolation. To distribute d shares, a trusted dealer (the owner) chooses a large prime q', and selects a polynomial $p(x)$ of degree

$c - 1$ over $\mathbb{Z}_{q'}$ such that $p(0) = K$. The owner computes each share s_i such that $s_i = p(i) \bmod q'$, and securely transfers each s_i to each user i. Then, any group of c members who have their shares can recover the secret using the Lagrange interpolation formula: $p(x) = \sum_{i=1}^{c} s_i \lambda_i(x) \ (mod\ q')$, where $\lambda_i(x) = \prod_{j=1, j \neq i}^{c} \frac{x-j}{i-j} \ (mod\ q')$. Since $p(0) = K$, the secret is expressed as $K = \sum_{i=1}^{c} s_i \lambda_i(0) \ (mod\ q')$. Thus, K can be recovered only if at least c shares are combined. In other words, no coalition of less than c members yields any information about K.

To maintain the integrity of the policy, ensuring its authenticity and preventing non-authorized alterations, each polynomial $P_i(x)$ is accompanied by a certificate, $C_{P_i(x)}$. The functionality of this certificate is to prevent that any malicious holder can cheat by providing an incorrect polynomial without risk of detection. Specifically, this certificate contains the following information:

$$C_{P_i(x)} = [n_B, z_i, P_i(x), T_e] K_B^{-1}, \tag{7}$$

where T_e is a validity period for $C_{P_i(x)}$. This certificate contains all the information required to enforce access control. Since SETUP subprotocol is executed only once, we have omitted its complexity analysis in this paper.

5.2 JOIN Subprotocol

This subprotocol is initiated when a peer n_A desires a particular object O of a user n_B. Since user n_A may be still unknown by n_B, this sends the following information to n_B:

$$n_A \longrightarrow n_B : m_1 = [n_A, n_B, \text{JOIN\_REQ}] K_A^{-1}, \tag{8}$$

where JOIN_REQ is a request by which n_A formally expresses its desire to gain access to O. Upon reception, n_B verifies n_A's signature. If the owner accepts the request, then it assigns n_A to a class according to its criteria. If necessary, the owner can add a new class to the access hierarchy but this concern does not matter here. What it may happen, the owner sends the following data to the requester (through a secure channel):

$$n_B \longrightarrow n_A : C_j = [m_1, j, T_e] K_B^{-1}, s_{j1}, \{\text{CID}_{j1}, ..., \text{CID}_{jd}\} \tag{9}$$

where T_e is a limited validity period, j is the index of the polynomial (class identity) used to control access to object O, s_{j1} is the first of the two level-1 shares of class key S_j, and CID_{ji}, $1 \leq i \leq d$, is the class secret for the ith policy holder. The certificate C_j is used to ascertain that the requester has the capability to request access to an unknown object of class c_j, and is called *request certificate*. This certificate must be presented to policy holders to obtain the corresponding polynomial shares.

Complexity Analysis. Computational complexity is shown in Table 1. Communication complexity of this protocol is mainly dominated by the overhead of Pathak and Iftode's challenges. For a TG of size $k = 10$, Pathak and Iftode's protocol does not incur more than 100 messages. If the signers know each other, communication overhead basically depends on the certificate's length and the CIDs' length. Since each Pathak and Iftode's challenge requires at least two signature generations and their respective verifications, communication complexity is $\mathcal{O}(k)$.

Table 1. Worst-case efficiency analysis (computational effort)

Subprotocol	Stage	No. crypto operations	Total complexity
JOIN	1.1 n_A's JOIN_REQ	$1S$	$\mathcal{O}(k \log k)$
	1.2 n_B's checking	$1PI + 1V$	
	1.3 Permission generation	$1S$	
ACCESS	1.1. n_A's ACCESS_REQ	$1S$	$\mathcal{O}(d\,k \log k)$
	1.2 Holders' checking	$d(PI + V)$	
	2.1 n_A's checking	dV	
	2.1 Share computation	dPE	
	3.1 Key reconstruction	SR	
REVOCATION	1.1 Key and shares' generation	$h_G(K + 2SG + dSG)$	$\mathcal{O}(h_G\,n^2 d)$
	1.2 Polynomial update	$h_G\,dPG$	
	1.3 Policy certificate generation	$h_G\,dS$	

h_G, *height of the hierarchy; S, signature generation; V, signature verification; k, no. of signers;*
PI, *Pathak and Iftode's protocol; K, symmetric key generation; SG, secret sharing generation;*
SR, *secret sharing reconstruction; PG, polynomial generation; PE, polynomial evaluation;*
n, *no. of terms*

5.3   ACCESS Subprotocol

The protocol starts when a user n_A desires to access an object O from a user n_B. Since O is published encrypted using a symmetric key S_j, the requesters must have a set of at least c valid CIDs to access O. To ease exposition, we consider that O belongs to class c_j, i.e., $O \in o(c_j)$. We describe the input and output for this operation as follows.

Input. As introduced in Section 5.1, the access policy for object O is hidden to policy holders by combining the ACP scheme with secret sharing. As input, each policy holder h_i stores a certificate $C_{P_i(x)}$ called *policy certificate*, which contains polynomial share $P_i(x)$. The requester n_A has a request certificate and a set of presumably legal CIDs.

Output. The requester learns a level-2 share $ss_{j2,i}$ for each policy holder only if CID_{ji} is valid, $1 \le i \le d$, or a random number otherwise. Finally, class key S_j is reconstructed by combining share s_{j1} with any selection of c level-2 shares.

Protocol. The protocol is as follows.

1. For each policy holder h_i, n_A sends an ACCESS_REQ which formally expresses its desire to access O:

$$n_A \longrightarrow h_i : m_2 = [n_A, h_i, C_j, \text{ACCESS\_REQ}]\, K_A^{-1}. \qquad (10)$$

Upon reception of the ACCESS_REQ, h_i checks the signature of m_2. If the signature matches, the ownership of C_j must be ascertained. This prevents users to skip JOIN subprotocol and request access directly. If it matches, h_i finally responds to n_A with the policy certificate $C_{P_i(x)}$ corresponding to class c_j.

2. For each received certificate $C_{P_i(x)}$, n_A first verifies that the signature comes from the owner of O. If the signature is valid, then n_A extracts $P_i(x)$ and z_i from $C_{P_i(x)}$. Finally, from z_i and CID_{ji}, n_A obtains the level-2 share $ss_{2j,i}$ by:

$$ss_{2j,i} = P_i(f(CID_{ji}, z_i)), \tag{11}$$

We observe that only a valid CID makes $A_i(f(CID_{ji}, z_i)) = 0$, and thus to recover the share; otherwise, $P_i(f(CID_{ji}, z_i))$ returns a random value that does not yield any information about S_j (provided that q is sufficiently large).

3. Finally, if the requester obtains at least c shares, he can reconstruct S_j (by applying the Lagrange interpolation formula).

Complexity Analysis. Computational complexity is shown in Table 1. Communication overhead is the following. For each policy holder, the protocol requires the requester to submit an ACCESS_REQ. Since each ACCESS_REQ is verified by means of Pathak and Iftode's protocol, the communication overhead is $\mathcal{O}(dk)$. If the requester knows each policy holder and vice versa, communication cost depends on the transmission of the d polynomial shares. In this case, communication complexity is $\mathcal{O}(d)$.

5.4 REVOCATION Subprotocol

The owner of an object, O, can revoke user n_A's permissions for it. Let c_j be the class in the hierarchy from which user n_A is deleted. There are two cases to consider:

- *Revocation from a leaf class.* If the revocation is from a leaf class, the steps are the following:
  1. The owner revokes symmetric key S_j if he wants to prevent n_A to read O until it is overwritten and re-encrypted. In this case, the owner generates a new key and its corresponding shares as described in Section 5.1.
  2. The owner generates d new CIDs and recomputes polynomials $A_i(x)$, $1 \le i \le d$, including the CIDs of all its ancestors.
  3. Finally, the owner issues a new policy certificate for each polynomial share and forwards it to each policy holder h_i (through a secure channel).
- *Revocation from an internal class.* As above, the owner performs steps $1 - 3$ to update class c_j. Unfortunately, it is required more computation in this case: the old CIDs must be replaced with the new set of c_j's CIDs in the ACPs of all descendant classes. For each descendant class, the owner also generates a new key. Once the key is changed, future access from the leaving users will be effectively disabled.

Complexity Analysis. Computational complexity of this subprotocol is tabulated in Table 1. The communication overhead of REVOCATION subprotocol is mainly due to the transmission of the updated polynomials to the policy holders.

6 Security Analysis

Due to space constraints, we restrict our analysis to the proof that our protocol is secure according to Definition 1. By Assumption 2, it can be easily shown that our protocol is secure against eavesdropping, impersonation and message modification attacks. The major weakness comes from the public key authentication mechanism. At some stages of the protocol, both parties are required to authenticate the other's public key in order to verify the signatures exchanged. However, Pathak and Iftode's could fail due to the impossibility of getting an honest majority. Next, we prove that a legal user can obtain the correct output if he owns the corresponding permission.

Theorem 1. *For each policy holder* h_i, *a requester can learn* $ss_{2,i}$ *if and only if he has a valid* CID$_i$ *and nothing otherwise.*

Proof. To derive share-share $ss_{2,i}$, the requester first contacts h_i. If this policy holder is honest, the requester will receive the ith polynomial share; otherwise, he will obtain no response because the policy certificate prevents any alteration of the polynomial share by part of h_i. If $P_i(x)$ is received, there are two cases to consider. If the requester owns CID$_i$, then he will be able to recover $ss_{2,i}$ by plugging CID$_i$ into $P_i(x)$. Otherwise, he will learn no information about the share. Concretely, we will obtain a random integer less than q. This claim holds thanks to the security properties of the ACP scheme.   □

Theorem 2. *A requester learns how many rules are in the access policy and policy holders learn only the class where the requested object belongs to.*

Proof. A requester obtains a polynomial share for each responding policy holder. Since the degree of each polynomial share is equal to the number of access rules (if there are no pseudo terms), the requester learns the number of rules in the access policy. By this claim and Theorem 1, we can conclude the first part of the proof.

When requesting the polynomial shares, the requester encloses the class where the desired object belongs to. This reveals to policy holders the users that presumably have access to objects of a particular class. This is the unique information that policy holders obtain about the users. Observe that CIDs are never revealed to the policy holders.   □

7   Conclusions

In this paper we proposed an access control protocol targeted to P2P collaborative systems, which are environments characterized by the lack of a central control. Our protocol does not a require a trusted third party and provides privacy-protection for sensitive policies and sensitive permissions using the innovative concept of Access Control Polynomials. We showed how our protocol can accommodate hierarchical access control and key management. We also analyzed its security and performance.

Due to the space constraints, we omitted the comparison with existing schemes and illustrative examples. For future work, this could be done in conjunction with a real evaluation on an existing P2P network.

References

1. Kallahalla, M., Riedel, E., Swaminathan, R., Wang, Q., Fu, K.: Plutus: Scalable secure file sharing on untrusted storage. In: FAST 2003, pp. 29–42 (2003)
2. Goh, E.J., Shacham, H., Modadugu, N., Boneh, D.: SiRiUS: Securing Remote Untrusted Storage. In: NDSS 2003, Internet Society (ISOC), February 2003, pp. 131–145 (2003)

3. Pathak, V., Iftode, L.: Byzantine fault tolerant public key authentication in peer-to-peer systems. Computer Networks Journal 50(4), 579–596 (2006)
4. Crispo, B., Sivasubramanian, S., Mazzoleni, P., Bertino, E.: P-hera: Scalable fine-grained access control for p2p infrastructures. In: ICPADS 2005, pp. 585–591 (2005)
5. Gaheni, A., Chandra, C.: Parameterized access control: from design to prototype. In: SecureComm 2008, pp. 1–8 (2008)
6. Palomar, E., Tapiador, J.M.E., Hernandez-Castro, J.C., Ribagorda, A.: Secure content access and replication in pure p2p networks. Comput. Commun. 31(2), 266–279 (2008)
7. Zou, X., Dai, Y.S., Bertino, E.: A practical and flexible key management mechanism for trusted collaborative computing. In: INFOCOM 2008, pp. 1211–1219 (2008)
8. Artigas, M., et al.: A novel methodology for constructing secure multipath overlays. IEEE Internet Computing 9(6), 50–57 (2005)
9. Castro, M., et al.: Secure routing for structured peer-to-peer overlay networks. SIGOPS Oper. Syst. Rev. 36(SI), 299–314 (2002)
10. Saxena, N., Tsudik, G., Yi, J.H.: Threshold cryptography in p2p and manets: The case of access control. Computer Networks 51(12), 3632–3649 (2007)
11. Menezes, A.J., Vanstone, S.A., Oorschot, P.C.V.: Handbook of Applied Cryptography. CRC Press, Inc., Boca Raton (1996)

Customized and Optimized Service Selection with ProtocolDB

Zoé Lacroix[1,2], Maria-Esther Vidal[3], and Christophe R.L. Legendre[2]

[1] Translational Genomics Research Institute (TGen), Scottsdale, Arizona, USA
[2] Arizona State University, Tempe, Arizona, USA
[3] Universidad Simón Bolívar, Caracas, Venezuela

Abstract. Infrastructures that support reasoning on services and their composition into workflows are critical to evaluate and improve performance. In this paper we present ProtocolDB, a system that supports process design and analysis. The approach allows the description of a workflow with alternate implementations thus, allowing reasoning on workflow performance with respect to service selection during the rewriting phase. We illustrate the approach with the analysis and evaluation of a scientific workflow with respect to two measures: cost and quality.

1 Introduction

The composition of services into workflows serves as a foundation for modeling various cross-industry activities. Although workflows are often used to optimize the orchestration of tasks and for quality assessment, little has been done to support in a single system a vector of performance metrics. In this paper we present ProtocolDB a system that supports the design of workflows and the analysis of their performance with respect to a set of criteria defined by the user. This approach allows the analysis of the workflow in terms of the cost of the evaluation of services that comprise the workflow and the identification of alternate services that may produce a more efficient workflow. The approach exploits the knowledge encoded in a domain ontology and in the mappings between the services and the ontology concepts and relationships; thus, characterization of similar resources is supported. We illustrate our approach in the context of a scientific workflow evaluated for cost and quality. Workflow design and implementation with ProtocolDB are described in Sections 2 and 4, respectively. Service and metadata representation are discussed in Section 3. The performance of each workflow implementation with respect to the selected services is addressed in Section 5. Section 6 is devoted to related work whereas Section 7 concludes the paper.

2 Workflow Design

In ProtocolDB workflows are first expressed in terms of a domain ontology where each task expresses a specific aim [10]. A *design protocol* (or workflow) is defined in a top-down fashion from a conceptual design task that describes the workflow as a whole. The conceptual design is defined in terms of input and

A. Hameurlain and A M. Tjoa (Eds.): Globe 2009, LNCS 5697, pp. 112–123, 2009.

output parameters which are expressed as complex conceptual types (collections of concept variables). Each design task may be split either sequentially or in parallel into two design tasks. Each design protocol is mapped to one or more implementation protocols. Design protocols enable reasoning on workflows at a conceptual level. A critical component of the ProtocolDB architecture is the ontology. The ontology can be specified prior to the workflow design or generated from the entry of the design protocol. The first step of the workflow design consists of the specification of the input and output of the protocol as a whole. The input and output are respectively expressed as complex types (record, set, list) in terms of the concepts of the ontology. This step allows the characterization of the dataflow. The user may either select concepts already entered in the domain ontology or the concepts used to describe the input and output of the workflow will be entered as new concepts in the workflow ontology. The splitting process (successor or parallel) is constrained by the dataflow already defined. That is if a workflow W has an input I and output O and is split with a succession $W_1 \otimes W_2$, then the input of W_1 is automatically assigned to I and the output of W_2 is automatically assigned to O. Similarly, if W is split with two parallel tasks W_1 and W_2, then the input (resp. output) of W_1 (resp. W_2) is included[1] in I (resp. O).

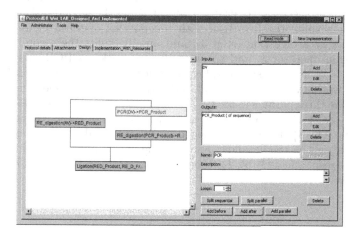

Fig. 1. Sub-cloning Design Workflow

We illustrate the process of workflow design as modeled in ProtocolDB with a scientific workflow. The aim of the *sub-cloning workflow* is to transfer a sequence of interest presented in a vector (donor vector) into another vector (acceptor vector). The design workflow entered in ProtocolDB is shown on the left side of the ProtocolDB interface displayed in Figure 1. The input (resp. output) of the workflow is a plasmid construct containing a sequence of interest, i.e., insert (resp. another plasmid construct which has accepted the insertion of the sequence of interest). The first design task is a PCR step that aims at producing

---

[1] Here 'inclusion' refers to sub-typing.

large amounts of material and verifying the quality of the donor vector (DV). Starting with a small amount of DV material, a PCR is conducted in order to amplify the DV-integrated sequence of interest (or insert). Then, a digestion step is performed using the same enzymes to cut both the acceptor vector (AV) and the insert. A gel extraction of the digested products is performed (filtering task) in order to get rid of small sequences generated by the last enzymatic reaction and because they will spoil the ligation step. The two final extracted products, i.e., AV and sequence of interest, are linked together using the T4 Ligase enzyme (ligation step). The product of the ligation is run on an electrophoresis gel in order to check whether the expected vector is present or not in the mix of the final reaction. If it is, the newly formed vector (AV + sequence of interest) has to be amplified for further usage. The bacterial transformation is used again for the final step of the sub-cloning protocol. The workflow design is thus composed of four design tasks: PCR, two tasks of digestion, and a ligation. The dataflow of the workflow is composed of the translational flow (here sequences) and the various parameters needed to implement each task. These parameters are not specified at the design level but will be specified at implementation when the services are selected.

The internal representation of the workflow corresponds to a binary tree as illustrated in Figure 2. To obtain this design, the user first registers the workflow (step 1), uses the succession operator $\otimes$ and specifies the second task as a ligation (step 2), then splits the first task with the parallel operator $\oplus$ and specifies the first task as a digestion (step 3), and, finally, splits the second task with the succession operator $\otimes$ and specifies the two tasks as PCR and digestion, respectively. We define a structural equivalence relationship for workflows that is used for workflow comparison and optimization. For example, there are two ways to define three parallel tasks T_1, T_2, and T_3: $T_1 \oplus (T_2 \oplus T_3)$ and $(T_1 \oplus T_2) \oplus T_3$. Because of the structural equivalence, we denote any of these compositions by $T_1 \oplus T_2 \oplus T_3$. This structural equivalence can be extended to semantic rules that handle variations on the dataflow. For example, if the input (resp. output) of T_1 is not used (resp. affected) by T_3, then $(T_1 \oplus T_2) \otimes T_3 \approx T_1 \oplus (T_2 \otimes T_3)$.

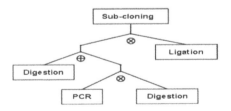

Fig. 2. Workflow Tree

3   Representing Services

Services are represented as basic implementation tasks with a name, input, and output description. Each service is also mapped to the ontology. Its input (resp. output) is expressed in terms of concepts and the service itself may be mapped to an existing conceptual relationship. For example, the thermocycler device available at the laboratory requires eight reagents: RNase/DNase free water, PCR buffer, $MgCl_2^{++}$, mix of dNTP (diNucleotide TriPhosphate), Taq polymerase, Primers Forward and Reverse, and finally, the template (sequence). The complex datatype that describes the input of the thermocycler is expressed in terms of four concepts in the ontology: solvent, ion, sequence, enzyme, and as follows:

[solvent,solvent,ion,sequence,enzyme,[sequence,sequence],sequence]

Its output is a set of sequences or {sequence}. While the input sequence corresponds to the input of the workflow, the other inputs: RNase/DNase free water, PCR buffer, $MgCl_2^{++}$, mix of dNTP (diNucleotide TriPhosphate), Taq polymerase, Primers Forward and Reverse of respective conceptual type solvent, solvent, ion, sequence, enzyme, and [sequence, sequence] are outputs of service providers such as BioLabs and Invitrogen. The *service graph* contains the domain ontology composed of concepts and extended to complex conceptual types. Each resource is represented as a labeled directed edge from the conceptual representation of its input to the conceptual representation of its output. For example the service graph illustrated in Figure 3 is composed of four concepts and two complex conceptual types represented by ovals and fifteen services represented by rounded rectangles.

Each service is annotated with metadata or parameters that capture various characteristics of interest to the user or the quality of the result obtained by evaluating the service. Usually these parameters are known as Quality of Service parameters or QoS. Some of QoS parameters can capture the cost of a service, the response time or time required for completing the task and receiving the results, the quality of the service, the expected size of its output, etc. QoS parameters may be used to select resources that best meet the users' needs. Note that ProtocolID allows the annotation of services and the optimization of their selection with respect to any measurable characteristics.

We illustrate our approach with metadata associated with the services in the service graph illustrated in Figure 3. Each service is represented as a pair

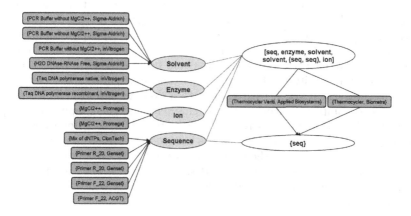

Fig. 3. Service Graph

provider/product[2] because, providers typically offer a variety of products. In this example, we use two annotations to document the services: quality and cost. Quality is a score from 1 (poor) to 5 (excellent) entered by the workflow designer; it expresses the user's confidence in the expected performance of the service. This score may be reflecting the performance of the service in other past workflows as well as preliminary tests. The cost, given in US dollars ($), corresponds to a specific product volume and concentration extracted from lists and databases of the different products, supplies, and devices published by the providers. The metadata associated with the thermocycler may capture its electrical consumption or depreciation price or other charges. The preparation of the PCR mix reaction requires the use of tubes, cones, micropipettes, non-provided solute, etc. The amplification number ($\mathbf{A}$) corresponds to the number of amplifications that can be performed by each service. Finally, performance criteria are defined for each service. In our example, the two performance criteria are $\mathbf{Q}$ (quality) and $\mathbf{C}$ (cost). Quality is defined as the value of the metadata quality in the service metadata table, when $\mathbf{C}$ is defined by the following equation: $C(N) = P\lceil \frac{N}{A} \rceil$, where, N is the number of target sequences on which the workflow is run, and $\lceil \ \rceil$ denotes the ceiling function. This constitutes the metadata for each service associated with PCR.

4   Selecting Services

A design protocol is mapped to one (or more) *implementation protocols* (workflows) as follows. Each design task is mapped to an implementation protocol. The composition mechanism of implementation protocols is similar to the design one: they are either, a service, a succession of two implementation tasks, or a parallel composition of two implementation tasks. Basic implementation tasks are *services*. The implementation of the design task PCR is achieved as follows. The design task links two complex conceptual types [sequence] and {sequence} as illustrated in Figure 1. Therefore a workflow that implements the design task PCR receives a sequence as input and produces a set of sequences. The workflow is composed of nine services. The design task PCR is linked to its implementation as follows $T_{PCR} \equiv S_1 \oplus S_2 \oplus S_3 \oplus S_4 \oplus S_5 \oplus S_6 \oplus S_7 \oplus S_8 \otimes S_9$ where S_9 is the thermocycler service. Each selection of services corresponds an implementation. The sub-cloning workflow was implemented at TGen with the laboratory thermocycler, however, the other services could be selected with respect to their ability to optimize criteria of interest, e.g., cost and quality. Services are registered in the service graph with respect to a domain ontology. This mapping of services to complex conceptual types characterized their input and output, and it provides a semantic description of their functionality. Moreover, services may be linked to conceptual relationships between the same complex conceptual types as the ones describing their input and output. By extending the mapping of services to the domain ontology, each design workflow W may be linked to several implementations I_1, I_2, etc. This defines a semantic equivalence of services and implementations as follows.

---

[2] In case of a digital service we use the Web Service formalism.

Definition 1. Semantic Equivalence of Services

Two services S_1 and S_2 are semantically equivalent, denoted by $S_1 \cong S_2$, if they are linked to the same conceptual relationship (or design task).

Definition 2. Semantic Equivalence of Implementations

Two implementations I_1 and I_2 are semantically equivalent, denoted by $I_1 \cong I_2$, if they are linked to the same conceptual relationship (or design task).

The semantic equivalence is extended to workflows as follows. If $W = W_1 \oplus W_2$, $W_1 \equiv I_1$, and $W_2 \equiv I_2$, where $I_1 \cong I_1'$ and $I_2 \cong I_2'$ then $I_1 \oplus I_2 \cong I_1' \oplus I_2'$ and $I_1' \oplus I_2'$ is a suitable implementation of W, that is $W \equiv I_1' \oplus I_2'$. A similar rule applies for the succession operator $\otimes$. Semantic equivalence is used to support service discovery and service reasoning.

5 Reasoning on Services

The selection of services may significantly affect the outcome of a task, and in consequence, the performance of the whole workflow. The ProtocolDB approach aims at guiding users in the selection of resources that may best meet their needs. The metadata specifying the services, or QoS parameters, are exploited to rank the possible implementations. For example, a user who is looking forward to implementing a workflow at the lowest cost, will be returned the list of workflow plans ranked from the lower associated cost. This approach was demonstrated in BioNavigation [13,14,15,7] where each service of a linear implementation path was characterized by various statistics used to predict the execution costs.The reasoning component of ProtocolDB is designed to support workflows that are not limited to successive compositions of services; it also supports multi-criteria evaluation.

The approach consists in (1) discovering suitable services in the service graph to implement each task of the design workflow and (2) ranking them with respect to the selected criteria. We illustrate the approach with the sub-cloning workflow and two criteria: the cost (price) of the execution and the quality of the result. In previous papers [7,15,16], we presented the algorithm *ESearch* that performs a Breath-First strategy, and traverses the service graph to enumerate the service paths that implement each design path of a workflow. Here each design path corresponds to a path from the input of the workflow to its output. For example, the sub-cloning design workflow displayed in Figure 1 contains two design paths: Digestion⊗Ligation and PCR⊗Digestion⊗Ligation. *ESearch* identifies suitable services to implement each design task contained in each design path of the design workflow. The result of each selection is a workflow implementation. We compute a vector of cost for each workflow implementation as follows. For each QoS parameter m selected for optimization, $C(W, I)$ corresponds to the total cost of an implementation workflow W on an input I; it is defined as the sum of the cost of each service S that comprises W, i.e., $C(W, I) = \sum_{S \in W} C(S, I_S)$. *ESearch* performs an exhaustive search on the space of the service paths in the source graph that may be used to rewrite the workflow. Then, it scans the complete set of paths to compute the metric values; finally, it ranks the complete set of paths.

ESearch uses a Deterministic Finite Automaton (DFA) that represents the design workflow to traverse the space of possible service paths, and returns the service paths that correspond to implementations of the design paths accepted by the DFA. It runs in polynomial time in the size of the service graph, if the graph is cycle-free and all paths are cycle-free, i.e., the service graph is a tree. If s is the maximum number of services that can precede a service in the service graph, and l is the maximum length of (cycle free) paths satisfying the regular expression, then $O(s^l)$ is an upper bound for *ESearch*. Because the search space of service paths may be large, an exhaustive enumeration of the whole set of paths may be very unefficient, thus unaceptable. Furthermore, for general service graphs and design workflows, *ESearch* can be time exponential on the size of the graph. In the future, we plan to implement search techniques to identify efficiently source paths with the highest QoS parameter scores.

We illustrate the approach with the scientific workflow and the two performance criteria **Q** and **C**. Each design task of the workflow design can be implemented by several services, but each service has a score for **Q** and **C** computed from the service metadata table shown in Figure 4. There are 96 possible implementations of the sub-cloning workflow, among them implementations A, B, and C.

The quality scores of the services composing each implementation are recorded in Figure 5. The overall quality score assigned to the whole sub-cloning implementation is the average of the quality score of each service. Unlike the quality score, the cost depends on the size of the input. The input of the PCR workflow is a sequence, and an amplification is performed for each input sequence. The cost of each implementation is reported in Figure 6.

SERVICES		METADATA				
Product	Provider	Service quality	Price (US $)	Product size	Product concentration	Amplification number
Taq DNA polymerase recombinant	inVitrogen	3	59	100 U	2 U / µl	200
Taq DNA polymerase native	inVitrogen	4	65	100 U	2 U / µl	200
PCR Buffer without MgCl$_2$$^{++}$	Sigma-Aldrich	2	25.6	1.5 ml	10 X	300
PCR Buffer without MgCl$_2$$^{++}$	Sigma-Aldrich	2	45	5 ml	10 X	1000
PCR Buffer without MgCl$_2$$^{++}$	inVitrogen	1	30	1 ml	5 X	100
MgCl$_2$$^{++}$	Promega	2	30	1.5 ml	25 mM	75000
MgCl$_2$$^{++}$	Promega	5	40	25 ml	25 mM	1250000
H$_2$O DNAse-RNAse Free	Sigma-Aldrich	5	41.11	1000 ml	N.A.	23795
Mix of dNTPs	ClonTech	4	250	250 µl	100 mM each dNTP	250
Primer R_20	Genset	4	80.7	250 µl	10 mM	250
Primer R_20	ACGT	2	60	200 µl	18 mM	560
Primer F_22	Genset	4	84.3	250 µl	22 mM	550
Primer F_22	ACGT	2	63.4	200 µl	14 mM	280
Thermocycler Veriti ™ 60-Well Thermal Cycler	Applied Biosystems	4	3000	1 U	N.A.	1
Thermocycler 3 blocks for 20 x 0.5 ml tubes	Biometra	3	8000	1 U	N.A.	1

Fig. 4. Service Metadata (QoS parameters)

SERVICES		IMPLEMENTATIONS		
Product	Provider	A	B	C
Taq DNA polymerase recombinant	inVitrogen	2	2	2
Taq DNA polymerase native	inVitrogen			
PCR Buffer without MgCl₂$^{++}$	Sigma-Aldrich			2
PCR Buffer without MgCl₂$^{++}$	Sigma-Aldrich	2		
PCR Buffer without MgCl₂$^{++}$	inVitrogen		1	
MgCl₂$^{++}$	Promega		2	
MgCl₂$^{++}$	Promega	5		5
H₂O DNAse-RNAse Free	Sigma-Aldrich	5	5	5
Mix of dNTPs	ClonTech	4	4	4
Primer R_20	Genset		4	4
Primer R_20	ACGT	3		3
Primer F_22	Genset	4		
Primer F_22	ACGT		3	
Thermocycler Veriti™ 60-Well Thermal Cycler	Applied Biosystems	4		4
Thermocycler 3 blocks for 20 x 0.5 ml tubes	Biometra		2	
	Overall Quality	4	3	4

Fig. 5. Selection and Quality Score of Services

	IMPLEMENTATIONS		
Amplification Number	A	B	C
1	550	573	550
2	550	573	550
50	550	573	550
100	550	573	550
125	580	573	550
150	580	573	550
200	580	573	550
250	669	632	609
300	1059	882	940
350	1089	882	966
400	1089	882	966
500	1178	941	1025
800	2047	1639	1825
1100	2645	2052	2299
5000	10722	8110	9091
10000	21373	16055	18102
20000	42675	31944	36096
50000	106604	79695	90189

Fig. 6. Cost of Implementations (with respect to input size)

Implementation A corresponds to a selection of retail providers offering small volumes, whereas the services selected in implementation B can be seen as bulk providers offering large quantities at more competitive prices. Implementation C is a mix of retail and bulk services. Not surprisingly the cost prediction varies significantly with respect to the input size. A user wishing to run the most cost effective workflow implementation for one single input sequence will select the services used in A. However, a user wishing to run the workflow on large input sizes such as 50,000 sequences, will select the services of B for a cost 25% less than A. The approach supports multi-dimensional performance optimization by allowing multi-criteria comparison. For example, a user can specify a quality and cost threshold and select the combination of services that best meet ones needs. Service selection is made more critical for scientific workflows with the advent of high-throughput scientific workflows that perform millions of biochemical or genetic tests. But the problem is not limited to scientific workflows. As Web services are becoming more available and semantically wrapped for better use and integration, the problem of selecting a service that best meets the user needs is a challenge.

The ProtocolDB approach supports alternative ways to improve the performance of a workflow. For example, by reasoning on the domain ontology the system can relax some constraints regarding the specificity of the service. Indeed, if a class C_1 is a sub-class of class C_2 in the ontology, if a design task T requires a service that takes C_1 and returns output C, if there is no service available with input C_1, and if there is a service S with input C_2 and output C, then the service S can be selected to implement T. This is the reasoning approach of BiOnMap [1,2,3] that uses a deductive database to record the service graph and ontology in the extensional database, and the reasoning rules against the ontology as the intentional database. Finally, ProtocolDB supports the design of a simulation workflow that will mimic the workflow and predict the feasibility and expected quality of the execution. For example, one can design a simulation of the sub-cloning workflow *in silico* [12]. This latter approach combines implementations that are experimental (in the wet lab) and digital.

6   Related Work

Laboratory Information Management Systems (LIMS) [21] support the integration of different functionalities in a laboratory, such as sample tracking (invoicing/quoting), integrated bar-coding, instrument integration, personnel and equipment management, etc. LIMS typically support *wet* workflows that coordinate the management of tasks, samples, and instruments and allow reasoning on business-like parameters such as, ordering (e.g., invoicing) and organization (automation and optimization); however, they do not offer resource planning with respect to a customized set of metrics. In contrast, the ProtocolDB approach offers the ability to select the services that best meet the users' needs by evaluating the performance of each service in the workflow and by ranking the options; thus, users can select the services that best meet their needs.

Scientific workflow systems such as Kepler [17] or Taverna [19] describe the scientific process from experiment design, data capture, integration, processing, and analysis that leads to scientific discovery. They typically express *digital* workflows and execute them on platforms such as grids. Workflows systems do not provide resource discovery functionalities as the ones presented in this paper, where service composition plans are ranked with respect to a customized metrics. In addition, a large amount of scientific workflows mix wet and digital tasks. Experiments are first designed and simulated with digital resources in order to predict the quality of the result or to identify the parameters suitable for the expected outcome. The ProtocolDB approach can provide service discovery and planning for any kind of workflows, even those that mix manual (wet) tasks and the digital ones.

Service discovery systems typically support the identification of services suitable to implement a specific task. Criteria for discovery are typically syntactic expressions that represent user functional requirements, for example, the input or output format of a Web service, or what the service does. On the other hand, the problem of identifying a set of concrete services that implement a design workflow and best meet a set of QoS parameters is known as the QoS-aware service composition problem, and has been shown to be NP-hard [23]. A survey of existing approaches can be found in [9,24]. This problem is a combinatorial optimization problem and several heuristics have been proposed to find a relatively good solution in a reasonably short period of time [4,6,5,8,11,20,23]. The proposed solutions vary from logic-based techniques [4,5,6], hybrid algorithms that combine the tabu search and simulating annealing meta-heuristics [11], and a multi-objective optimization solution that uses a genetic based algorithm to identify a set of non-dominated service compositions that best meet a set of QoS parameters [23]. Although all these solutions are able to solve the optimization problem efficiently and scale up to a large number of abstract processes, they have mainly focused on quality [18,22,25,26,27]. In contrast, the ProtocolDB approach aims at supporting multi-dimensional performance criteria based on a variety of metadata attached to services. This approach offers multiple views of the workflow and provides the ability to compare different implementations.

7 Conclusion

The ProtocolDB[3] approach presented in this paper supports workflow design, analysis, and optimization. Workflows are modeled at two levels: a *design* that captures the workflow aim in terms of a domain ontology linked to one or more *implementations* that specify the services selected for its implementation. We define a *structural equivalence* relationship for workflows that expresses the equivalence of alternate workflow designs and a *semantic equivalence* that captures alternate workflow implementations. Both relationships are used to analyze workflows and identify alternate implementations that optimize customized performance criteria evaluated against various service metadata registered in a *service graph*. We illustrate the approach with the analysis of a fusion protein construct workflow developed at the Translational Genomics Research Institute (TGen). Future work includes the integration of the BiOnMap service to increase the

---

[3] ProtocolDB, currently under development at Arizona State University, is available at http://bioinformatics.eas.asu.edu/siteProtocolDB/indexProtocolDB.htm

reasoning ability of the approach and the ability to index datasets produced by the workflow execution to support data provenance analysis.

Acknowledgment

We thank Piotr Wlodarczyk for the implementation of the first ProtocolDB prototype. We acknowledge the Pharmaceutical Genomics Division at TGen, and in particular Drs. Tuzmen and Mousses. This research was partially supported by the National Science Foundation[4] (grants IIS 0431174, IIS 0551444, IIS 0612273, IIS 0738906, IIS 0832551, and CNS 0849980).

References

1. Ayadi, N.Y., Lacroix, Z., Vidal, M.-E.: A Deductive Approach for Resource Interoperability and Well-Defined Workflows. In: Meersman, R., Tari, Z., Herrero, P. (eds.) OTM-WS 2008. LNCS, vol. 5333, pp. 998–1009. Springer, Heidelberg (2008)
2. Ayadi, N.Y., Lacroix, Z., Vidal, M.-E.: BiOnMap: A Deductive Approach for Resource Discovery. In: 1st International Workshop On Resource Discovery, pp. 477–482. ACM, New York (2008)
3. Ayadi, N.Y., Lacroix, Z., Vidal, M.-E., Ruckhaus, E.: Deductive Web Services: An Ontology-Driven Approach for Service Interoperability in Life Science. In: Meersman, R., Tari, Z., Herrero, P. (eds.) OTM-WS 2007, Part II. LNCS, vol. 4806, pp. 1338–1347. Springer, Heidelberg (2007)
4. Berardi, D., Calvanese, D., Giacomo, G.D., Hull, R., Mecella, M.: Automatic Composition of Transition-based Semantic Web Services with Messaging. In: 31st International Conference on Very Large Data Bases (VLDB), pp. 613–624 (2005)
5. Berardi, D., Cheikh, F., Giacomo, G.D., Patrizi, F.: Automatic Service Composition via Simulation. International Journal of Foundations of Computing Science 19(2), 429–451 (2008)
6. Berardi, D., Giacomo, G.D., Mecella, M., Calvanese, D.: Composing Web Services with Nondeterministic Behavior. In: IEEE International Conference on Web Services, pp. 909–912 (2006)
7. Bleiholder, J., Naumann, F., Lacroix, Z., Raschid, L., Murthy, H., Vidal, M.-E.: BioFast: challenges in exploring linked life sciences sources. SIGMOD Record 33(2), 72–77 (2004)
8. Cardellini, V., Casalicchio, E., Grassi, V., Presti, F.L.: Flow-Based Service Selection for Web Service Composition Supporting Multiple QoS Classes. In: IEEE International Conference on Web Services, pp. 743–750 (2007)
9. Claro, D.B., Albers, P., Hao, J.-K.: Web Services Composition. In: Semantic Web Services, Processes and Applications, pp. 195–225 (2006)
10. Kinsy, M., Lacroix, Z., Legendre, C., Wlodarczyk, P., Yacoubi Ayadi, N.: ProtocolDB: Storing Scientific Protocols with a Domain Ontology. In: Weske, M., Hacid, M.-S., Godart, C. (eds.) WISE Workshops 2007. LNCS, vol. 4832, pp. 17–28. Springer, Heidelberg (2007)
11. Ko, J.M., Kim, C.O., Kwon, I.-H.: Quality-of-Service Oriented Web Service Composition Algorithm and Planning Architecture. Journal of Systems and Software 81(11), 2079–2090 (2008)

---

[4] Any opinion, finding, and conclusion or recommendation expressed in this material are those of the authors and do not necessarily reflect the views of the National Science Foundation.

12. Lacroix, Z., Legendre, C., Tuzmen, C.: Reasoning on Scientific Workflows. In: 3rd International Workshop On Scientific Workflows (July 2009) (to be published by IEEE)
13. Lacroix, Z., Morris, T., Parekh, K., Raschid, L., Vidal, M.-E.: Exploiting Multiple Paths to Express Scientific Queries. In: 16th International Conference on Scientific and Statistical Database Management, pp. 357–360. IEEE, Los Alamitos (2004)
14. Lacroix, Z., Parekh, K., Vidal, M.-E., Cardenas, M., Marquez, N.: BioNavigation: Selecting Optimum Paths through Biological Resources to Evaluate Ontological Navigational Queries. In: Ludäscher, B., Raschid, L. (eds.) DILS 2005. LNCS (LNBI), vol. 3615, pp. 275–283. Springer, Heidelberg (2005)
15. Lacroix, Z., Raschid, L., Vidal, M.-E.: Efficient Techniques to Explore and Rank Paths in Life Science Data Sources. In: Rahm, E. (ed.) DILS 2004. LNCS (LNBI), vol. 2994, pp. 187–202. Springer, Heidelberg (2004)
16. Lacroix, Z., Raschid, L., Vidal, M.-E.: Semantic Model to Integrate Biological Resources. In: 22nd International Conference on Data Engineering Workshops, p. 63. IEEE, Los Alamitos (2006)
17. Ludascher, B., Altintas, I., Berkley, C., Higgins, D., Jaeger, E., Jones, M., Lee, E.A., Tao, J., Zhao, Y.: Scientific Workflow Management and the KEPLER System. Concurrency and Computation: Practice and Experience, Special Issue on Scientific Workflows 18(10), 1039–1065 (2005)
18. Makripoulias, Y., Makris, C., Panagis, Y., Sakkopoulos, E., Adamopoulou, P., Tsakalidis, A.: Web Service discovery based on Quality of Service. In: IEEE International Conference on Computer Systems and Applications, pp. 196–199 (2006)
19. Oinn, T., Addis, M., Ferris, J., Marvin, D., Senger, M., Greenwood, M., Carver, T., Glover, K., Pocock, M.R., Wipat, A., Li, P.: Taverna: a tool for the composition and enactment of bioinformatics workflows. Bioinformatics 20(17), 3045–3054 (2004)
20. Rahmani, H., GhasemSani, G., Abolhassani, H.: Automatic Web Service Composition Considering User Non-functional Preferences. In: 4th International Conference on Next Generation Web Services Practices, pp. 33–38. IEEE, Los Alamitos (2008)
21. Townsend, N., Waugh, M., Flattery, M., Mansfield, P.: LIMS: Meeting the challenge of modern business. American Laboratory 33(6), 34–40 (2001)
22. Ukor, R., Carpenter, A.: On Modelled Flexibility and Service Selection Optimisation. In: 9th Workshop on Business Process Modeling, Development and Support, Montpellier, France (June 2008)
23. Wada, H., Champrasert, P., Suzuki, J., Oba, K.: Multiobjective Optimization of SLA-aware Service Composition. In: IEEE Congress on Services - Part I, pp. 368–375 (2008)
24. Yu, H.Q., Reiff-Marganiec, S.: Non-functional Property-based Service Selection: A survey and classification of approaches. In: Non-Functional Properties and Service Level Agreements in Service Oriented Computing Workshop co-located with The 6th IEEE European Conference on Web Services, vol. 411 (2008)
25. Yu, T., Zhang, Y., Lin, K.-J.: Efficient algorithms for Web services selection with end-to-end QoS constraints. ACM Transactions on the Web 1(1), 6–32 (2007)
26. Zeng, L., Benatallah, B., Ngu, A.H.H., Dumas, M., Kalagnanam, J., Chang, H.: QoS-Aware Middleware for Web Services Composition. IEEE Transactions on Software Engineering 30(5), 311–327 (2004)
27. Zhang, W., Yang, Y., Tang, S., Fang, L.: QoS-driven Service Selection Optimization Model and Algorithms for Composite Web Services. In: 31st Annual International Computer Software and Applications Conference, vol. 2, pp. 425–431. IEEE, Los Alamitos (2007)

A Semantic-Based Ontology Matching Process for PDMS

Carlos Eduardo Pires[1], Damires Souza[1,2], Thiago Pachêco[1],
and Ana Carolina Salgado[1]

[1] Federal University of Pernambuco (UFPE), Center for Informatics, Av. Prof. Luiz Freire,
s/n, 50740-540 Recife, PE, Brazil
[2] Federal Institute of Education, Science and Technology of Paraiba - IFPB, Brazil
{cesp,dysf,tpap,acs}@cin.ufpe.br

Abstract. In Peer Data Management Systems (PDMS), ontology matching can be employed to reconcile peer ontologies and find correspondences between their elements. However, traditional approaches to ontology matching mainly rely on linguistic and/or structural techniques. In this paper, we propose a semantic-based ontology matching process which tries to overcome the limitations of traditional approaches by using semantics. To this end, we present a semantic matcher which identifies, besides the common types of correspondences (equivalence), some other ones (e.g., closeness). We also present an approach for determining a global similarity measure between two peer ontologies based on the identified similarity value of each correspondence. To clarify matters, we provide an example illustrating how the proposed approach can be used in a PDMS and some obtained experimental results.

Keywords: Ontology Matching, Semantic Matching, Semantic Correspondences, Similarity Measure, PDMS.

1 Introduction

The increasing use of computers and the development of communication infrastructures have led to a wide range of data sources being available through networks such as Peer Data Management Systems (PDMS) [1]. In PDMS, each peer is an autonomous source that makes available a local schema. Sources manage their data locally, revealing part of their original schemas to other peers. Schema mappings, i.e., correspondences between schema elements, are generated to allow information exchange between peers. To help matters, ontologies have been considered as a basis for making explicit the content of these data sources (referred here as peer ontologies) and, consequently, as a means for enhancing information integration [1].

Peer ontologies are designed and developed autonomously, what entails several forms of heterogeneity between them, even between those on the same domain [2]. Reconciling such ontologies and finding correspondences between their elements (concepts or properties) is still a relevant research issue, mainly in distributed environments such as PDMS. Ontology matching techniques are required to deal with the diverse concept meanings existing in the peer ontologies. Resulting correspondences between peer ontologies are usually associated with a similarity

A. Hameurlain and A M. Tjoa (Eds.): Globe 2009, LNCS 5697, pp. 124–135, 2009.

value which expresses the level of confidence on the correspondence between the elements. Besides, in a PDMS, it is relevant to have a global measure representing the overall similarity degree between two peer ontologies (and not only between their elements) to determine if these peers should be stated as semantic neighbors in the overlay network.

In order to identify correspondences between the elements of a source ontology with elements of a target one, some works have used additional semantic descriptions, called background knowledge [3]. The common objective is to complement current matching techniques which fail in some cases (e.g., linguistic matching) [4]. To this end, a domain ontology can be used to allow the identification of additional semantic relationships (e.g., subsumption or part-of) between the ontology elements.

In this paper, we present a semantic-based ontology matching process which has been instantiated in a PDMS. Our contribution is twofold: (i) identifying semantic correspondences between two given peer ontologies taking into account a domain ontology as background knowledge; and (ii) proposing a global similarity measure between these two ontologies. In the former, the basic idea is to use the existing relationships of the domain ontology to derive semantic correspondences between the source and target ontologies' elements. In the latter, the semantic correspondences are used in conjunction with linguistic and structural correspondences to produce a global similarity measure between the ontologies. To clarify matters, we provide an example showing how the approach can be used and some results obtained from experiments.

This paper is organized as follows: Section 2 discusses ontology matching in PDMS; Section 3 presents our approach for identifying semantic correspondences; Section 4 provides an overview of the semantic-based matching process; Section 5 shows our approach for determining the global similarity measure; Section 6 presents some experimental results. Related work is discussed in Section 7. Finally, Section 8 draws our conclusions and points out some future work.

2 Ontology Matching in PDMS

So far, several ontology matching definitions have been proposed [2, 5]. According to [2], ontology matching is the process of finding correspondences between elements of different ontologies, normally describing the same or similar domains. An element can be a concept, a property, or an instance. The output of such process is called alignment which contains a set of correspondences indicating which elements of two ontologies (denoted O_1 and O_2) logically correspond to each other. A correspondence can be defined as a 4-tuple $\langle e_i, e_j, r, n \rangle$, where e_i and e_j are the two matched ontology elements (with $e_i \in O_1$ and $e_j \in O_2$); r is the relationship holding between e_i and e_j; and n expresses the level of confidence underlying such correspondence. The correspondences can be produced by one or more algorithms (matchers) which are executed sequentially or in parallel. These matchers are classified into four approaches [2]: linguistic, structural, semantic, and extensional. Examples of existing ontology matching tools are: COMA++ [6], H-Match [7], and Falcon-AO [8].

In this work, we deal with the problem of ontology matching in a PDMS. In our system, ontologies are used as a uniform conceptual representation of exported schemas. Peer ontologies belong to the same knowledge domain (e.g., *Education* or

Health) and an ontology describing the domain is available to be used as background knowledge. Correspondences between peers' ontologies are established to provide a common understanding of their data sources and enable query answering. Correspondences are determined between pairs of peers and are used to compute the global similarity measure between the involved peers in order to determine if they should be considered as semantic neighbors in the overlay network. Two peers are semantic neighbors if their global similarity is higher than a certain threshold.

Considering this setting, we introduce a working scenario composed by two peers P_1 and P_2 which belong to the *Education* knowledge domain. In this scenario, peers have complementary data about academic people and their works (e.g., Research) from different institutions. Each peer is described by an ontology – O_1 (*Semiport.owl*) and O_2 (*UnivBench.owl*). We have considered as background knowledge a Domain Ontology (*DO*) named *UnivCSCMO.owl*[1]. Since terminological normalization is a pre-matching step in which the initial representation of two ontologies are transformed into a common format suitable for similarity computation, we have normalized both ontologies O_1 and O_2 to a uniform representation format according to the *DO*. In this scenario, we are interested in identifying semantic correspondences between O_1 and O_2 elements and in determining if P_1 and P_2 are semantic neighbors.

3   Using a Domain Ontology to Define Semantic Correspondences

In our work, we consider domain ontologies (DO) as reliable references that are made available on the Web. We use them in order to bridge the conceptual differences or similarities between two peer ontologies. In this sense, first concepts and properties from the two peer ontologies are mapped to equivalent concepts/properties in the DO and then their semantic correspondence is inferred based on the existing semantic relationship between the DO elements. Figure 1 shows an overview of our approach for specifying the semantics of the correspondences between peer ontologies. In this

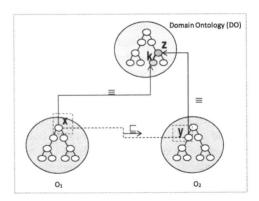

Fig. 1. Specifying semantic correspondences between peer ontologies

---

[1] The complete ontologies are available at our project's web site: http://www.cin.ufpe.br/~speed /SemMatch/index.htm

overview, $O_1:x \equiv DO:k$ and $O_2:y \equiv DO:z$. Since k is subsumed by z in the DO, we infer that the same relationship occurs between x and y. Then, we conclude that $O_1:x$ is subsumed by $O_2:y$, denoted by $O_1.x \xrightarrow{\sqsubseteq} O_2.y$.

To specify the correspondences, we take into account four aspects: (i) the semantic knowledge found in the DO; (ii) if the peer ontology concepts share super-concepts in the DO; (iii) if these super-concepts are different from the root concept and; (iv) the depth of concepts measured in number of nodes. Next, we present the definition of semantic correspondences together with the set of rules that identify their types. The notation we use is based on Distributed Description Logics (DDL), which has been designed to formalize multiple ontologies interconnected by mappings [9]. Since our approach is not concerned with proposing new algorithms for DL or DDL, we rely on existing equivalence and subsumption ones [10] as the basis for our definitions.

Definition 1 - Semantic Correspondence. A semantic correspondence is represented by one of the following expressions:

1. $O_1:x \xrightarrow{\equiv} O_2:y$, an *isEquivalentTo* correspondence
2. $O_1:x \xrightarrow{\sqsubseteq} O_2:y$, an *isSubConceptOf* correspondence
3. $O_1:x \xrightarrow{\sqsupseteq} O_2:y$, an *isSuperConceptOf* correspondence
4. $O_1:x \xrightarrow{\triangleright} O_2:y$, an *isPartOf* correspondence
5. $O_1:x \xrightarrow{\triangleleft} O_2:y$, an *isWholeOf* correspondence
6. $O_1:x \xrightarrow{\approx} O_2:y$, an *isCloseTo* correspondence
7. $O_1:x \xrightarrow{\perp} O_2:y$, an *isDisjointWith* correspondence

where x and y are elements (concepts/properties) belonging to the peer ontologies.
Each correspondence type is defined as follows:

Equivalence: An element $O_1:x$ *isEquivalentTo* $O_2:y$ if $O_1:x \equiv DO:k$ and $O_2:y \equiv DO:k$. This correspondence is represented by $O_1:x \xrightarrow{\equiv} O_2:y$ and means that both concepts/properties (x and y) describe the same real world concept/property.

Specialization: An element $O_1:x$ *isSubConceptOf* $O_2:y$ if $O_1:x \equiv DO:k$ and $O_2:y \equiv DO:z$ and $DO:k \sqsubseteq DO:z$. Such correspondence is represented by $O_1:x \xrightarrow{\sqsubseteq} O_2:y$ and means that $O_1:x$ is less general than $O_2:y$.

Generalization: An element $O_1:x$ *isSuperConceptOf* $O_2:y$ if $O_1:x \equiv DO:k$ and $O_2:y \equiv DO:z$ and $DO:k \sqsupseteq DO:z$. This correspondence is represented by $O_1:x \xrightarrow{\sqsupseteq} O_2:y$ and expresses that $O_1:x$ is more general than $O_2:y$.

Closeness: An element $O_1:x$ *isCloseTo* $O_2:y$ if $(O_1:x \equiv DO:k$ and $O_2:y \equiv DO:z)$ and $(DO:k \sqsubseteq DO:a$ and $DO:z \sqsubseteq DO:a)$ and $DO:a \neq \top$ and $(depth(DO:a, DO:\top) \geqslant treshold Root)$ and $\neg(DO:k \perp DO:z)$ and $(depth(DO:k, DO:a) \leqslant thresholdCommonAncestor)$ and $depth(DO:z, DO:a) \leqslant thresholdCommonAncestor)$. This correspondence is represented by $O_1:x \xrightarrow{\approx} O_2:y$. Considering the DO, the nearest common ancestor of two concepts is used to determine the closeness degree between them. Two concepts are close if they are perceived as belonging to a common relevant meaning, i.e., they are under the same real world concept. The *thresholdRoot* and the *thresholdCommonAncestor* are dependent on the current DO's granularity and size: the former provides a limit for the position of the common ancestor in relation to the root; the latter provides a limit for the position of each matching concept in relation to the common ancestor. Thereby, we state that two concepts k and z are close if (i) they share a common ancestor in the DO; (ii) this common ancestor is not the root ($\top$); (iii) the concepts do not hold any subsumption nor disjointness relationship between themselves and (iv) the measured depths are evaluated to true, according to the referred thresholds. For example, considering that the concepts *cat* and *lion* (each one belonging to a different peer ontology) are sub-concepts of a common ancestor *feloidae* (in a given DO), and the closeness conditions are evaluated to true (e.g., the depth between each concept and the common ancestor is lower than the corresponding threshold), we can infer that *cat* and *lion* are close concepts.

Aggregation – PartOf: An element $O_1{:}x$ *isPartOf* $O_2{:}y$ if $O_1{:}x \equiv DO{:}k$ and $O_2{:}y \equiv DO{:}z$ and $DO{:}k \rhd DO{:}z$ (isPartOf). This correspondence is represented by $O_1{:}x \overset{\rhd}{\to} O_2{:}y$ and states that $O_1{:}x$ is a part or component of $O_2{:}y$.

Aggregation – WholeOf: An element $O_1{:}x$ *isWholeOf* $O_2{:}y$ if $O_1{:}x \equiv DO{:}k$ and $O_2{:}y \equiv DO{:}z$ and $DO{:}k \lhd DO{:}z$ (isWholeOf). This correspondence is represented by $O_1{:}x \overset{\lhd}{\to} O_2{:}y$ and means that, $O_1{:}x$ is an aggregate of $O_2{:}y$, i.e., x is composed by y.

Disjointness: An element $O_1{:}x$ *isDisjointWith* $O_2{:}y$ if $O_1{:}x \equiv DO{:}k$ and $O_2{:}y \equiv DO{:}z$ and $DO{:}k \perp DO{:}z$. This is represented by $O_1{:}x \overset{\perp}{\to} O_2{:}y$ and states that $O_1{:}x$ does not overlap with $O_2{:}y$.

Considering the scenario introduced in Section 2, in order to identify the semantic correspondences between O_1 and O_2, first, our matching tool found out the equivalences between concepts of O_1 and concepts in the DO, and the equivalences between concepts of O_2 with their related ones in the DO. Then, the set of rules described in this section was applied. As a result, the set of semantic correspondences between O_1 and O_2 was identified. We present examples of this set concerning the concept *Faculty* (from O_1) with some related concepts in O_2 in Table 1.

Table 1. Some semantic correspondences between O_1 and O_2

Correspondences for O_1:Faculty	
O_1:Faculty $\overset{\equiv}{\to}$ O_2:Faculty	O_1:Faculty $\overset{\rhd}{\to}$ O_2:PostDoc
O_1:Faculty $\overset{\sqsubseteq}{\to}$ O_2:Worker	O_1:Faculty $\overset{\approx}{\to}$ O_2:Assistant
O_1:Faculty $\overset{\sqsupseteq}{\to}$ O_2:Professor	O_1:Faculty $\overset{\approx}{\to}$ O_2:AdministrativeStaff

In this illustrative set, we can see the equivalence correspondence between *Faculty* in O_1 and O_2. Equivalence is an example of a commonly identified correspondence type in traditional ontology matching approaches. Taking into account the semantics underlying the DO, we can also identify other unusual correspondences. In this fragment, *Faculty* has been identified as: (i) sub-concept of *Worker*; (ii) super-concept of *Professor* and *PostDoc*; and (iii) close to *Assistant* and *AdministrativeStaff*.

4 The Semantic-Based Ontology Matching Process

The Ontology Matching Process brings together a combination of already defined strategies with our semantic-based approach. In this process, linguistic-structural and semantic matchers are executed in parallel, and their individual similarity values are aggregated into combined similarity ones. As shown in Figure 2, the process receives as input two matching ontologies (O_1 and O_2) and a domain ontology DO to be used as background knowledge. As output, it may produce one or two alignments (A_{CO} and/or A_{12}), according to the following two possible goals in the process instantiation:

A. *Generating only the alignment A_{CO}*: in this option (phase 1), only the resulting set of correspondences identified by the linguistic-structural and semantic matchers is considered. In this set, a correspondence is defined between an element $e_i \in O_1$ and some matching elements $e_1,...,e_j \in O_2$, considering the kind of semantic correspondence between them and its respective similarity value. Such alignment is useful for query answering purposes [11];

B. *Calculating the global similarity measure*: in this case, both phases 1 and 2 are performed, i.e., both alignments A_{CO} and A_{12} are generated. Correspondences in A_{12} are defined between an element $e_i \in O_1$ and their best matching element $e_j \in O_2$ (i.e., the element e_j having the highest similarity value with e_i). Resulting correspondences are ranked according to the combined similarity value and a filter strategy is applied to select the most suitable correspondences. Based on the similarity value of each correspondence, the global measure is calculated.

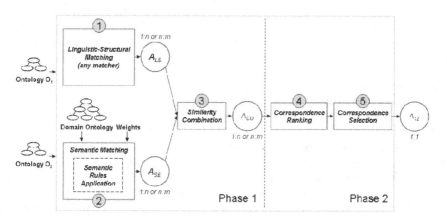

Fig. 2. The general ontology matching process

The main steps carried out by the semantic-based ontology matching process are:

(1) Linguistic-Structural Matching
In this step, any existing ontology matching tool including linguistic and/or structural matchers can be used. Such linguistic and structural matchers are handled as a hybrid matcher, i.e., as a fixed combination of simple matchers. The combination of their similarity values depends on the composition strategy of the ontology matching tool

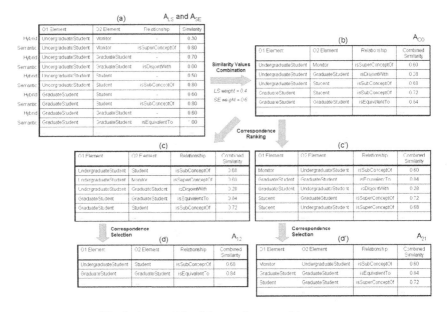

Fig. 3. An example of the ontology matching process

that has been used. The alignment produced by the hybrid matcher is denoted by A_{LS}. Correspondences in A_{LS} are stated as: $\langle e_i, e_j, n \rangle$, as defined in Section 2. Figure 3 shows the process instantiation for the ontologies O_1 and O_2 described in Section 2. For the sake of space, only a limited number of linguistic-structural correspondences are depicted in Figure 3a. Among them, for instance, the similarity value generated by the hybrid matcher for the pair of elements (*UndergraduateStudent, Monitor*) is 0.30.

(2) Semantic Matching
Using a DO, the semantic matcher applies the set of semantic rules described in Section 3 to derive the type of semantic correspondences between O_1 and O_2. Each type is associated with a weight which corresponds to the level of confidence of such correspondence, as follows: isEquivalentTo (1.0), isSubConceptOf (0.8), isSuperConceptOf (0.8), isCloseTo (0.7), isPartOf (0.3), isWholeOf (0.3) and isDisjointWith (0.0). The resulting alignment is denoted by A_{SE}, and correspondences are stated as: $\langle e_i, e_j, r, n \rangle$. Figure 3a shows some semantic correspondences between O_1 and O_2. For instance, O_1:*UndergraduateStudent isSuperConceptof* O_2:*Monitor*, what implies that the semantic similarity value between them is 0.80.

(3) Similarity Combination
The individual similarity values of the correspondences produced by the hybrid matcher and the semantic matcher are associated in a combined similarity one, through a weighted average of the values generated by the individual matchers. The weights are attributed according to the relevance of each matcher. The combined alignment set is stated as A_{CO} and correspondences are denoted as: $\langle e_i, e_j, r, n \rangle$. The

similarity value of each correspondence in A_{CO} takes into account the linguistic, structural, and semantic features of the involved elements.

A weighted average is used because matchers may produce opposing similarity values. For example, a linguistic matcher can find a low similarity value for two elements because their labels are different. On the other hand, a semantic matcher can detect that the same elements are related by a strong relationship (e.g., equivalence) and assign a high similarity value. Regarding our example, the similarity values generated by the hybrid and the semantic matchers for the pair of elements (*UndergraduateStudent, Monitor*) are 0.30 and 0.80, respectively. We assume that the weights associated to the hybrid and semantic matchers are 0.4 and 0.6, respectively. Thus, the combined similarity value for the pair is 0.60 (Figure 3b).

(4) Correspondence Ranking
Elements of O_1 are ranked (in descending order) according to the elements of O_2. In Figure 3c, O_1:*UndergraduateStudent* is ranked according to O_2:*Monitor*, O_2:*GraduateStudent*, and O_2:*Student*.

(5) Correspondence Selection
Finally, a filter strategy is applied to choose the most suitable correspondence for each O_1 element. The strategy consists in selecting the correspondence with the highest combined similarity. As a result, an alignment A_{12} is generated. Each correspondence in A_{12} is defined as: $\langle e_i, e_j, r, n \rangle$. In Figure 4c, given the concept *UndergraduateStudent*, the correspondence (*UndergraduateStudent, Student*) is chosen since its combined similarity value (0.68) is higher than the other two ones involving *UndergraduateStudent*. A fragment of A_{12} is shown in Figure 3d.

Steps 4 and 5 are also executed in the opposite direction. The elements of O_2 are ranked according to the elements of O_1 (Figure 3c') and the filter strategy is applied (Figure 3d'). An alignment A_{21} is then produced. For the final alignment set, an O_1 and an O_2 element are only accepted as a matching correspondence if they are identified as such in both directions. Next, we will present our approach for determining the global similarity measure.

5   Calculating the Global Similarity Measure

The evaluation of the overall similarity between the ontologies O_1 and O_2 is an additional step in the proposed ontology matching process. This step uses the produced alignment sets A_{12} and A_{21} (Step 5) as input to calculate such similarity value. This value indicates the global similarity degree between the ontologies.

Existing similarity measures such as *dice* [6], *weighted* [12] and *overlap* [13] can be adapted to calculate such global similarity degree. They consider the size of the input ontologies. In our work, the size of an ontology is determined by the number of its elements and is denoted by |O|. As opposed to the *dice measure*, the global similarity degree computed by the *weighted average measure* is influenced by the individual similarity values. Hence, the *dice measure* returns higher similarity values than the *weighted average measure*. With all element similarities set to 1.0, both measures return the same similarity. However, in general not all correspondences are evaluated to the maximum level of confidence (1.0). Regarding the *overlap measure*, it is mostly used when the input ontologies are close to each other and have similar sizes. In practice, it is common to match ontologies with different sizes. Considering that, in this work we use the *weighted average measure* to evaluate the global similarity degree between O_1 and O_2. The selected measure is determined as follows:

$$Weighted\ Average(O_1, O_2) = \frac{\sum_{i=1}^{|A12|} n + \sum_{j=1}^{|A21|} n}{|O_1| + |O_2|}$$

Considering the ontologies *Semiport.owl* (O_1) and *UnivBench.owl* (O_2) presented in Section 2, the global similarity measure between them is 0.77. For more details, a full description of the calculus can be found at our project's web site.

6   Experiments and Results

The semantic-based ontology matching tool has been implemented in Java. Jena[2] has been used to provide ontology manipulation and reasoning. In this version, we have used H-Match [7] as the hybrid matcher, and we have restricted the correspondence identification to concepts (not including properties). The tool's main window (Figure 4) is split into three parts: (i) an area for choosing the matching ontologies; (ii) an area for depicting the resulting semantic correspondences; and (iii) an area for executing the main options (e.g., identifying the semantic correspondences).

The goal of our experiments is to check if we can obtain a higher precision/recall [13] considering our matching process. Precision and recall are defined as the ratio of the number of true positive ($|R \cap A|$) and retrieved correspondences ($|A|$) or those to be retrieved ($|R|$), where R is a reference alignment and A is an alignment produced by any ontology matching tool.

We invited expert users (knowledgeable about the *Education* domain) to produce a manual alignment between O_1 and O_2. This "gold standard" alignment was used against our produced alignments. We used the ontology matching tools (COMA++, H-Match, and Falcon-AO) to match the ontologies *Semiport.owl* and *UnivBench.owl*. Afterwards, we used recall and precision to measure the agreement between the resulting alignments and the manual alignment. Next, we combined the (linguistic-structural) alignments produced by each ontology matching tool with the semantic alignments produced by our ontology matching tool. Again, recall and precision were applied to measure the agreement between the resulting alignments and the manual alignment. For both comparisons, we applied the filter strategy described in Section 4 (i.e., for each concept in O_1, we selected the correspondence with the highest combined similarity). The comparison results are illustrated in Figure 5. According to them, we can see that when the semantic matcher is applied both measures (recall and precision) are increased. The reason for such improvement is that incorrect correspondences are removed from the resulting alignments while missing but still relevant correspondences are introduced.

---

[2] Jena, http://jena.sourceforge.net/

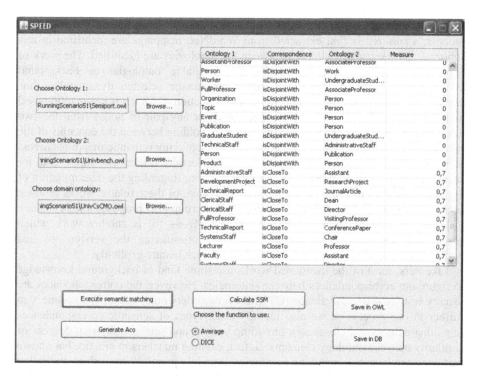

Fig. 4. The semantic matching tool interface

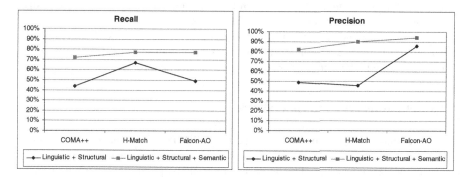

Fig. 5. Evaluation of resulting alignments

7 Related Work

A few semantic-based approaches have considered the use of background knowledge as a way to improve the determination of correspondences between two ontologies. Aleksovski and his group [14] use the DICE ontology as background knowledge and present a matching case where the source and the target ontology are of poor semantics (flat lists). The work described by Reynaud and Safar [4] makes use of

WordNet and implements a system named *TaxoMap* which performs the following process: a sub-tree is first extracted from WordNet, mappings are identified in this sub-tree, and the correspondences between the ontologies are identified. The work of Sabou et al. [3], differently, uses online available ontologies as background knowledge. The idea is that these ontologies can be selected dynamically, thus circumventing the need for a manual ontology selection. S-Match is a semantic-based matching tool [15] which takes two trees, and for any pair of nodes from the two trees, it computes the strongest semantic relation holding between the concepts of the two nodes. CTXMatch [16] is an algorithm for discovering semantic mappings across hierarchical classifications (HCs) using logical deduction. It takes two inputs and, for each pair of concepts, returns their semantic relation. Regarding the determination of a global similarity measure between ontologies, none of these related works produce such measure. Only the work of Castano and her group [12] proposes a kind of such measure, but concerned with ER schemas. COMA++ [6] is another work which argues that calculates a global measure, but, considering the version we had performed our tests, we were not able to find out such feature explicitly.

Like ours, most of the mentioned works use some kind of background knowledge to figure out correspondences between ontologies. However, the correspondences are usually restricted to equivalence (CTXMatch considers other ones). We go one step further in our process as we also identify other types of semantic correspondences (e.g., disjointness and closeness), providing various and semantically-rich degrees of similarity between ontology elements. In fact, existing matchers in practice has shown that concepts from two matching ontologies are rarely precisely equivalent, but rather have some semantic overlap. Consequently, finding such degree of semantic overlap (or not, in case of disjointness) seems more useful for tasks such as query answering (e.g., disjointness, for more details, we refer [11]) or similarity measurement than finding only precise equivalences. To the best of our knowledge, closeness is a type of semantic correspondence that is not found in any related work. Concerning the global similarity measure, our work, differently, provides such innovation, as an additional feature in the semantic-based ontology matching process.

8   Conclusions and Further Work

In environments which are highly dynamic (e.g., PDMS), the semantics surrounding correspondences among ontologies is rather important for tasks such as query answering or peer clustering. This work has presented an ontology matching process which tries to overcome the limitations of existing approaches by using domain ontologies as background knowledge. To this end, we have developed a semantic matcher which identifies, besides the traditional types of correspondences (equivalence), some other ones (e.g., closeness and disjointness). Furthermore, as a result of the overall process, we have introduced the determination of a global similarity measure between the matching ontologies which is calculated considering the identified similarity value of each identified correspondence. Such measure has been used to semantically cluster peers in our PDMS.

Experiments carried out have shown that the combination of the proposed semantic matcher with linguistic-structural matchers can improve the alignments produced by existing ontology matchings tools, by taking out incorrect or meaningless correspondences and including some relevant ones. These additional correspondences are useful for query answering and for the determination of the global measure. Currently we are expanding the experiments with additional scenarios. As further work, we will extend our tool considering properties both in the correspondences identification and in the determination of the global similarity measure.

References

1. Adjiman, P., Goasdoué, F., Rousset, M.-C.: SomeRDFS in the Semantic Web. In: Spaccapietra, S., Atzeni, P., Fages, F., Hacid, M.-S., Kifer, M., Mylopoulos, J., Pernici, B., Shvaiko, P., Trujillo, J., Zaihrayeu, I. (eds.) Journal on Data Semantics VIII. LNCS, vol. 4380, pp. 158–181. Springer, Heidelberg (2007)
2. Euzenat, J., Shvaiko, P.: Ontology Matching. Springer, Heidelberg (2007)
3. Sabou M., D'Aquin M., Motta E.: Using the Semantic Web as Background Knowledge for Ontology Mapping, In: ISWC 2006 Ontology Matching WS (2006)
4. Reynaud, C., Safar, B.: Exploiting WordNet as Background Knowledge. In: International ISWC 2007 Ontology Matching (OM 2007) Workshop, Busan, Korea (2007)
5. Ehrig, M., Sure, Y.: FOAM - Framework for Ontology Alignment and Mapping. In: Workshop on Integrating Ontologies, vol. 156, pp. 72–76 (2005)
6. Aumüller, D., Do, H.H., Massmann, S., Rahm, E.: Schema and ontology matching with COMA++. In: International Conference on Management of Data (SIGMOD), Software Demonstration (2005)
7. Castano, S., Ferrara, A., Montanelli, S.: Matching ontologies in open networked systems: Techniques and applications. Journal on Data Semantics V, 25–63 (2006)
8. Hu, W., Qu, Y.: Falcon-AO: a practical ontology matching system. Journal of Web Semantics 6(3), 237–239 (2008)
9. Borgida, A., Serafini, L.: Distributed description logics: Assimilating information from peer sources. In: Spaccapietra, S., March, S., Aberer, K. (eds.) Journal on Data Semantics I. LNCS, vol. 2800, pp. 153–184. Springer, Heidelberg (2003)
10. Baader, F., Calvanese, D., McGuinness, D., Nardi, D., Patel-Schneider, P.: The Description Logic Handbook: Theory, Implementation and Applications. Cambridge University Press, Cambridge (2003)
11. Souza, D., Arruda, T., Salgado, A.C., Tedesco, P., Kedad, Z.: Using Semantics to Enhance Query Reformulation in Dynamic Environments. To Appear in the Proceedings of the 13th East European Conference on Advances in Databases and Information Systems, Riga, Latvia (2009)
12. Castano, S., Antonellis, V., Fugini, M.G., Pernici, B.: Conceptual Schema Analysis: Techniques and Applications. ACM Transactions on Database Systems 23(3), 286–333 (1998)
13. Rijsbergen, C.J.: Information Retrieval. Stoneham, MA: Butterworths, 2nd edn (1979), http://www.dcs.gla.ac.uk/Keith/Preface.html
14. Aleksovski, Z., Klein, M., Katen, W., Harmelen, F.: Matching Unstructured Vocabularies using a Background Ontology. In: Staab, S., Svátek, V. (eds.) EKAW 2006. LNCS (LNAI), vol. 4248, pp. 182–197. Springer, Heidelberg (2006)
15. Giunchiglia, F., Shvaiko, P., Yatskevich, M.: S-match: an algorithm and an implementation of semantic matching. In: Bussler, C.J., Davies, J., Fensel, D., Studer, R. (eds.) ESWS 2004. LNCS, vol. 3053, pp. 61–75. Springer, Heidelberg (2004)
16. Serafini, L., Zanobini, S., Sceffer, S., Bouquet, P.: Matching Hierarchical Classifications with Attributes. In: Sure, Y., Domingue, J. (eds.) ESWC 2006. LNCS, vol. 4011, pp. 4–18. Springer, Heidelberg (2006)

An In-Database Streaming Solution
to Multi-camera Fusion

Qiming Chen[1], Qinghu Li[2], Meichun Hsu[1], and Tao Yu[2]

[1] Hewlett Packard Co.,
HP Labs Palo Alto, California, USA
[2] Hewlett Packard Co.,
HP Labs, Beijing, China
`{qiming.chen,qinghu.li,meichun.hsu,tao.yu}@hp.com`

Abstract. Multi-camera based video object tracking is a multi-stream data fusion and analysis problem. With the current technology, video analysis software architecture generally separates the analytics layer from the data management layer, which has become the performance bottleneck because of large scaled data transfer, inefficient data access and duplicate data buffering and management. Motivated by providing a convergent platform, we use user-defined Relation Valued Functions (RVFs) to have visual data computation naturally integrated to SQL queries, and pushed down to the database engine; we model complex applications with general graph based data-flows and control-flows at the process level where "actions" are performed by RVFs and "linked" in SQL queries. We further introduce Stream Query Process with stream data input and continuous execution. Our solutions to multi-camera video surveillance also include a new tracking method that is based on P2P time-synchronization of video streams and P2P target fusion.

These techniques represent a major shift in process management from one-time execution to data stream driven, open-ended execution, and constitute a novel step to the use of a query engine for running processes, towards the "In-DB Streaming" paradigm.

We have prototyped the proposed approaches by extending the open-sourced database engine Postgres, and plan to transfer the implementation to a commercial and proprietary parallel database system. The empirical study in a surveillance setting reveals their advantages in scalability, real-time performance and simplicity.

1 Introduction

Video surveillance has three phases: *event detection*, *event representation*, and *event recognition*. The *detection* phase deals with multi-sourced spatio-temporal data fusion for effectively and reliably extracting motion trajectories from video streams. Using multi-cameras can solve the spatial occlusion problem, where the objects observed from multiple cameras are integrated to spatio-temporal patterns corresponding to 3-dimensional views of the real-world locations of the detected objects. Sensor-data fusion from multiple cameras is an important topic for many applications such as aerial-photography, remote-sensing, cartography, etc. The focus of this research is not

A. Hameurlain and A M. Tjoa (Eds.): Globe 2009, LNCS 5697, pp. 136–149, 2009.

to introduce yet another algorithm, but to support it as a kind of data-intensive computation directly by the database engine for efficiency and scalability.

1.1 The Problems

The present video analytics applications generally fail to scale. A major reason is that almost all the video processing platforms treat database merely as a storage engine rather than a computation engine. As a result,

- the transfer of massive amount of video data between the database platform and the computation platform causes serious problem in performance and scalability;
- as video data is sizable, the video analytics layer again is burdened with many generic data management issues which the data management layer excels at but now need to be duplicated or handled ad hoc at the application layer;
- the opportunity to balance resource utilization between data management and video processing is lost when these two layers are distinctively separated, as they are now.

To solve the above problem, the next generation video analytics system will be characterized by having analytics executed inside the DB engine, by

- using User Defined Functions (UDFs) to reach those applications which are beyond the standard relational database operations, and
- using SQL to construct the data-flows of the applications.

However, for that, both the UDF technology and the SQL framework have limitations.

- The limitation of UDF lies in the lack of formal support of relational input and output. The existent scalar, aggregate and table UDFs are not relation-schema aware, unable to model complex applications, and cannot be composed with relational operators in a SQL query.
- The limitation of SQL lies in the inability of supporting applications at the process level with graph based data-flows and control-flows which are more complicated than query trees.

1.2 Related Work

Embedding data-intensive analytics in the database layer using SQL and UDFs is an active research field [4,8] but not seen in video analysis, due to the problems listed above. Using multiple SQL queries to model complex applications were supported by the existent commercial database systems at the script programming level rather than at the process level, and not tightly integrated with query processing. Pig Latin [11] developed at Yahoo Research combines the high-level declarative querying in the spirit of SQL, and low-level procedural programming, but it is characterized by decomposing a query into multiple expressions rather than composing multiple queries into a process. Business process management (BPM) addresses the issue of building middleware on top of, rather than integrating into, the data management layer [5,6,7]. Finally, the existing Data Stream Management Systems (DSMSs) such as Aurora[1], Eddies[3], STREAM[2] typically focus on tuple-oriented stream data processing, specific applications (e.g. TelegraphCQ) and standalone operations, rather than set-oriented stream data elements, generic solution, and process level semantics as required by video analytics. To the best of our knowledge, combining analytics computation and data management by constructing a graph-based dataflow process in SQL and executing it with a query engine, has not been addressed so far.

1.3 Our Solutions

Our solutions to scalable and efficient object location recognition problem in multi-camera video surveillance includes the following.

– We provide a convergent platform by pushing down multi-camera data fusion and other video analytics to the DB engine.
– We extend UDFs to *Relation-Valued Functions (RVFs)* for wrapping complex video analytics applications and composing them using SQL.
– We formulate the data-continuous semantics of queries and RVFs under streamed input/output, towards the notion of Stream Query Process (Stream QP).
– We proposed a new multi-camera tracking method that is based on P2P time-synchronization of video streams and P2P target fusion. .

These techniques constitute a novel step to use a query engine for running dataflow processes in the "In-DB Streaming" paradigm, and represent a major shift in process management from one-time execution to data stream driven, open-ended execution.

Through empirical study in a surveillance setting, the proposed approach shows its advantages in scalability, real-time performance and simplicity.

The rest of this paper is organized as follows: Section 2 outlines the fusion of multi-camera data; Section 3 discusses the notion of Stream QP with queries and RVFs; Section 4 discloses our implementation techniques; Section 5 shows experiment results; Section 6 concludes.

2   Stream Processing in Multi-cameras Based Human Tracking

Object tracking [15] can be defined as the problem of estimating the trajectory of an object in the video image plane as it moves around a scene, based on background subtraction [12]. In order to deal with objects occlusion, multiple cameras are utilized. The multi-camera data fusion can be triggered by any peer camera system; multiple, but minimal number of, input streams are joined on timestamp, and processed for deriving the real-world locations of the detected objects. The results are kept in the database for other analysis tasks to look-up. The multi-camera object tracking is based on processing distributed video streams with the following techniques.

– Identify moving objects (Human in this work) through background subtraction (BGS) and correlating the foreground objects in a stream of video frames. BGS is the basic operation in object tracking algorithms, which allows foreground objects to be segmented from the background in a camera view, and represented as bounding boxes.

- Calculate the real world position of each bounding box of the detected object based on the extrinsic and intrinsic parameters of the stationary calibrated camera. For human tracking, the midpoint of the bottom line of the bounding box is used as its location in the image plane.
- Fusion multi-camera data, as depicted in Fig 1 (a), with a single camera, the BGS algorithms often cannot figure out accurate foot location. This leads to error magnification in real world position calculation. As a result, multiple cameras are used to improve the accuracy of object tracking.

 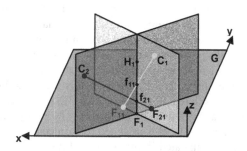

Fig. 1. (a): Foot location error by single camera;   (b): Multi-camera position adjustment

The information flows and derivations in multi-camera object tracking can be briefly described as below.

2.1 Media Stream Generation

Each camera is assigned a Media Server (MS) to receive the captured video stream and deliver the frames with timestamps to the corresponding human tracking operation. The MS also periodically performs P2P synchronization between neighboring cameras, namely, the cameras having overlapping view fields.

2.2 Single Camera-Based Human Tracking

In this phase the video frames delivered from each designated Media Server is processed by a human tracker; that performs its own tracking and keeps its own tracks for each target person. A person is detected based on background subtraction, and is represented by a bounding box; the midpoint of the bottom line of the bonding box is transformed into the real world position based on the extrinsic and intrinsic camera parameters.

Establishing the correspondences between detected persons in the consequent frames is a basic challenge in human tracking. This task is to determine whether the bounding boxes in the consecutive frames represent the same person or not. The operation is generally referred to as *Single Camera based Consistent Labeling* (SCCL). We implemented SCCL using OpenCV [13], an open source library.

A Human Tracker continuously outputs a stream of tuples with schema like (camera-id, timestamp, human-label, position), which are delivered to the corresponding Trajectory Merger.

2.3 Trajectory Merging

In this phase, output streams from a set of single camera based trackers are combined for deriving the merged trajectory of each detected person that is actually captured by multiple cameras. The major stream processing operations in this phase include *Multi-Cameras based Consistent Labeling* and *Position Adjustment,* as described below.

Multi-Cameras Based Consistent Labeling (MCCL). This is to establish correspondence between detected persons in different camera views. We assume that all cameras are calibrated and they share the same dominant plane, the real world ground plane. Therefore, a detected human location $p(x, y)$ (midpoint of the bottom line in the detected bounding box) in the image plane of a camera can be transformed into a 3D position $P(X, Y, 0)$ in the ground plane. The persons with similar 3D positions will be assigned the same label. That is, for two 3D positions P_1 and P_2 with the same timestamp, if $|P_1-P_2|<d$ (d is the predefined distance threshold), then P_1 and P_2 are considered as two projected 3D positions of the same person. This checking process has been done by a Trajectory Merger periodically.

When a new label is assigned to a trajectory from a Human Tracker by a Trajectory Merger, the updated information will be sent to all the other Trajectory Mergers that process the output from the same Human Tracker. This P2P-style information exchange only occurs between neighbored Trajectory Mergers. The scalability of the whole system will not break down.

Position Adjustment (PA). In the MCCL method mentioned above, we have assumed that the employed BGS algorithm could figure out accurate foot location. But in reality few BGS algorithms can meet the assumption. This leads to error magnification in the projection which transforms a 2D point in the image plane into a 3D position in the ground plane.

We propose a multi-camera tracking method for P2P adjustment of the projected position, named VLMSD (Vertical Line with Minimal Sum of Distances).

The fundamentals of VLMSD are depicted in Fig 1(b) with following notations:

- G: the ground plane (with $Z=0$);
- C_1: projection center of 1st camera;
- C_2: projection center of 2nd camera;
- H_1: the head of a person;
- F_1: the real foot of a person;
- f_{11}: the foot detected by the Human Tracker attached to the 1st camera;
- F_{11}: the projected foot position by f_{11} and parameters of the 1st camera;
- f_{21}: the foot detected by the Human Tracker attached to the 2nd camera;
- F_{21}: the projected foot position by f_{21} and parameters of the 2nd camera.

In VLMSD, we model a person as a line vertical to the ground G. For each detected person with the same timestamp from different cameras, we can get projective lines in the world coordinate, e.g. C_1F_{11} and C_2F_{21} in Fig 1(b).

On the contrary, given any projective lines from two different cameras like C_1F_{11} and C_2F_{21}, we can figure out a vertical line F_1H_1 intersected with both C_1F_{11} and C_2F_{21}. Then we compute the sum of distances $sd(C_1F_{11}, C_2F_{21})=|F_1F_{11}|+|F_1F_{21}|$. For

C_1F_{11}, without loss of generality, if $sd(C_1F_{11}, C_2F_{21})$ is the minimal one in all $sd(C_1F_{11}, C_2F_{2i})$, the same label is assigned to the corresponding two detected persons and F_1 is taken as his/her final 3D position after adjustment.

The data-flows in multi-cameras tracking is depicted in Fig 2 where cameras A and B are neighboring, meaning that they have overlapping visual fields; B and C are also neighboring, but A and C are not neighboring. The media servers generate video streams with timestamps; the SCCLs derive single camera based bounding box streams; these streams are merged in MCCLs, with further Peer-to-Peer position adjustment by the PAs.

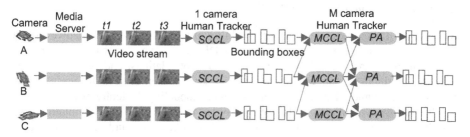

Fig. 2. Peer-to-Peer Streaming in Multi-Camera Tracking

For avoiding unnecessary communication and computation costs, the flows of video streams to the fusion center is automatically controlled. For supporting real-time response, we regularly use only minimal number of camera data streams in determining the real-world location of detected objects, but if the result is non-deterministic, take into account the data streams from more cameras.

In order to push down such data intensive computation to the database layer for fast data access and reduced data transfer, we proposed the "In-DB Streaming" approach.

3 Stream SQL Process

3.1 Handle Video Streaming Inside Database Engine

Video analysis applications constitute continuous multi-modal metadata extraction from video streams. The support to real-time, efficient data derivation has given rise to the need of handling such dataflow processes inside the database engine. Fig. 3 illustrates "In-DB streaming" where the data-flows in multi-camera human tracking are controlled by SQL query processing, and the computations are performed by UDFs.

To automate stepwise In-DB streaming, we introduce a new kind of dataflow process – Stream Query Process (Stream QP). A Stream QP is data-stream driven and continuously running; it is modeled as a graph of stationed operators – relation queries and UDFs with relation valued input and return; the connections of these operators are expressed by SQL phrases.

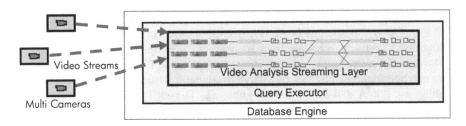

Fig. 3. In-DB Video Streaming by SQL and computation by UDFs

3.2 Relation Valued Function (RVF)

We rely on UDFs to extend the action capability of the database engine. However, the conventional scalar, aggregate and table UDFs are unable to express relational transformations since their inputs or outputs are not relations, and hence cannot be composed with other relational operators in a query. Further, these UDFs are typically processed with tuple-wise input which may incur modeling difficulty or performance penalty for large applications [4,5,9]. In order to overcome these limitations we introduce the kind of UDFs with input as a list of relations and return value as a relation, called Relation Valued Functions (RVFs). Adding RVFs to the UDF family has several advantages:

- an RVF can operate on a set of tuples, thus can accommodate more general applications which cannot be defined on a single tuple;
- applied to a set of tuples, rather than tuple-by-tuple, avoids repeatedly feeding in the initial data required for processing each tuple;
- operating on tuple sets opens the potential of batch and parallel processing using multi-cores or GPUs;
- an RVF derives a relation (although it can have database update effects in the function body) just like a standard relational operator, thus can be naturally composed with other relational operators or sub-queries in a SQL query (Fig 4).

SELECT * FROM rfv_1 (Q_1, Q_2(Q_3, rvf_2));

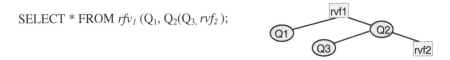

Fig. 4. Integrating applications to query using RVFs

In general, RVFs provide means to wrap complex applications and to integrate them to SQL queries.

3.3 Stream Query Process

Aiming to support video processing and other complex data-intensive applications efficiently inside the database engine, we need to model DAG (Directed Acyclic Graph) based data-flows to reach process level semantics – using SQL as the *control framework* and RVFs as the *actors*.

However, a single SQL query can only represent a tree, rather than a general graph; the query result at a step cannot be forked to more than one destination; the data-flows additional to control-flows are not allowed; and there is no notion for keeping an intermediate result to be used later than the immediate successive step.

Our solution to represent DAG based data-flows at the process level is based on multiple SQL queries connected in sequential, concurrent or nested fashion (for simplicity we omit certain details such as conditional branch). These inter-connected queries form a *Query Process* (QP). A component query of a QP may invoke RVFs, and takes the results of its predecessors as its data sources.

We further extend QP to deal with data streams by introducing the notion of Stream Query Process (Stream QP). A stream QP runs continuously with streamed input data and then generates streamed data-flows throughout the process. This notion can be further described as follows.

- A stream element is a schema-preserved relation (a set of tuples) rather than a single tuple; the set of tuples forming a stream element are identifiable by the same stream-key or filterable by a range condition (typically based on time delta). This distinguishes Stream QP from the existent stream processing systems [1,2,3] which look at data tuple-by-tuple.
- The basic operations of a Steam QP are queries and RVFs, which can be triggered repeatedly by *stream inputs*, *timers* or *event-conditions*, and parameterized by a stream-key or value range (e.g. time delta). An operation takes the results its predecessors as its data sources; the sequence of executions of it generates a data *stream*.
- Operations are "stationed" and asynchronous communicated. When two operations are consecutive in the dataflow, a *pipe* (or queue) from the upstream one to the downstream one is implied. Multiple pipes with replicated return elements must be provided for linking an operation to multiple successors, assuming that a queued data element can only be de-queued once. A pipe is defined with a *relation schema* for holding type-preserved steam elements, and with a *stream-key* or a value range for identifying the stream elements. A pipe is an abstract object that can be implemented by a queue, a relation (in-memory or on disk), etc.
- If a station has multiple successor stations, then (conceptually) its output is to be replicated and sent to all its successor stations as input (fork).
- If a station has multiple predecessor stations, then it is eligible for execution when all its predecessors have produced output (join).

Further, the control-flows of a QP are derivable from its data-flows. In a QP, a control-flow path implies a data-flow path but not vice versa. In Fig 5, for example, the data flow path from Q to Q_1 and Q_2 are additional to the control-flows. However, given the data dependencies between operations and the DAG constraint, the control-flows are derivable. In this example, the control-flows can be expressed by a nested sequence $<Q, f, [Q_1, Q_2]>$ (not necessarily unique) meaning that Q should be executed before f, and $[Q_1, Q_2]$ can be executed in any order but after f. Deriving a control-sequence from data-dependencies ensures the involved query Q and RVF f to be executed only once.

The components of a Stream QP - stationed operations connected by FIFO pipes, are conceptually different from the "steps" and "links" found in the one-time executed business processes.

An application is modeled by a query Q, followed by RVF f that takes Q's results as input, then followed by Q_1 and Q_2 which take f's as well as Q's results as input. The data flows and control flows are not coincident.

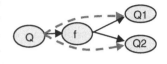

Fig. 5. A simple query process with separate data-flows and control flows

A simplified example for multi-camera human tracking is given in Fig. 6. The video frames are captured by the media servers of multiple camera systems, where the input frames are segmented into *slots* (like cuts); each slot contains multiple video frames with timestamps, and therefore identifiable by a time range. The consecutive slots can have different numbers of frames and therefore different lengths of time-span. For the Stream QP outlined below,

- the stream elements are slots identifiable by a time-range;
- the Stream QP is executed once and once again upon the availability of stream data inputs, i.e. the time-range identified slots containing video frames;
- the time-range serves as the parameters of the QP, meaning that its component queries may be *parameterized*.

This process has the following operations.

- Queries Q_1, Q_2, Q_3 captures video frame streams from the media servers of three camera systems, which are in the unified format with synchronized timestamps;
- RVFs F_1, F_2, F_3 are single-camera based human trackers (SCCL); they take the above video streams as input, and output continuous sequence of tuples with attributes camera-id, human-id, timestamp, 2D-bounding-box;
- RVFs F_4 deals with *multi*-camera based human trajectory merge (MCCL) incorporating with certain context knowledge; it outputs continuous sequence of tuples with attributes consistent-human-id, timestamp, 3D-position;
- RVFs F_5 and F_6 generate two kinds trajectory analysis reports, based on the information delivered from F_4.

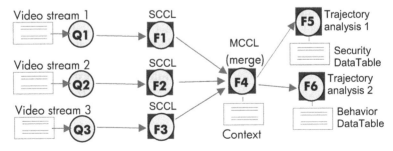

Fig. 6. A Query Dataflow Process for multi-camera human tracking

The pseudo specification of this QP is illustrated below where the definitions of operation F_4 use "in-line" specification for the input data source. The process is marked TRANSIENT meaning that it is executed in-memory.

```
Create Query Process Multi_Camera_Tracking (int t1, int t2) {

  Source: FrameStream1, FrameStream2, FrameStream3, Context;
  TRANSIENT;

  Define Operation Q₁ As                              /* Q₂ and Q₃ are similar */
  SELECT * FROM FrameSream1 WHERE timestamp >= t1 AND timestamp < t2;

  Define Operation F₁ As                              /* F₂ and F₃ are similar */
  SELECT timestamp, person_id, 2D_bounding_box FROM SCCL(SELECT * FROM Q₁);
    InputMode: BLOCK, ReturnMode: SET;

  Define              Operation              F₄                          As
  SELECT timestamp, final_person_id, 3D_position FROM MCCL(F₁,F₂, F₃, Context );
    InputMode: BLOCK, ReturnMode: SET;

  Define              Operation              F₅                          As
  SELECT * FROM trajectory_analysis1 (F₄, SecurityDataTable),
    InputMode: BLOCK, ReturnMode: SET;

  Define              Operation              F₆                          As
  SELECT * FROM trajectory_analysis2 (F₄, BehaviorDataTable),
    InputMode: BLOCK, ReturnMode: SET;
}
```

From the above example, we can see the basic characteristics of a QP: correlated queries and RVFs, graph based data-flows, and constructed by SQL. In a QP pipeline, the data flowed through operations can be "ETLed" by SQL queries, and the RVFs are streamlined in the SQL queries.

4 Implementation of Stream QP

We have provided the preliminary support to Stream QP by extending the Postgres query engine by plugging in an RVF manager and a light-weight QP Management System (QPMS). Here we concentrate to the QPMS implementation.

A QP is made of the queries and RVFs executable by the query engine. A QPMS is a "*middleware inside query engine*" for handling multiple QPs with interleaved operation executions; it can be launched by the query executor in the similar way as the Postgres Function Manager. The QPMS has two major components:

- QPM – i.e. Query Process Manager for creating and managing QP instances, and for scheduling operations;
- OLM – i.e. Operation List Handler for launching queries (possibly involving RVFs) using the Postgres internal SPI query facility.

The execution of a QP is controlled by the QPM and OLM services. The component queries, the data-flows, as well as the control-flows derived from data-dependencies, represent the static properties, or *template*, of the QP. We distinguish two modes of QP executions.

Poke Mode QP Execution. A Stream QP execution can be triggered by the arrival of a stream element, and the continuous supply of stream elements causes a sequence of individual QP executions. Under the *poke mode*, each execution is controlled in the following way.

- Based on the template of a QP, the QPM creates a *QP instance* and derives one control-sequence of its operations. A QP instance has several states (ready, in-progress, complete/fail) maintained by the QPM. A QP instance object is persisted after each use unless the process is specified as TRANSIENT, so are the operation instances and pipes.
- The QPM creates the start operation instances based on the control-sequence. An operation instance also has states (ready, in-progress, complete/fail).
- For running every operation including the start ones, the QPM identifies the incoming pipes, creates the outgoing pipes, generates a corresponding *operation-item*, and puts it to the *operation queue*. At the minimum, an operation item includes the process-instance-ID, the operation-instance-ID, the query (may involve RVFs), and the references to incoming and outgoing pipes. The operation items, once put in the operation queue, can be executed in any order, and in fact they are de-queued in pipeline and executed by individual, time-overlapping threads.
- The OLM runs as a separate thread of the QPM, it de-queues the operation items one by one; for each item, it launches a thread to execute the query associated with that item, using the high-efficient Postgres internal SPI facility, then puts the returned query result into the outgoing pipes, and sends a return value, *rv*, to the QPM. The return value is a message that contains, at the minimum, the process-instance-ID, the operation-instance-ID, the query execution status returned from the Postgres query engine, and the references to outgoing pipes.
- Upon receipt of the *rv*, the QPM updates the corresponding operation instance and process instance, checks the control-sequence and triggering condition or timer, then selects the next eligible operation or operations to run, rolling forward the process instance, towards the end of it.

A sequence of stream elements causes a sequence of such one-time QP executions.

Poll Mode QP Execution. This mode of control is used to run the kind of Stream QPs with different paced operations which are typically activated by timers. For instance, a set of video frames are summarized minute by minute but analyzed hour by hour. In this case the process boundary becomes vague and it has to be executed in the poll mode. While such a process is continuously running, the statuses of it and its component operations are traced by the QPM that polls the operation instances, checks the availability of input data and the timers, then picks the ready-to-run operations and sends the corresponding operation items to the operation queue. The execution of an operation (query or query invoking RVFs) is still handled by the OLM in the way described above. Introducing process level control allows the system to deal with the inter-relationship of the operations. For instance, if an hourly analysis is failed (by exception, timeout, etc) it can be re-run at the next hour, depending on the policies specified at the process level.

To remark, our QPMS differs from the DSMSs in several aspects: it takes a relation rather than a single tuple as a stream element; it relies on the queries parameterized by *element-key* or *value-delta* to retrieve the set of tuples for a stream element; it manages operations in the schema-aware and process-aware way.

5   Experiments

We tested our approach by using the extended Postgres database engine to run the Stream QP shown in Fig. 6, inside the database engine with direct data access (in terms of Postgres SPI facility) and at the client side with ODBC based data access and server-client data transfer. For simplicity, we ignored operations F5 and F6, and compare the performance on a single execution of the process on an input stream element containing multiple video frames. We used the camera calibration method from [16] and employed an open source tool box [14]. The BGS algorithm is based on [13] in OpenCV.

We did the experiments in two situations: tracking 5 persons in a sequence of frames, and tracking 10 persons in a sequence of frames. The number of frames ranges from 30 – 180 (30, 60, 90, 120, 150, 180) - as the frame rate is 30 frames/second, that means the process is executed every 1, 2, 3, 4, 5 or 6 seconds. The 5 people tracking results are shown in Fig. 7, and the 10 people tracking results are shown in Fig. 8.

Number of frames	30	60	90	120	150	180
Inside	4	4	5	6	8	10
Outside	111	139	152	177	180	210

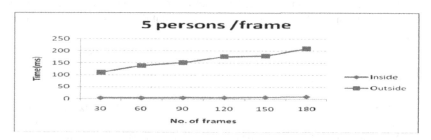

Fig. 7. Inside DB / Outside DB streaming performance comparison on 5 people tracking

Number of frames	30	60	90	120	150	180
Inside	5	9	18	23	29	36
Outside	137	182	226	258	292	342

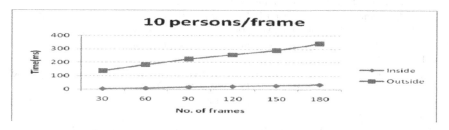

Fig. 8. Inside DB / Outside DB streaming performance comparison on 10 people tracking

The performance difference between steaming inside and outside DB is obvious: the performance is enhanced more than 10 times if running inside the database engine. Most of the extra time in running at the client side is spent on loading the data from DB.

6 Conclusion

In this work we have proposed and implemented the In-DB streaming solution to the multi-camera data fusion application. For efficiency and scalability, we provided a convergent platform for video analysis and data management, extended UDFs to allow video analytics to be naturally integrated to SQL queries, introduced Stream Query Process to model complex applications with general graph based data-flows and control-flows, and further developed the QPMS for handling the continuous execution of Stream QPs. The "In-DB Streaming" represents a major shift in process management from one-time execution to data stream driven, open-ended execution, and a novel step to the use of a query engine for process management.

We have prototyped the proposed approaches by extending the open-sourced database engine Postgres, and plan to transfer the implementation to a commercial and proprietary parallel database system. We also developed a new P2P object tracking method.

The empirical study in a surveillance setting reveals the advantages of processing video streams inside the database engine in scalability, real-time performance and simplicity.

References

1. Arasu, B., Babcock, S., Babu, M., Datar, K., Ito, I., Nishizawa, J., Rosenstein, J.: STREAM: The Stanford Stream Data Manager. In: Proceedings of SIGMOD (2003)
2. Avnur, R., Hellerstein, J.M.: Eddies: Continuously adaptive query processing. In: ACM SIGMOD, Dallas, TX (May 2000)
3. Chen, J., DeWitt, D., Naughton, J.: Design and evaluation of alternative selection placement strategies in optimizing continuous queries. In: ICDE, CA (2002)
4. Chen, Q., Hsu, M.: Data-Continuous SQL Process Model. In: Meersman, R., Tari, Z. (eds.) OTM 2008, Part I. LNCS, vol. 5331, pp. 175–192. Springer, Heidelberg (2008)
5. Chen, Q., Hsu, M.: Inter-Enterprise Collaborative Business Process Management. In: Proc. of 17th Int'l Conf on Data Engineering (ICDE 2001), Germany (2001)
6. Chen, Q., Kambayashi, Y.: Nested Relation Based Database Knowledge Representation. In: Proc. of ACM SIGMOD 1991, vol. 20(2) (1991) (ACM SIGMOD Rec.)
7. Dayal, U., Hsu, M., Ladin, R.: A Transaction Model for Long-Running Activities. In: VLDB (1991)
8. Isard, M., Budiu, M., Yu, Y., Birrell, A., Fetterly, D.: Dryad: Distributed data-parallel programs from sequential building blocks. In: EuroSys 2007 (March 2007)
9. Jaedicke, M., Mitschang, B.: User-Defined Table Operators: Enhancing Extensibility of ORDBMS. In: VLDB (1999)
10. Jiao, L., Wu, G., Wu, Y., Chang, E.Y., Wang, Y.-F.: The Anatomy of A Multi-Camera Video Surveillance System

11. Olston, C., Reed, B., Srivastava, U., Kumar, R., Tomkins, A.: Pig Latin: A Not-So-Foreign Language for Data Processing. ACM SIGMOD (2008)
12. Li, L., Huang, W., Gu, I.Y.H., Tian, Q.: Foreground Object Detection from Videos Containing Complex Background. ACM Multimedia (2003)
13. Open Computer Vision Library,
    http://sourceforge.net/projects/opencvlibrary/
14. Vezhnevets, V., Velizhev, A.: GML C++ Camera Calibration Toolbox,
    http://research.graphicon.ru/calibration/
    gml-c++-camera-calibration-toolbox.html
15. Yilmaz, A., Javed, O., Shah, M.: Object Tracking: A Survey. ACM Journal of Computing Surveys (2006)
16. Zhang, Z.: A Flexible New Technique for Camera Calibration. Technical Report MSR-TR-98-71, Microsoft Research (1998)

Author Index